I0438965

MARRIAGES OF ORANGE COUNTY, FLORIDA
Volume 3: January 1, 1925 - August 20, 1934

Compiled and Edited by
Betty Jo Stockton and Mary Nardini

Central Florida Genealogical Society, Inc
1998
Reprint 2014

Additional copies of this publication
may be ordered from:

Central Florida Genealogical Society
PO Box 536309
Orlando, FL 32853-6309
or
www.cfgs.org
or through Amazon.com

©Central Florida Genealogical Society, In
1998
4th printing 2014

Foreword

With the opening of the new courthouse in Orange County and consolidation of office space, access to marriage records has greatly improved since the first volume of this series. Marriage records from 1869 through February 1998 are now held by the Records Management Office in the Orange County Court House and may be ordered from that office. The cost is $1.00 per page ($2.00 for a certified copy.) Include the name of bride and groom, the marriage date and the book and page where the marriage was recorded as part of your request for records. The office will also search for marriage records for $1.00 per year per name. Records may be ordered from:

Records Management Office
Room 150, Orange County Courthouse
425 N. Orange Ave, Orlando, FL 32801
(407) 836-6321

Additionally, almost all Orange County marriage books were filmed by the LDS Family History Library in 1972 and can be ordered through any Family History Center. Film numbers are given below.

In 1984, the Central Florida Genealogical Society published *Dated Index to Marriages 1869-1899, Orange County, Florida*, which is now out of print. *Orange County Marriage Book Volume I*, published in the fall of 1997, revised and expanded that earlier volume and included marriages through December 1909. *Orange County Marriage Book Volume II* continued, listing marriages from January 1910 through December 1924. This volume includes marriages from January, 1925 through August 23, 1934. Listing is alphabetical by surname of groom; every name is indexed. Volume and page of the original record is noted as 5/ 133 (volume 5, page 133.)

The amount of information included in the original records varied. For example, Marriage Books 5 and 6 usually included the residence of bride and groom; later volumes did not. Marriage Book 6 listed the race of the couple. In some cases, the actual marriage date was not listed; we have given the application or recording date and noted it as such. In a few cases, there was a substantial time lapse between application and recording date; both dates are given here — the marriage date obviously falls between the two, but the exact date is unknown.

Names are spelled exactly as given in the records. Where there was a doubt, it is noted with a ? and the possible alternative spelling given. Some names were difficult to decipher and may still be incorrect. Many seemed to be spelled phonetically — whether this was the correct spelling or simply what the clerk heard, we do not know.

The residence of bride and groom (when given) follows each name and is in brackets. All towns are in Florida unless otherwise noted. Where the race of the couple was indicated, it is noted as (B) Black or (W) White. No other designation of ethnic background was given.

Many records also list witnesses, the name of the person performing the marriage and the place of the marriage. These are not included in this volume but may be found on the original records or on Family History Library films which are on permanent loan at the Par Avenue Family History Center in Orlando or may be ordered through any Family History Center at a nominal cost. There are also applications for licenses for many of these couples (see film numbers below.) Some of these have a great deal of information; others very little.

Family History Library Film Numbers are:

Marriage Book Volume 5	(26 Dec 1921 - 30 May 1925)	#1887397	
Marriage Book Volume 6	(20 Jun 1925 - 17 Oct 1927)	#1887394	
Marriage Book Volume 7	(15 Oct 1927 - 9 May 1931)	#1887299	
Marriage Book Volume 8	(9 May 1931 - 20 Aug 1934)	#1887394	(also on #1887299)

Marriage Licenses	Volume 5 (1924-1925)	#0997574	
Marriage Licenses	Volume 6 (1925-1926)	#0997575	
Marriage Licenses	Volume 7-10 (1926-1928)	#1887398	
Marriage Licenses	Volume 11-12 (1930-1931)	#1887444	(Later ones may have not been filmed)

A

Abercrombie, Carl Dorsett [Jacksonville]	Yearty, Florence [Jacksonville]	16 Oct 1926	6/ 358
Abernathy, Walter [Orlando]	Gayle, Grace Eleanor [Orlando]	22 Aug 1925	6/ 216
Ace, Claude William [Orlando]	Diszell, Naomi [Orlando]	14 Mar 1927	6/ 474
Acree, Louis Eston [Fernandina]	Acree, Louise [Winter Haven]	18 Mar 1926	6/ 181
Adams, Cal [Orlando]	Anderson, Rosa Lee [Orlando]	23 Feb 1927	6/ 464
Adams, Charles Albert	Barker, Martha Elsie	12 Oct 1930	7/ 511
Adams, Charles Lowden [W] [Orlando]	Lathrop, Myrtle Ann [Orlando]	7 Jun 1925	5/ 594
Adams, Charlie	Price, Josephine	26 Jan 1929	7/ 239
Adams, Henry Willis [Orlando]	Field, Gaserlean [Orlando]	16 Oct 1926	6/ 354
Adams, John William [Apopka]	Goodwin, Helen Marie [Apopka]	12 Aug 1926	6/ 308
Adams, Lester	Haywood, Alberta	22 Feb 1930	7/ 418
Adams, Thomas Edward [W] [Orlando]	Lambert, Mary Elizabeth [Orlando]	3 Jun 1925	5/ 595
Adams, William	Liles, Alma	30 Apr 1930	7/ 446
Adams, Willie C.	Williams, Solona	12 May 1928	7/ 112
Adell, Martin	Blocker, Pota Belle	7 Apr 1934	8/ 456
Aderhold, Isaac Davis	Bennett, Alta Elizabeth	25 Nov 1931	8/ 80
Adkins, B. A.	Sharp, Janie Evelyn	26 Dec 1931	8/ 94
Adwell, Roy Hilton [Winter Park]	Jones, Martha [Orlando]	2 Oct 1925	6/ 56
Agey, Hoite Norton [Orlando]	Lewis, Eleanor Florence [Orlando]	6 Mar 1926	6/ 177
Ahern, C. Jerry	Smith, Eunice Thelma	29 Mar 1928	7/ 90
Ahik, Carl George [W] [Winter Park]	Webb, Abbie Alice [Demerest, GA]	24 Jun 1925	6/ 3
Aiken, Richard [B] [Sanford]	Harris, Vina [Sanford]	14 Dec 1925	6/ 101
Ailsworth, Arthur Carroll [Orlando]	Benson, Katherine [Orlando]	10 Aug 1927	6/ 577
Airhart, John Patton	Madden, Evelyn Brown	8 Oct 1927	6/ 597
Akerman, Joe A. [Orlando]	Norman, Frances Rachael [Orlando]	13 May 1927	6/ 521
Akers, Willie S. [Orlando]	Byrd, Amelia [Orlando]	14 May 1927	6/ 509
Akin, Claude Curtis [Orlando]	Johnson, Helen Elain [Jamestown, NY]	29 Jun 1926	6/ 253
Akins, Ira Newton	Odum, Susie Mae	13 Dec 1932	8/ 228
Akins, Roy Alexander	McFarland, Grace Moore	23 Jun 1934	8/ 449
Akins, Roy Alexander	McFarland, Grace Moore	23 Jun 1934	8/ 499
Albert, Arthur [Orlando]	Sloan, Lillian [Orlando]	9 May 1927	6/ 504
Albertson, George Fitz-Randolph	Maynard, Lena Pearl	28 Apr 1930	7/ 445
Alcorn, Thomas Brances	Duley, Mary Sally	14 Oct 1931	8/ 59
Aldrich, John Burton	Bandy, Lena McCown	11 Feb 1928	7/ 62
Allardice, William Duncan [Orlando]	Schweikert, Edna Wilhelmina [Orlando]	17 Feb 1926	6/ 159
Allen, Americus Calhoun	Davis, Idalene Mae	28 Aug 1928	7/ 178
Allen, Charlie [Orlando]	Love, Rosabell [Orlando]	4 Dec 1926	6/ 403
Allen, Clare B. [Orlando]	Crane, Bernice Pell [Orlando]	17 Apr 1926	6/ 222
Allen, Clifford H.	Goodman, Juliet Gould	3 Mar 1928	7/ 75
Allen, David Evans [W] [Syracuse NY]	White, Isabelle [Conway]	11 Feb 1925	5/ 529
Allen, Frank [Orlando]	Franklin, Willie [Orlando]	16 Oct 1926	6/ 355
Allen, John Curtis	Hernandez, Wilhelmina Landonia	22 Feb 1934	8/ 439
Allen, John William [Fairvilla]	Tullis, Bessie Mae [Fairvilla]	20 Mar 1926	6/ 184
Allen, Leonard Dell	Wright, Holly	28 Jan 1928	7/ 53
Allen, Linton E.	Ives, Helen C.	12 Apr 1928	7/ 98
Allen, Oliver Ray	Sutula, Helen Francine	2 Apr 1930	7/ 435
Allen, Ollie [B] [Orlando]	King, Hattie May [Winter Park]	27 Jun 1925	6/ 5
Allen, Robert S.	Mayberry, Josie	12 Nov 1929	7/ 372

Allen, Royal Vance [Benson Springs]	Tighe, Mary N. [Orlando]	18 Apr 1927	6/ 496
Allen, Sebron	Williams, Virginia Suffold	1 May 1928	7/ 111
Allen, Thomas	Brown, Georgia	25 Dec 1931	8/ 93
Allen, W. J. [B] [Winter Park]	Andrews, Angie [Winter Park]	24 Dec 1925	6/ 113
Allen, Willie	Rice, Willie B.	11 Jul 1928	7/ 159
Allman, Jasper [W] [Sanford]	Prosser, Edna Mirl [Sanford]	7 Jul 1925	6/ 11
Alls, Louis [B] [Winter Garden]	Roberson, Mary Ann [Oakland]	1 Jun 1925	5/ 597
Almond, Percival Clarmont [Orlando]	Reeme, Myrtis	28 Aug 1926	6/ 322
Almsted, Martin [Orlando]	McGuire, Lucile [Tampa]	11 Apr 1927	6/ 490
Altman, Roy Lee	Yates, Mary Alice	8 Jan 1932	8/ 102
Ambrose, Arthur	Tyson, Lillie	24 Sep 1927	6/ 590
Ambrose, Arthur	Mitchell, Virginia	19 Oct 1931	8/ 61
Ambrose, Charlie [Winter Park]	Green, Mary [Mt Dora]	12 May 1926	6/ 234
Ambrose, Edward	Brown, Rosa	9 Apr 1931	7/ 589
Amig, Rodney W.	Clark, Louise	13 Mar 1930	7/ 426
Amig, Rodney Whitcomb	Williams, Lois	15 Apr 1932	8/ 144
Amman, John	Williams, Anna H.	3 Apr 1929	7/ 271
Ammon, R. R.	Sulatycki, Ethel	19 Sep 1929	7/ 347
Anderson, Bryan George [W] [Orlando]	McKenney, Alice [Orlando]	8 Apr 1925	5/ 556
Anderson, Claude	Green, Serena May	6 Jan 1934	8/ 402
Anderson, Claude [Orlando]	Griffin, DeLorraine [Orlando]	15 Jul 1926	6/ 298
Anderson, Dave [Orlando]	Calhoun, Laura [Orlando]	22 Aug 1925	6/ 37
Anderson, Edward Lind	Gerhardt, Minnie Ethelind	8 Aug 1934	8/ 519
Anderson, George	Carter, Addie	9 Dec 1932	8/ 382
Anderson, Godfrey Theodore	Amerman, Gizella	11 Jun 1929	7/ 310
Anderson, Henry	Boyd, Retha	21 Jan 1928	7/ 50
Anderson, Holger Emil [Orlando]	Lizze, Tressia [Colorado Springs, CO]	25 Nov 1926	6/ 398
Anderson, Horace [B] [Orlando]	Riggens, Carrie [Orlando]	18 Jan 1926	6/ 140
Anderson, Howard Alfred	Miller, Ellen	11 Jun 1930	7/ 465
Anderson, Isaac	Taylor, Hannah	4 Nov 1929	7/ 366
Anderson, John Gerard [W] [New York NY]	Riess, Elizabeth Caroline [Melbourne]	6 Jun 1925	5/ 595
Anderson, John Ralph	Carmichael, Henriette	18 Apr 1931	7/ 582
Anderson, Lawrence [Winter Park]	Ambrose, Louise [Winter Park]	15 Apr 1926	6/ 210
Anderson, LeRoy	Toney, Carolyn Agnes	21 Dec 1932	8/ 101
Anderson, Loman Belton [Winter Garden]	McEachern, Myrtis Will [Winter Garden]	26 Apr 1927	6/ 498
Anderson, Louis Montjoy	Drake, Catherine Virginia	11 Jan 1932	8/ 103
Anderson, Matthews [Apopka]	Marshall, Sallie [Apopka]	17 Jan 1927	6/ 438
Anderson, Ralph	Hutchens, Victor	6 Apr 1929	7/ 274
Anderson, Wesley [Orlando]	Shelton, Queen Esther [Orlando]	6 Mar 1927	6/ 476
Anderson, Wilbert Seth [Orlando]	Dodson, Beatrice [Orlando]	23 Oct 1926	6/ 367
Anderson, William [B] [Orlando]	Major, Lucy [Orlando]	5 Dec 1925	6/ 104
Anderson, William L.	Lawrence, Maggie Louise	3 Jun 1929	7/ 302
Anderson, Willie	Neal, Callie	4 Feb 1928	7/ 56
Andralliski, Willie Lewis	Carter, Eula Lee	1 Aug 1929	7/ 327
Andrews, Bennie	Perry, Seretha	23 Oct 1931	8/ 64
Andrews, John William	Frank, Daisy Milton	22 Dec 1931	8/ 95
Andrews, Oakley [W] [Orlando]	Ferrell, Carrie Mae [Benhaden]	12 May 1925	5/ 572
Andrews, Scott [B] [Orlando]	Norris, Victoria [Orlando]	3 Jan 1926	6/ 130
Ange, Joseph Fenner, Jr [W] [Orlando]	Riddel, Dorothy Elizabeth [Orlando]	14 Oct 1925	6/ 88
Angier, Irving Oscar [Orlando]	Slates, Francis Kimberly [Orlando]	6 May 1926	6/ 232
Anglin, Cicero David	Joiner, Hazel Evelyn	28 May 1934	8/ 482
Anglin, Emory Estes	Harper, Ruby Lee	30 Sep 1929	7/ 350

Anvil, Albert Bryan [Orlando]	Kimball, Winifred [Orlando]	15 Feb 1927	6/ 459
Appleby, Oscar Thurmond [Winter Garden]	Cothran, Roxie Jimmie [Alachus]	25 Jul 1927	6/ 555
Arbuckle, Vernon Lawrence [W] [Orlando]	Cobb, Lillian Irene [Orlando]	15 Jan 1926	6/ 136
Archidiacono, Giovani	Ciuffo, Bridigo	2 Dec 1933	8/ 379
Archie, Moses James	Carr, Ira	20 Aug 1928	7/ 175
Ard, James Jackson	Godwin, Media Jane	14 Jun 1934	8/ 494
Argo, Virgil William	Helm, May Mildred	21 Dec 1933	8/ 388
Argrett, Leroy	Hooks, Lorraine	22 Jan 1934	8/ 416
Aring, Russel Owen [Apopka]	Mackey, Inez Hancock [Apopka]	22 Jan 1926	6/ 148
Arlene, Thomas Jefferson	Burgess, Lula Asenith	8 Nov 1927	7/ 10
Armistead, Henry [Orlando]	Daniels, Gertrude [Orlando]	3 May 1926	6/ 226
Armistead, West Humphrey	Belk, Lucile	20 Oct 1927	7/ 7
Armstrong, Clinton [Burlington, KS]	Kessler, Theta [St Louis, MO]	8 May 1926	6/ 231
Armstrong, Robert	Mack, Amanda	1 Dec 1933	8/ 387
Armstrong, Scott	Stevens, Dora	15 Apr 1933	8/ 284
Arnadorff, Hugh Jackson	Ferrell, Christine	7 Jun 1930	7/ 466
Arnert, Howard Ellis	Holland, Maud Mozell	20 Jun 1931	8/ 21
Arnett, Allen	Shaw, Evie	10 Oct 1932	8/ 209
Arnold, Forest Lester	Ralston, Mary Elizabeth	28 Nov 1928	7/ 209
Arnold, Fred	Jerry, Ida May	7 Jul 1931	8/ 30
Arnold, Willie	Allen, Catherine	18 Nov 1929	7/ 374
Arslanian, Kegham	Andressian, Cora	31 Dec 1928	7/ 227
Artford, Howard Authur	Ryals, Ethel	30 Jan 1928	7/ 58
Artie, Harvey Chester	Shaw, Hazel May	6 Aug 1930	7/ 485
Ash, Clemson	Lewis, Marie	13 Nov 1928	7/ 203
Ashby, Burt G. [Orlando]	Johnson, Dorothy [Orlando]	26 Apr 1927	6/ 503
Ashe, Caromerr [Orlando]	Jackson, Algrine [Orlando]	9 Aug 1926	6/ 314
Ashe, James	Bellamy, Sadie	25 Jul 1933	8/ 328
Ashe, Sammie [B] [Orlando]	Mack, Lillie Mae [Orlando]	3 Jan 1925	5/ 505
Ashford, Henry Daniel [Tampa]	McDermott, Willanette Whitehead	24 Feb 1926	6/ 169
Ashley, Thomas Grady	Wilson, Vera Inez	14 Apr 1929	7/ 281
Ashlock, Carl Johnson [Orlando]	Roach, Ruby Nina [Shreveport, LA]	28 May 1926	6/ 257
Ashmore, Glenn Russell	Bruce, Helen Gertrude	24 Dec 1927	7/ 33
Ashmore, James Rufus, Jr.	Fischer, Charlotte Helma	12 Aug 1933	8/ 334
Asne, Lonnie	Martin, Daisy	24 Jan 1932	8/ 106
Aspinwall, Palmer	DuBose, Sarah Louise	19 Jun 1929	7/ 313
Atkins, Charles	Allen, Marie	8 Jan 1934	8/ 405
Atkins, Charlie	Jerry, Julia	28 Jan 1933	8/ 250
Atkinson, Jeptha [Winter Park]	Jerrigan, Nannie Bertz [Winter Park]	21 May 1927	6/ 513
Aulls, Ernest Carlisle	Arnold, Christina Morton	4 Sep 1929	7/ 341
Austin, Ed	French, Jereline	15 Sep 1928	7/ 187
Austin, James [B] [Orlando]	Willis, Ophelia [Orlando]	22 Apr 1925	5/ 562
Austin, James Andrew [Orlando]	Davis, Loyale James [Orlando]	30 Jun 1927	6/ 563
Austin, James Richard	Wetherington, Johnnie Ruth	24 Dec 1930	7/ 533
Austin, John	Ross, Ossie	18 Feb 1929	7/ 246
Austin, Sam	Mims, Lillian	11 Jun 1932	8/ 168
Austin, Tommie	Harris, Malinda	25 Oct 1929	7/ 361
Avedisian, David [Orlando]	Baylarian, Veronica [Orlando]	13 Jun 1926	6/ 269
Averill, Kennerly M.	Carr, Marie I.	16 Jul 1929	7/ 324
Avery, Clarence	Keene, Louise	31 Aug 1929	7/ 337

Avery, James Askew	Pfeifer, Mary Rosalie	8 Jun 1928	7/ 133
Avery, Ray Wright	Williams, Olivia	4 Oct 1932	8/ 208
Awter, William Frederick [W] [Orlando]	Bennin, Henriette Louise [Gotha]	28 Jun 1925	6/ 9
Ayers, Marion	Stockwell, Luella Mae	30 Nov 1933	8/ 379
Ayers, Roy [Winter Garden]	Flowers, Thelma [Winter Garden]	2 Apr 1927	6/ 48

B

Babb, Millard Grady	Phillips, Elizabeth	30 Jun 1929	7/ 319
Babb, Willie [Orlando]	Jacobs, Octavius [Orlando]	12 Jan 1927	6/ 436
Babbitt, E. E.	Biggs, Olivette Hind	14 Nov 1929	7/ 372
Babbitt, Earl [Kissimmee]	Hedrick, Catherine [Orlando]	16 Apr 1926	6/ 210
Bachman, Richard [Taft]	Mueller, Lena [Orlando]	15 Jun 1926	6/ 273
Bachmann, Ernest Edward	Himler, Helen May	23 Oct 1931	8/ 63
Baggett, Earth Clayton	Dye, Beaula LaFrancis	2 Sep 1927	6/ 576
Baggett, Julian Herman [W] [Taft]	Sphaler, Dona Ola [Taft]	18 Jan 1925	5/ 514
Baidy, Arthur	Carawell, Clara	2 Feb 1931	7/ 551
Bailey, Arthur	Mark, Alberta	17 Dec 1927	7/ 31
Bailey, Benjamin Herman	Adcock, Frances Rives	28 Dec 1928	7/ 289
Bailey, Burrell Francis	Blue, Callie Vanevar	30 May 1931	8/ 10
Bailey, Dewey Asa	Burnette, Lillie Mae	23 Nov 1929	7/ 377
Bailey, Hance V. [Orlando]	McCowen, Gertrude [Orlando]	11 Dec 1926	6/ 407
Bailey, Henry William	Johns, Virginia Lucille	27 Apr 1931	7/ 587
Bailey, Robert [Orlando]	Perry, Annie [Orlando]	24 Dec 1926	6/ 416
Bailey, W. H., Jr [Winter Park]	Weldon, Edwina [Winter Park]	30 Jan 1926	6/ 145
Bailey, Walter Burton	Cartledge, Frossie Estelle	4 Jan 1930	7/ 397
Bailey, William Herbert	Holloway, Murnice	4 Apr 1928	7/ 92
Baines, Lucius	Pulley, Lucy	18 Aug 1928	7/ 173
Baines, Robert [Orlando]	Bryer, Lintha Mae [Orlando]	28 Dec 1926	6/ 421
Baity, Abraham Jeff [B] [Orlando]	Brooks, Lillie [Orlando]	9 Feb 1925	5/ 525
Baken, Jimmie Lee	Willis, Clara	13 Sep 1927	6/ 579
Baker, Albert J.	Canada, Ora	1 Oct 1927	6/ 588
Baker, Allen Nathaniel	Kinsey, Mary	11 Jan 1933	8/ 242
Baker, Esop Willie	Williams, Rosa Lee	31 Aug 1931	8/ 45
Baker, Hardy	Anderson, Lucile	18 Oct 1930	7/ 510
Baker, Harry Edward	Grandbouche, Lucille L.	25 Feb 1928	7/ 71
Baker, Horace Benjamin [B] [Orlando]	Heath, Thelma Ernestine [Orlando]	16 Jan 1925	5/ 513
Baker, Jake Granville	Beal, Esther LaVerne	16 Dec 1933	8/ 392
Baker, Jerry Lee [B] [Orlando]	Taylor, Clara [Orlando]	7 Dec 1925	6/ 96
Baker, John Caldwell	Mayfield, Ethyle Elizabeth	24 Apr 1929	7/ 283
Baker, John G. [Orlando]	Pedrick, Jesse [Orlando]	22 Jun 1927	6/ 528
Baker, Mozel	Harding, Bessie	4 Aug 1928	7/ 168
Baker, Raymond	Singleton, Lula Mae	1 Nov 1933	8/ 359
Baker, Ulyseese	Dixon, Hattie Mae	4 Jun 1932	8/ 165
Baker, Vernon E. [Winter Park]	Jackson, Eva [Winter Park]	4 Aug 1927	6/ 557
Baldo, Leslie Joseph	Martin, Iola	10 Apr 1930	7/ 437
Baldwin, Minor C.	Sproat, Louise G.	15 May 1928	7/ 117
Bales, Jack [orlando]	Walsh, Alma [Orlando]	5 Feb 1927	6/ 458
Balian, Hetoum [Orlando]	Baylarian, Haiguhie [Orlando]	31 Aug 1927	6/ 571
Ball, Hayward	Roberts, Ruby Mae	14 Jun 1934	8/ 494
Ball, J. F. [Orlando]	Avera, Bessie [Orlando]	12 Sep 1926	6/ 339
Ball, Lee	Williams, Evelyn	8 Mar 1928	7/ 77

Ball, Sidney C.	Lane, Lizzie	27 Dec 1928	7/ 222
Ballentine, Mattis	Rock, Ruby I.	31 May 1929	7/ 301
Bandy, Elmer Earl [W] [Orlando]	Driver, Mae [Orlando]	3 Jan 1925	5/ 508
Bandy, Olie Sherman	Whitmore, Florence Emily	1 Jun 1929	7/ 302
Bankley, Henry E.	Terrill, Emma	4 Aug 1928	7/ 168
Banknight, Adell Jackson	Yates, Margaret	26 Mar 1929	7/ 267
Banks, Caster [Winter Garden]	Evans, Maggie [Winter Garden]	28 Jun 1926	6/ 252
Banks, Elmer Gerard	Ponder, Christine Ada	21 Jun 1931	8/ 23
Bankston, Willie	Munford, Mildred	24 Jan 1931	7/ 547
Barber, Aubrey DeWitt	Price, Louise Ernestine	18 Dec 1932	8/ 244
Barber, John William [Apopka]	Linton, Mary Ellen [Apopka]	22 Dec 1926	6/ 413
Barber, William	MacFarlane, Clara	8 Dec 1932	8/ 226
Barden, Howard Walton	Lowe, Beatrice	17 May 1934	8/ 477
Barfield, Lathan James [Orlando]	McClain, Ruby Pearl [Orlando]	7 Aug 1926	6/ 309
Barham, Leslie LeRoy [Orlando]	Schilling, Jaunita Salina [Orlando]	30 Jun 1926	6/ 292
Barker, Fred Robert	True, Florence	22 Mar 1928	7/ 85
Barkley, Freeman Emerson	Gambrell, Louise	17 Jan 1928	7/ 47
Barks, David Leon [Ocoee]	Childs, Myrtis Voncee [Ocoee]	25 Jun 1927	6/ 529
Barksdale, Charlie	Demps, Carrie	22 Dec 1928	7/ 220
Barlow, Lester Milton	Burns, Beryl Virginia	5 May 1933	8/ 295
Barlow, Ralph Wilson	Howell, Oza Louise	15 Oct 1929	7/ 359
Barnes, Clarence Wilson	Nettles, Maybelle	8 Apr 1934	8/ 459
Barnes, James Alexander [Orlando]	Williams, Abagail [Orlando]	16 Jun 1926	6/ 246
Barnes, John Wm., Jr.	Bordes, Raymond	20 Sep 1927	7/ 16
Barnes, Merlin C.	Wilson, Hildred Lavinia	3 Jul 1931	8/ 27
Barnes, William Shuford	Parham, Lois	19 May 1932	8/ 158
Barnes, William T. Lincoln, Jr.	Southerland, Elizabeth	16 Jun 1934	8/ 495
Barnes, William [Orlando]	Hobson, Inez [Orlando]	27 Feb 1926	6/ 165
Barnett, Willie Rogers	Williams, Leslie Mae	24 Jun 1930	7/ 471
Barnsley, William Henry [Apopka]	Eldredge, Mabel [Apopka]	29 Jul 1926	6/ 295
Barr, George Macdonald	Winslow, Blanche	12 Dec 1932	8/ 227
Barr, Robert Graham	Robinson, Theresa McCain	17 Nov 1933	8/ 371
Barrington, Whitfield	Scott, Lucy	11 Apr 1928	7/ 96
Barron, Arnice E. [W] [Leesburg]	Harris, Grace Lee [Leesburg]	14 Nov 1925	6/ 90
Barry, Edward [W] [Orlando]	Brannan, Mary [Pinecastle]	6 Apr 1925	5/ 554
Barry, Walter X.	Schniddi, Emma Catherine	30 Dec 1930	7/ 536
Barter, Harmond O.	Jennings, Ruby Beatrice	13 Jun 1929	7/ 309
Bartlett, Guy [W] [Jacksonville]	Douglas, Buine [Orlando]	10 Apr 1925	5/ 559
Bartlett, John Albert	Tice, Rose Emma	11 Apr 1932	8/ 140
Bartlett, William H.	Burmeister, Emma	22 Jan 1930	7/ 403
Barton, Bloomer Franklin	Elliott Catherine Clayton	1 Jun 1931	8/ 10
Barton, Elija	Smart, Rossie	11 Feb 1928	7/ 62
Baskin, James	Milton, Leila	1 Dec 1930	7/ 531
Bass, Albert Pope	Cowart, Nellie Mae	3 Mar 1934	8/ 441
Bass, Amos Fletcher	Byrd, Marie	23 Nov 1930	7/ 523
Bass, Hobson B.	Prescott, Jeanette	5 Mar 1929	7/ 257
Bass, James William [W] [Orlando]	Dozen, Lucile	1 Feb 1926	6/ 150
Bass, Stephen [Orlando]	Brown, Willie [Orlando]	22 May 1926	6/ 244
Bass, Walter C. [Kiss]	Rosenberg, Ethel [Orlando]	16 Dec 1926	6/ 408
Bass, William Moseley	Woodburn, Adele	2 Feb 1930	7/ 410

Bassett, Alfred [Orlando]	Crawford, Cathrine [Orlando]	17 Dec 1926	6/ 421
Bassett, Ellwworth Watson	Popoe, Ione Frances	18 Feb 1930	7/ 416
Bassett, Harold Henry	Frost, Emma Margaret	8 May 1933	8/ 292
Bateman, M. F. [Plymouth]	Barks, Willie Mae [Plymouth]	4 Sep 1926	6/ 329
Bates, Charles David	Stephens, Nellie Drew	28 Feb 1933	8/ 263
Bates, Edwin Thomas [Orlando]	Ogden, Virginia Patricia [Orlando]	20 Mar 1926	6/ 190
Bates, James	Pringley, Beatrice	20 Dec 1928	7/ 226
Batey, Sam [Oakland]	Glover, Sallie [Oakland]	11 Feb 1926	6/ 153
Batman, Joseph	Williams, Carrie	19 Jan 1931	7/ 545
Batte, Otto	Adern, Mary Bell	24 Dec 1927	7/ 32
Batten, Calvin Austin	Campbell, Maurine Claire	7 May 1933	8/ 291
Batten, Irvin Evan [Orlando]	Wycke, Martha Camallia	30 Jun 1926	6/ 291
Battie, Tom [B] [Orlando]	Joiner, Udell [Orlando]	28 Feb 1925	5/ 532
Battle Arthur	Wallace, Pinkie	31 May 1931	8/ 9
Battle, Oscar	Banks, Rosa	27 Dec 1933	8/ 397
Battle, Willie	Johnson, Nora	9 Mar 1929	7/ 258
Baughan, Edward Shirley	Teague, Catherine Perritt	4 Oct 1930	7/ 503
Bavar, Max Louie	Wetherbee, Lillian Katherine	1 Oct 1932	8/ 211
Beach, John Lawson	Rouse, Lori Louise	16 Mar 1929	7/ 264
Beach, John Milton	Rosser, Mary Margaret	4 Dec 1933	8/ 380
Beal, Samuel Walter [Sanford]	Vickery, Lourine Ayara [Sanford]	30 Jul 1926	6/ 294
Bean, John Elliot [W] [Apopka]	Whitfield, Eleanor [Apopka]	11 Jul 1925	6/ 16
Bearden, Guy R.	Pugh, Inez Emerita	22 Dec 1929	7/ 388
Beasley, Fred LeRoy	Williams, Mamie	21 Feb 1928	7/ 68
Beasley, Louis [Fort Pierce]	Pollard, Myrtle [Fort Pierce]	19 Sep 1925	6/ 47
Beasley, Richard	William, Ada	23 Feb 1929	7/ 253
Beatty, John Watson [Orlando]	Miller, Bessie Lee [Orlando]	2 Apr 1927	6/ 491
Beatty, William Henry	Jackson, Maxine	4 Nov 1931	8/ 70
Beauford, John	Cherry, Annie	14 Nov 1928	7/ 206
Beaver, Charles Levi	Fish, Lavernie	4 Jan 1933	8/ 237
Becton/Boston, Leon Omega	Langston, Agnes	1 Sep 1928	7/ 181
Beddie, Dock [Eatonville]	Everett, Ella Louise [Eatonville]	5 Jun 1927	6/ 525
BeDoit, Eugene Julius [Orlando]	Ragland, Ruth Francella [Winter Park]	30 Oct 1926	6/ 368
Bedworth, Francis Ernest [W] [Ilion NY]	Minx, Lillian Minta [Orlando]	10 Feb 1925	5/ 526
Beebe, George [Orlando]	Hughes, Lizzie May [Humboldt, TN]	24 Nov 1926	6/ 394
Beebe, Richard Edward	Rounds, Bessie Violet	18 Aug 1931	8/ 42
Beery, Stuart R.	Merrill, Bessie Irene	25 Apr 1931	7/ 590
Begin, Albert	Murray, Levia May	26 Feb 1929	7/ 251
Belcher, Johnnie Lester	Posey, Mamie Thelma	13 Jul 1930	7/ 480
Belin, Fred	Harvey, Alice	27 Jul 1930	7/ 486
Bell, Bennie	Jenkins, Mary	16 Apr 1934	8/ 463
Bell, Clarence [Orlando]	Wilson, Julia [Orlando]	5 Aug 1926	6/ 324
Bell, Clifton [B] [Orlando]	Linton, Amanda [Orlando]	9 Jan 1926	6/ 137
Bell, Emanuel	Green, Sophie	3 Jan 1930	7/ 397
Bell, Ernest	Scott, Ruby Lee	11 May 1932	8/ 156
Bell, Henry [B] [Orlando]	Irvin, Alberta [Orlando]	25 Feb 1925	5/ 531
Bell, Ike Junior	Lockett, Lavound	27 Jun 1934	8/ 500
Bell, J. D.	Kleckley, Marietta	1 Oct 1927	6/ 589
Bell, James [Lockhart]	Downs, Nettie [Lockhart]	20 Aug 1927	6/ 567
Bell, Joel Hartwell	Rewis, Christine Mary	22 Apr 1934	8/ 468
Bell, John	Crockett, Martha Lee	6 Jun 1932	8/ 165
Bell, John Charles	Seller, Leah Myrtle	22 Apr 1929	7/ 282

Bell, John Sheldon	Lamp, Lucille Anna	24 Aug 1930	7/ 490
Bell, Leslie	King, Ada	8 Sep 1927	6/ 578
Bell, Lewis [Orlando]	Corthran, Ruth [Orlando]	22 May 1926	6/ 243
Bell, Nathaniel	Williams, Mary	25 Apr 1934	8/ 468
Bell, Paul Eugene	Hunter, Wilhelmina	20 Oct 1933	8/ 352
Bell, Robert	Tillman, Mamie	16 Jun 1928	7/ 140
Bell, Warren Beagle	Nutt, Ruth Adelle	10 Oct 1927	6/ 592
Bell, Willie	Culpepper, Janie	22 Oct 1933	8/ 353
Belote, Henry Fowler	Bradford, Calla Anna	2 Jan 1932	8/ 98
Belote, William Alton	Mathews, Anne Elizabeth	12 Jun 1933	8/ 324
Belton, David	Nixon, Thelma	25 Apr 1928	7/ 105
Benaman, Oscar	Hill, Margaret Mae	16 Feb 1928	7/ 65
Benbow, John Byron [W] [Orlando]	Burnette, Lovey Raucker [Orlando]	4 Dec 1925	6/ 97
Benbow, Richard P. [W] [Orlando]	Johnston, Virginia [Milton IL]	11 May 1925	5/ 573
Benjamin, Albert [Orlando]	Smith, Ellen [Orlando]	9 Jul 1927	6/ 547
Bennett, James Q.	Bulgar, Katherine	29 Apr 1929	7/ 285
Bennett, Jay Lee	Danforth, Julia Verlon	24 Jun 1933	8/ 316
Bennett, John Robert	Jones, Luvada	5 Dec 1927	7/ 20
Bennett, Lee R.	Futch, Anna Mae	5 Jun 1932	8/ 166
Bennett, Son	Bracy, Queen	25 Mar 1933	8/ 276
Benson, Charlie	Bradley, Laura	7 Oct 1929	7/ 355
Bentley, James LeRoy	Parks, Dora Mae	6 Dec 1927	7/ 22
Berchoefer, Paul Joseph [Plant City]	Perry, Beulah Mizell [Orlando]	5 May 1926	6/ 230
Berg, Mathis [Orlando]	Nelson, Anna C. [Orlando]	11 May 1926	6/ 233
Berkins, Joseph	Ferguson, Gertrude	29 Jun 1929	7/ 316
Bermundy, Joe	Garcis, Encarnasiuon	5 Feb 1928	7/ 60
Berner, Frederick, Garrett, Jr.	Lancy, Evelyn Ross	11 Jan 1930	7/ 398
Berrin, Horace	Comadore, Carrie	19 Jan 1930	7/ 402
Berry, Frank	Kuhn, Carlene Ethel	3 Feb 1934	8/ 423
Bessent, Johnnie Adrant	Parrish, Mary Ona	1 Nov 1931	8/ 68
Bethell, Thomas [B] [Orlando]	Gary, Martha Lee [Orlando]	16 Jul 1925	6/ 18
Bettes, James Jerome [Orlando]	Sligh, Mallie Glasgow [Orlando]	20 Apr 1926	6/ 214
Betts, Archie Lucius	Betts, Mabel Hand	25 Mar 1932	8/ 132
Bickers, Elijah Lang [W] [Orlando]	Wade, Blanche [Orlando]	3 Jan 1925	5/ 506
Bien, Max Robert [Orlando] [lic. 12 May 1926; recorded 17 May 1926]	Jordan, Thelma Jeannette [Orlando]	12 May 1926	6/ 239
Billings, Herman Wesley	Whiteman, Lavonne	13 Jan 1934	8/ 409
Bing, Robert Louis	Toney, Rosa Lee	7 Sep 1932	8/ 196
Birchofsberger, Julius [Orlando]	Wade, Ophilia Thereas [Orlando]	7 Jun 1927	6/ 530
Birdsong, Henry	Marshall, Rosetta	28 Sep 1931	8/ 54
Biro, Anton [Orlando]	Rainwater, Hazel [Orlando]	2 Oct 1926	6/ 352
Bishop, Everett Cecil	Borden, Wilhelmina	13 Feb 1928	7/ 63
Bishop, W. Edward [Orlando]	Wrates, Dorothy E. [Sodus, NY]	6 Sep 1926	6/ 351
Bitzer, Emery West [Tampa]	Hocker, Mary Elizabeth [Ocala]	27 Feb 1927	6/ 466
Bivens, James [B] [Orlando]	Lamar, Annie Louise [Orlando]	27 Jan 1926	6/ 142
Black, Albert	Jordan, Marcedes	29 Aug 1929	7/ 338
Black, Albert Pierce	McNeely, Bessie	4 May 1931	7/ 594
Black, Andrew	Bullard, Ethel	9 Mar 1933	8/ 267
Black, Fred Clyde	Holley, Ruth Marie	21 Jun 1932	8/ 172
Black, John Alexander, Jr.	Shafer, Ola	20 Oct 1928	7/ 200

Blackburn, Rupert Gordon	Watson, Roma Frances	17 May 1934	8/ 477
Blackman, Clinton [B] [Winter Park]	Cogwell, Rosa Lee [Winter Park]	26 May 1925	5/ 580
Blackman, Ernest [B] [Apopka]	McKinzie, Henrietta [Apopka]	9 Mar 1925	5/ 537
Blackshear, Henry [Orlando]	Owens, Ida [Orlando]	23 Oct 1926	6/ 360
Blackwood, Herman Nash	Normandeall, Dorothea Louise	11 Oct 1930	7/ 507
Blain, Marvin Odie [Sanford]	Mosley, Falby [Winter Garden]	14 Jul 1926	6/ 301
Blair, Ellis [Orlando]	Hallman, Elsie [Orlando]	29 Dec 1926	6/ 426
Blair, Fred Johnson	Paul, Cora Helen	28 Jul 1931	8/ 38
Blair, John Henry	McCrae, Ruby Virtle	22 Jun 1930	7/ 470
Blair, Luther Clark	Sharp, Mabel Louise	30 Dec 1933	8/ 399
Blair, Richard	Strickland, Ida	23 Jun 1930	7/ 470
Blair, Willie Edmond [Winter Garden]	Meridith, Vera Gertrude [Winter Garden]	3 Jun 1926	6/ 256
Blakeley, Carey Thomas [W] [Orlando]	Hurkmer, Milderedge Elizabeth [Eustis]	1 Aug 1925	6/ 28
Blalock, J. F., Jr [Orlando]	Lewis, Iris Jewell [Orlando]	26 Jan 1926	6/ 148
Blanchard, Harry M. [Jacksonville]	Mullins, Willie S. [Jacksonville]	8 May 1926	6/ 233
Bland, Allen Eli	Bekemeyer, Nellie Louise	24 Dec 1933	8/ 396
Bland, John	Williams, Lulu	7 Jan 1932	8/ 104
Blanton, Caulie Columbus	Harrell, Janie Elizabeth	25 Aug 1932	8/ 188
Blanton, George Grady [Orlando]	Moore, Tillie [Orlando]	2 Feb 1927	6/ 449
Bleakley, Frank Elbert	Cooper, Maude Leslie	7 Mar 1929	7/ 259
Bledsoe, Gim [W] [Winter Park]	Prevall, Effie [Winter Park]	14 Nov 1925	6/ 83
Bligh, Joseph DeSails [Orlando]	Arnold, Sarah Marguerite [Orlando]	17 Mar 1926	6/ 180
Blocker, Amzie	Evans, Potabelle	24 Nov 1929	7/ 378
Blodgett, Stephen	Iseminger, Myrtle	10 Oct 1930	7/ 515
Bloothworth, Johnney William	Webb, Maudie Pearl	4 Apr 1931	7/ 580
Blount, Archie	Haynes, Mary Magdelene	12 Jan 1933	8/ 244
Blount, Jordan	Wilmore, Maggie Lee	7 Aug 1930	7/ 487
Blue, Harry G.	Mallory, Elizabeth	15 Jun 1929	7/ 311
Blue, John Richards	Stubbs, Marcia	23 Sep 1927	6/ 582
Blunt, Archie	Williams, Sophie	7 Dec 1931	8/ 84
Blunt, David	McLendon, Annie Belle	23 Nov 1929	7/ 375
Blunt, George [Orlando]	Nelson, Elizabeth [Orlando]	1 Apr 1926	6/ 196
Blunt, Nathaniel [B] [Eatonville]	Young, Lettie [Eatonville]	25 Apr 1925	5/ 564
Blunt, Walter Murray	McGee, Elizabeth Walker	6 Mar 1934	8/ 443
Blye, James	Felton, Amelia	14 Feb 1934	8/ 432
Boatright, John	Jaskin, Jessie Mae	17 Oct 1927	6/ 594
Bobo, Charles Clayton	Still, Vallie Estell	13 Jan 1934	8/ 412
Boddy, James E. [W] [Center Hill]	Johnston, Carrie [Winter Garden]	14 Jan 1925	5/ 512
Boettcher, Justus George	Graham, Rosella Cecilia	18 Nov 1929	7/ 374
Boger, Ernest Page [Winter Park]	Frison, Rosa Marie [Winter Park]	14 Jun 1926	6/ 268
Boggs, Ralph Thomas	Bolkler, Mary Etta	16 Jan 1928	7/ 51
Bohlmann, Emil Frederick	Mills, Lillian Lorraine	16 Jun 1934	8/ 495
Boles, Dan [B] [Orlando]	Strickland, Isabel [Orlando]	21 Dec 1925	6/ 109
Boles, William Lester	Livingston, Annie Merle	24 Dec 1927	7/ 33
Bond, Perry Ethan	Tanner, Mary Louise	8 Jan 1933	8/ 246
Bonnichsen, Leo Wilfred	Speer, Shirley Irene	21 Nov 1931	8/ 77
Book, Morris Butler	Brannon, Connie Elizabeth	24 Jan 1932	8/ 107
Boone, Eugene Minchew [Orlando]	Eck, Olive Victoria	4 Jun 1927	6/ 531
Booth, Charles Edgar	Millard, Bessie Lila	21 Nov 1932	8/ 223
Booth, Joel R.	Mishow, Maggie	2 Mar 1931	7/ 562
Booth, Leady	Darden, Allie Mae	29 Jun 1933	8/ 323
Booth, Melvin Wilson	Berg, Virginia Lee	18 Feb 1931	7/ 558

Boothe, Hilton Lewis	Carey, Frances Kerchebal	24 May 1933	8/ 308
Borden, Ira C. [W] [Lewiston, IL]	Desmond, Mildred [Lewiston, IL]	6 Nov 1925	6/ 76
Borgard, Hazel Clyde	Joiner, Mildred Inez	18 Apr 1931	7/ 583
Borgeau, Joseph Patrick	Gilbert, Agatha Mae	24 Jun 1931	8/ 24
Bostic, Clarence	Smith, Josephine	1 Apr 1930	7/ 434
Boston, Rufus Braxton [Orlando]	Macon, Lovie Lee [Orlando]	19 Feb 1926	6/ 164
Botsford, H. Gordon [W] [Orlando]	Hinson, Gladys [Orlando]	4 Apr 1925	5/ 553
Bouldin, Donald Lee	Kemp, Daisie	31 Dec 1928	7/ 225
Bourgeau, Emile [Orlando]	Katz, Juanita [Orlando]	9 Jun 1927	6/ 534
Bourne, Harold	DuPree, Elizabeth Henry	17 Mar 1933	8/ 274
Bowden, Bryant	Gary, Margaret	24 Jan 1930	7/ 404
Bowen, Charles E.	Van Duzor, Gertrude P.	1 May 1929	7/ 300
Bowen, Louis Richard	Sadler, Myra	10 Aug 1934	8/ 522
Bower, Dallas	Jenson, Lillian	1 Sep 1928	7/ 183
Bowling, Ernest Preston [W] [Plymouth]	Jones, Clarissia [Plymouth]	23 Dec 1925	6/ 115
Bowling, Robert	Portner, Alice	19 Aug 1931	8/ 42
Bowman, Edison	Scott, Mable	29 Apr 1933	8/ 288
Bowman, Lucius [Orlando]	Gibson, Clara Estella [Orlando]	22 Mar 1927	6/ 485
Bowman, William	Smith, Gussie	13 Mar 1930	7/ 429
Bowron, Leonard Milton	Lee, Alta Lucile	20 Dec 1932	8/ 231
Box, Henry	Faircloth, Johnnie	28 Oct 1929	7/ 363
Boyce, James [W] [Apopka]	Lynch, Lorena [Apopka]	16 Jun 1925	6/ 7
Boyd, Harold Audrey [Fayetteville, AR]	Gandy, Sarah Louise [Taft]	2 Jul 1926	6/ 303
Boyd, James	Stokes, Nettie Lee	27 May 1929	7/ 298
Boyd, Osborn	Morgan, Idella	2 Mar 1929	7/ 255
Boyd, William	Anderson, Lillie Mae	3 Mar 1928	7/ 74
Boyer, William Heckman [Miami]	Adams, Helen [Travers]	12 Aug 1927	6/ 563
Boykin, Clyde Byron	Jamison, Molly Lorraine	17 Apr 1934	8/ 464
Boykin, Ernest R.	Young, Sophia	26 Dec 1931	8/ 98
Boylen, Herbert Tandy	Walker, Mabelle Love	10 May 1929	7/ 294
Bozarth, Ralph Edward	Keck, Jessie Evelyn	11 Jun 1930	7/ 464
Brack, Arlie [Orlando]	Eagerton, Jennie [Orlando]	20 Aug 1925	6/ 40
Braddy, Julian H. [Orlando]	Dickerson, Elear [Columbus, OH]	2 Oct 1925	6/ 55
Bradford, Jesse Lavert [W] [Winter Garden]	Green, Gertrude Odessa [Winter Garden]	2 Jun 1925	5/ 585
Bradley, Felix	Golding, Beatice	11 Dec 1927	7/ 24
Bradley, Frank Eugene [W] [Sanford]	Echols, Pauline [Apopka]	1 Feb 1926	6/ 146
Bradley, Julius	Evans, Gertrude	18 Jun 1928	7/ 141
Bradley, William	Polen, Lizzie	7 Nov 1932	8/ 215
Bradwell, Sam	Murray, Mattie Lou	13 May 1929	7/ 293
Bramble, Willard Lee	McFarland, Florence Isabel	28 Mar 1933	8/ 278
Branch, Charles Washington	Jones, Charlotte	4 Sep 1931	8/ 46
Branch, John Lawrence [Plant City]	Boyette, Edrie Hazel [Tampa]	19 Jun 1926	6/ 281
Branch, Wesley	Baines, Emma Jane	8 Feb 1931	7/ 553
Branch, Will	Minor, Vassie Lee	15 Apr 1932	8/ 142
Brand, Alva	Webb, Mavis	5 Mar 1934	8/ 442
Branham, Leiper Gerhard [Orlando]	McDonough, Alice Pearl [Orlando]	16 Aug 1927	6/ 567
Brannin, Roy Curtis	Roach, Lynda Ford	1 Apr 1932	8/ 139
Brannon, Thomas Perry [Orlando]	Lott, Ethel Enola [Orlando]	6 Sep 1926	6/ 332
Brantley, James Oral	Brantley, Mary Blanche	30 Jun 1928	7/ 152
Brasnahan, Harry W. [Orlando]	Alfred, Mary C. [Orlando]	3 Dec 1926	6/ 397

Brass, Basil Franklin [W] [Daytona]	Hines, Louise Tucker [Orlando]	7 Mar 1925	5/ 536
Brauche, Millard Lancelot	Orteen, Vera	7 Mar 1928	7/ 78
Brawdy, Irvin	Oliver, Leona	18 Mar 1928	7/ 84
Brawley, John McKenzie	Hayes, Rena Mae	15 Nov 1927	7/ 12
Bray, Patrick	Broom, Lillian Rogers	26 Oct 1932	8/ 208
Brazell, Eugene	Smith, Estella	30 Oct 1933	8/ 358
Brennan, Thomas J.	McKnight, Mary Lucille Kennaday	7 Aug 1934	8/ 519
Brennan, Thomas Joseph	Eastman, Kit Mae	12 Jun 1930	7/ 465
Brewer, Harry Roger [Guilford, CT]	Stone, Lillian Estelle [Winter Park]	25 Dec 1926	6/ 422
Brewer, Joseph Greeley [W] [Orlando]	Laycock, Edith [Jacksonville]	11 Jun 1925	5/ 588
Brewer, Willie Lee	Jones, Lillie	20 Jan 1931	7/ 564
Brewington, James [Plant City]	Mathews, Rachel [Plant City]	9 Jun 1927	6/ 527
Brewington, Joe	Peterson, Gladys	6 Nov 1933	8/ 360
Brewton, Fred Douglas	Smith, Annie Mae	8 Sep 1930	7/ 495
Brice, Marshall [B] [Bridgeport, CT]	Mallory, Lillie [Columbus, GA]	7 Dec 1925	6/ 97
Bridges, Claude	Solomon, Nora	25 Mar 1928	7/ 88
Bridges, Edward I.	Cranshaw, Margaret C.	29 Mar 1930	7/ 464
Brierley, Vincent [Windermere]	Armstrong, Edna [Windemere]	22 Dec 1926	6/ 416
Briethaupt, Chas. Jefferson [W] [Montgomery AL]	Landers, Emilie [Orlando]	24 Dec 1925	6/ 118
Briggs, Randall [Winter Garden]	Green, Rhoda [Winter Garden]	17 May 1926	6/ 236
Bright, Willie [B] [Orlando]	Donaldson, Marie [Orlando]	21 Dec 1925	6/ 108
Brightwell, Ted	Richardson, Regie	29 Sep 1930	7/ 500
Briley, Homer Griffith	Mason, Harriet Elizabeth	11 Jul 1931	8/ 33
Brinamon, Theron Grant	Graham, Virginia Lee	3 Jun 1929	7/ 301
Brinkley, George Persal	Hardy, Irma Alfreda	12 Jan 1932	8/ 103
Brinson, William [Orlando]	Grathers, Janie Belle [Orlando]	1 Sep 1926	6/ 328
Britt, Edgar Hollis	Parker, Martha Annie	7 Nov 1931	8/ 71
Britt, James Curtis	Pope, Irene	15 Feb 1930	7/ 416
Britt, James Henry	Brown, Victoria	7 Dec 1927	7/ 20
Britt, James Henry	Boone, Geneva	30 Jul 1933	8/ 331
Britt, W. F. [W] [Orlando]	Rogers, Agnes [Orlando]	28 Jul 1925	6/ 26
Britt, Willard Neal	Rines, Elizabeth	23 Aug 1930	7/ 490
Britt, Willis Buren [W] [Ocoee]	Hurst, Effie [Ocoee]	20 Jun 1925	6/
Broadwater, Roy	Schmitt, Katie	11 May 1931	8/ 1
Broadwell, Willis Hampton	Brooks, Pearl McDaniel	5 Nov 1927	7/ 8
Brock, Gregory Lee [Sanford]	Dieterich, Gladys Tone [Sanford]	9 Jon 1926	6/ 266
Brockman, Holmes Gardner	Wetherbee, Ethel Muriel	1 May 1933	8/ 297
Brocksmith, Frederick William	Drawdy, Victoria	18 Nov 1933	8/ 368
Bronson, George	Fields, Sarah	19 Nov 1928	7/ 217
Bronson, John Nathan [Orlando]	Gaynor, Mary [Orlando]	1 Sep 1926	6/ 326
Bronson, Leonard Cox	Myers, Gladys Lucile	19 Jul 1931	8/ 34
Brook, Basil Henry	Poquette, Mary Jane	7 Jun 1934	8/ 489
Brooker, James Withers	Bollinger, Agnes Beatrice	27 Dec 1928	7/ 224
Brookins, Stanley Clifford	Lawrence, Ida	16 May 1930	7/ 455
Brooks, Alto [B] [Orlando]	Standmire, Clare [Orlando]	4 Jul 1925	6/ 13
Brooks, Arthur Washington [Atlanta, GA]	Smith, Elsie Louise [Orlando]	6 Jul 1927	6/ 551
Brooks, Earl John	Dunford, Alma	5 Apr 1934	8/ 455
Brooks, George	Anderson, Lillie Mae	16 Jul 1930	7/ 480
Brooks, James Sherwood [Griffin, GA]	Towns, Rosalie [Griffin, GA]	30 Dec 1926	6/ 423
Brooks, LeRoy	Tyson, Maud	9 Dec 1933	8/ 382
Brooks, Mack	Bailey, Eva	22 Jun 1932	8/ 173

Brooks, Mose [B] [Orlando]	Blackshear, Ida [Orlando] [lic. says Mattie Green]	1 Feb 1926	6/ 144
Brooks, Nela [Orlando]	Emmons, Earnestine [Orlando]	1 Dec 1926	6/ 396
Brooks, Rezo	Rexford, Bertha Gertrude	20 May 1933	8/ 300
Brooks, Richard	Redding, Alberta	2 Jul 1932	8/ 175
Brooks, Sam John	McNish, Gussie Mae	31 May 1933	8/ 308
Broughman, Russell	Jackson, Minnie Bosick	15 Feb 1930	7/ 414
Browder, Cledis [Winter Garden]	Blair, Russell [Winter Garden]	24 Apr 1926	6/ 218
Brown, Amory Loring [Orlando]	Nelson, Buelah Burchette	12 Sep 1926	6/ 337
Brown, Amos	Taylor, Cora	20 Nov 1927	7/ 16
Brown, Andrew	Hines, Beulah	19 Apr 1928	7/ 100
Brown, Arthur	Kennedy, Celia	19 May 1928	7/ 115
Brown, Ben [Maitland]	Williams, Mattie [Maitland]	19 Sep 1925	6/ 48
Brown, Bishop [Orlando]	Patterson, May Belle [Orlando]	16 Aug 1926	6/ 307
Brown, Carey	Stewart, Ernestine	16 Apr 1929	7/ 279
Brown, Charlie	McCoy, Ruth	28 Jul 1928	7/ 167
Brown, Charlie	Kelley, Alica	25 Oct 1930	7/ 513
Brown, Chesley [Orlando]	Wilson, Ruby [Orlando]	30 Oct 1926	6/ 369
Brown, Chester A. [Orlando]	Dukart, Alice [Orlando]	26 Feb 1927	6/ 466
Brown, David	Fitz, Seppie	7 Apr 1931	7/ 575
Brown, David [Orlando]	Scruggs, Charlotte [Orlando]	23 May 1927	6/ 514
Brown, Dewey	Randolph, Jessie	23 Oct 1930	7/ 515
Brown, Edward	Boyd, E. Maggie	14 Jun 1928	7/ 140
Brown, Elmo G. [Winter Garden]	Warren, Catherine	24 Dec 1926	6/ 416
Brown, Elmore	Jones, Genie Lue	22 Nov 1927	7/ 15
Brown, Else	Huffman, Minnie	10 Oct 1930	7/ 505
Brown, Elsie	Maultsby, Annie	3 Aug 1929	7/ 328
Brown, Fletcher	Lockhard, Sophie	21 Jul 1928	7/ 163
Brown, Frank	Wallace, Belle	18 Nov 1933	8/ 371
Brown, Frank	Morgan, Loraine	6 Feb 1932	8/ 135
Brown, Frank Milton [Sanford]	Woods, Adele Elizabeth [Sanford]	2 Apr 1926	6/ 200
Brown, George	Harris, Charlotte	27 Feb 1933	8/ 262
Brown, George [Altamonte Springs]	Smith, Julia [Altamonte Springs]	5 Jun 1926	6/ 258
Brown, Hardy Lee	Wright, Madeline	3 Mar 1933	8/ 271
Brown, Hardy Lee	Harris, Annie Lee	11 Jun 1928	7/ 137
Brown, Harley Colbuth [W] [Orlando]	Foss, Marian Abbie [Orlando]	23 Jul 1925	6/ 26
Brown, Harry [W] [Lakeland]	Conoley, Mary D. [Orlando]	13 Jun 1925	5/ 588
Brown, Henry	Parrish, Clara May	10 Feb 1932	8/ 114
Brown, Henry	Daniels, Aline	15 Jan 1930	7/ 399
Brown, Henry [Orlando]	Willis, Mattie [Orlando]	12 Feb 1927	6/ 455
Brown, Herbert	Anderson, Leola	11 Jun 1928	7/ 135
Brown, J. W.	Grier, Mamie	1 Jun 1929	7/ 304
Brown, James	Leorn, Elizabeth	12 Mar 1934	8/ 450
Brown, James [Orlando]	Lockett, Rosa [Orlando]	8 Apr 1927	6/ 489
Brown, James [Orlando]	Patten, Ruthanna [Orlando]	31 Aug 1926	6/ 325
Brown, James [Tampa]	Clutts, Alice [Clermont]	18 Oct 1925	6/ 74
Brown, James A. [W] [Maitland]	Martin, Edna [Maitland]	6 Jun 1925	5/ 597
Brown, James Allen, Jr.	Cheek, Josephine Alice	2 Mar 1933	8/ 264
Brown, James Lawrence	Richmond, Althea Irene	20 Mar 1930	7/ 430
Brown, James Lester	Harrison, Clara Pauline	7 Aug 1932	8/ 182

11

Brown, Jim [Orlando]	Fort, Elmira [Orlando]	30 May 1926	6/ 248
Brown, Joe [Orlando]	Levitt, Winnie Belle [Orlando]	12 Feb 1926	6/ 187
Brown, John	Morgan, Mary	9 Nov 1927	7/ 9
Brown, John William	Hall, Myrtle	8 Jun 1934	8/ 490
Brown, Joseph	Jackson, Ellen Vida	30 May 1932	8/ 162
Brown, Joseph [B] [Orlando] [gives address]	Smith, Lela [Orlando] [gives address]	21 Nov 1925	6/ 87
Brown, Joseph [B] [Taft]	Straughter, Rosa Etta [Taft]	14 Dec 1925	6/ 100
Brown, Keneth	Leavatt, Ida Mae	2 Mar 1929	7/ 255
Brown, Lee	Baker, Fannie	31 Oct 1927	7/ 4
Brown, Leslie [Winter Park]	Lucas, Adele [Winter Park]	13 Dec 1926	6/ 413
Brown, Lester	Williams, Lillian	28 Sep 1929	7/ 350
Brown, Lewis [W] [Orlando]	Jackson, Maggie [Orlando]	11 Apr 1925	5/ 558
Brown, Orville Runals [W] [Winter Garden]	Flowers, Trudie [Winter Garden]	19 May 1925	5/ 575
Brown, Oscar	Wright, Teretha	14 Nov 1931	8/ 74
Brown, Pearlie	Brown, Lola Easter	30 Sep 1929	7/ 351
Brown, Ridgely Rhodes [Orlando]	Brown, Mary Louise	27 Aug 1927	6/ 579
Brown, Robert Albert	Samuel, Vivian Emily	2 Nov 1931	8/ 69
Brown, Robert Boyd [Columbia, SC]	Phillips, Viola [Orlando]	7 Jun 1927	6/ 550
Brown, Robert Vance [Asheville, NC]	Hitchcock, Ethel Jean [Dvenport,IA]	5 Feb 1927	6/ 454
Brown, Robert Wm. [Orlando]	Bankston, Susie [Orlando]	1 May 1926	6/ 224
Brown, Roscoe	Irving, Armetta	10 Feb 1929	7/ 243
Brown, Roscoe	Marshall, Ruth	18 Mar 1933	8/ 271
Brown, Rufus [Orlando]	Woodley, Mattie [Orlando]	21 Apr 1926	6/ 206
Brown, Sam	Barrett, Sarah	10 Dec 1928	7/ 214
Brown, Samuel Henry [W] [Shelbyville KY]	Moorman, Luada/Louada [Maitland	22 Apr 1925	5/ 564
Brown, Sherman	Lloyd, Phylis	1 Dec 1929	7/ 379
Brown, Sidney [Orlando]	Payne, Francis [Orlando]	27 Mar 1926	6/ 191
Brown, Sydney [Orlando]	Walden, Mollie [Orlando]	12 May 1927	6/ 506
Brown, Thomas Lloyd	Quattlebaum, Jane Ann	20 May 1933	8/ 301
Brown, Will	Reed, Princell	11 Sep 1933	8/ 346
Brown, Will [Orlando]	Taylor, Lon [Orlando]	17 Oct 1925	6/ 67
Brown, William	Williams, Daisey	20 Jun 1931	8/ 23
Brown, William	Brown, Willie Mae	16 Jan 1934	8/ 413
Brown, William [Ft.Meyers]	Vandergriff, Tempy	5 Jan 1927	6/ 429
Brown, William [Orlando]	May, Mary L. [Orlando]	29 May 1926	6/ 248
Brown, William A.	Green, Mary E.	29 Sep 1927	6/ 588
Brown, William Andrew [Orlando]	Howard, Thelma Blanche [Baltimore, MD]	16 May 1927	6/ 507
Brown, William Henry [Oviedo]	Shuman, Nannie Mae	18 May 1926	6/ 240
Brown, Willie	Woosley, Mamie	12 Jan 1929	7/ 229
Brown, Yancey	Turner, Marie Catherine	23 Dec 1931	8/ 92
Browning, Eddie [Plant City]	Cliborn, Leora [Plant City]	14 Oct 1926	6/ 353
Browning, James Troy [Haynesville]	Striplin, Sara Ruth [Orlando]	30 Jun 1927	6/ 545
Brubaker, James Donald	DeWitt, Pauline	11 Feb 1931	7/ 555
Bruenson, Walter Leslie [Orlando]	Lott, Frances [Sanford]	14 Jan 1927	6/ 439
Brumbaugh, Russell Ewing	Hutchins, Helene Irene	23 Jul 1933	8/ 329
Brumberg, Fred Guthrie	Wilson, Eleanor Marie	28 Dec 1932	8/ 347
Bruner, Thomas Heyward	Russell, Gladys Elenor	23 Jun 1934	8/ 501
Brunner, Lens [Kissimmee]	Johnson, Jennie May [Orlando]	6 Sep 1925	6/ 53
Brunson, Will	Johnson, Anna	1 Mar 1933	8/ 264
Bruton, Carl C. [Sanford]	Knight, Ruth [Lake Monroe]	31 Aug 1927	6/ 571
Bruton, Edward Rupert	Still, Margaret Elouise	24 May 1928	7/ 119
Bruton, Fred	Jenkins, Senora	12 Dec 1928	7/ 215

Bruton, Richard	Potter, Essie Will	12 May 1928	7/ 124
Bryan, Edward Joseph	Brown, Myrthe Gloria	26 Oct 1930	7/ 514
Bryan, Paul William	Holcomb, Opal	19 Oct 1929	7/ 365
Bryant, Charley	Scrivan, Cora Lee	2 Oct 1930	7/ 502
Bryant, Isaiah	Sipp, Ethel Mae	15 Mar 1931	7/ 570
Bryant, LeRoy	Chester, Queenie	2 Nov 1929	7/ 364
Bryant, Leroy	Calhoun, Mattie Lou	29 Jan 1934	8/ 419
Bryant, Lewis Benjamine [Winter Park]	Smith, Lula [Winter Park]	12 Nov 1926	6/ 383
Bryant, Marshall	Hunter, Bertha	22 Oct 1932	8/ 207
Bryant, Robert	Goolsby, Velma	5 Dec 1930	7/ 527
Bryant, Robert James	Ellis, Dorothy Edna	8 Feb 1933	8/ 256
Bryant, Thomas Archer	Stanfill, Ola Ida	7 Sep 1931	8/ 47
Bryant, Tip	Tice, Delorise	19 May 1934	8/ 479
Bryars, William Alfred	Chestang, Nancy Evelyn	9 Nov 1931	8/ 72
Bryce, Robert Earle	Reynolds, Cecile Lillian	9 Jan 1934	8/ 407
Buchan, Arthur Ralph	Anderson, Anna Belle	18 Apr 1928	7/ 104
Buchan, Elliott Cole	Helms, Lillie	25 Nov 1931	8/ 83
Buchan, Homer Lee [Orlando]	Horn, Vivian O'Resse [Orlando]	18 Jul 1926	6/ 297
Buchan, Jack Simpson	Shutz, Laura Edna May	14 Dec 1931	8/ 87
Buchanan, Duncan [Conway Road, Orlando]	Exum, Mittie [Orlando]	16 Oct 1926	6/ 354
Buchanan, Howard [Orlando]	Tice, Jonnie Mae [Orlando]	8 Mar 1926	6/ 171
Buchanan, Leslie Worby	Miller, Grace Elizabeth	1 May 1929	7/ 286
Buchanan, Oliver E. [W] [Orlando]	Johnson, Ellen [Orlando]	22 Mar 1925	5/ 546
Buchanan, Oscar	Forte, Lena	12 Feb 1929	7/ 244
Buckler, Jessie James [B] [Winter Park]	Blackman, Lucille [Winter Park]	21 Dec 1925	6/ 108
Buckner, Roy Nelson	Aymard, Abbie Viola	22 Sep 1927	6/ 583
Budowski, Johnny Antony	Redding, Eva Mae	9 Jan 1928	7/ 42
Buffington, Clifford D. [Winter Garden]	Kilgor, Clyde [Winter Garden]	12 Feb 1927	6/ 454
Bufford, Howard	Hills, Rosa Lee	30 Jun 1934	8/ 504
Bufort, Manual	Brinson, Mattie	12 Jun 1932	8/ 170
Bugg, Eugene Jeanings	Radford, Maribel	4 Aug 1928	7/ 170
Bujac, Etinne deVellissier, Jr [Carlsbad ,NM]	Smith, Grace Mary Mather [Oakland]	31 Dec 1926	6/ 427
Bullingham, James Norman	Busbee, Missouri Elizabeth	2 May 1931	7/ 595
Bundy, Donald Davis [Orlando]	Prosser, Tulsa Isabelle [Orlando]	23 Nov 1926	6/ 390
Burch, Arthur Eugene, Jr. [St. Petersburg]	Oviatt, Dorothy Nell [Kansas City, MO]	30 Jun 1926	6/ 300
Burchfield, Coleman	Lunn, Ethel Agnes	27 May 1933	8/ 305
Burdick, Frank Cortez	Gardner, Olive Mae	5 Apr 1934	8/ 455
Burdick, Mauarice Dudley [Orlando]	Smith, Ruth Dorcan [Orlando]	24 Dec 1926	6/ 422
Burke, Clarence Wilmer	Elliott, Eva	10 Feb 1934	8/ 426
Burke, Joseph Willis [Orlando]	Stotler, Mary Ella [Orlando]	20 May 1926	6/ 243
Burkett, George Mathew [Orlando]	Rone, Lorene [Orlando]	23 Jun 1927	6/ 528
Burkette, William Horatio [Tampa]	Duncan, Ernestine [Sanford]	14 Oct 1926	6/ 358
Burkhalter, Ikie	Waters, Christine	8 Jan 1933	8/ 241
Burley, Joseph Nathaniel	Jackson, Josephine Louise	28 Oct 1933	8/ 356
Burlingham, Holland Yates	Casity, Myrtle Mae	18 Mar 1933	8/ 271
Burn, Frank Randall [Orlando]	Raiford, Howell Lodell/Ladel [Orlando]	1 May 1926	6/ 225
Burnap, Howard Milton	Downs, Ruby	30 Oct 1929	7/ 363
Burnett, Mostyn Clyde	Smith, Bertha	14 Jan 1933	8/ 247
Burney, Robert Thedoe [B] [Orlando]	Adams, Louie [Orlando]	18 Nov 1925	6/ 85
Burns, Edward Matthew	Marlor, Mary Belle	20 Nov 1929	7/ 374

Burns, Frederick Robert [W] [Orlando]	Sullivan, Beuhal Ethelyn [Orlando]	20 Jul 1925	6/ 21
Burns, John F.	William, Dorothy Louise	3 Sep 1928	7/ 180
Burns, Joseph Eugene	Macy, Myrtle	2 May 1928	7/ 110
Burnsed, Harold Dickson	White, Juliet	23 Apr 1932	8/ 147
Burnsed, Henry	Boddy, Lillie Mae	27 Jul 1928	7/ 165
Burnsed, Peter Everett	Thompson, Marjorie Marie	30 Apr 1932	8/ 149
Burnsed, Robert Carl	Barks, Myrtice	18 May 1929	7/ 295
Burrell, John Franklin	Miller, Rosetta	19 Sep 1932	8/ 197
Burroughs, Mervin	Tyson, Ruby	18 Nov 1933	8/ 369
Burrows, Felix Arthur	Gaskin, Laura Ethel	14 Dec 1932	8/ 229
Burton, Horace Franklin	Wall, Della Ernestine	21 Jun 1928	7/ 146
Burton, Jimmie [Orlando]	Harvey, Deelpha [Orlando]	5 Feb 1927	6/ 458
Busbee, Woodrow	Helms, Eunie Vae	2 Feb 1934	8/ 421
Busch, Lonnie Clarence [Orlando]	Byrd, Louise Agnes [Orlando]	2 May 1927	6/ 499
Bush, John Thomas [W] [Wauchula]	Smith, Alice Rebecca [Bushnell]	16 Jul 1925	6/ 18
Buskirk, George Abrham	Mathews, Josie Peters	15 Mar 1931	7/ 569
Buson, Harvey H. [Winter Park]	Wilkes, Elizabeth [Winter Park]	21 Aug 1927	6/ 568
Bussell, Elvin Thomas	Gemeinhardt, Elizabeth	1 Mar 1934	8/ 439
Butler, Burrell [Orlando]	Taylor, Addie Lou [Orlando]	24 Feb 1927	6/ 471
Butler, Charlie	Daniels, Johnnie Mae	19 Jun 1930	7/ 469
Butler, Ed	Mayo, Jeanette	2 Oct 1929	7/ 353
Butler, Eddie	Lewis, Marie	29 Apr 1934	8/ 470
Butler, Eddie Westly Williams [B] [Winter Garden]	Hayward, Florence M. [Apopka]	23 Dec 1925	6/ 112
Butler, John Albert [Orlando]	Ludlam, Marion Stewart [Orlando]	22 Jan 1927	6/ 446
Butler, Matthew	Rowe, Mauric	13 Oct 1928	7/ 196
Butler, Paul	Reed, Melvin	11 Apr 1931	7/ 578
Butler, Pierce	Robinson, Minnie	18 Jan 1930	7/ 400
Butler, Robert William [Dr]	Stowe, Minnie Riley	29 Apr 1931	7/ 588
Butler, Roy [Orlando]	Chupp, Bessie [Orlando]	12 May 1926	6/ 234
Butler, Wayman	Jordan, Allie May	17 DEc 1927	7/ 27
Butler, Willie [B] [Atlanta, GA]	Myers, Hattie [Moultrie, GA]	23 Mar 1925	5/ 546
Butler, Noble [Orlando]	Bailey, Eleanor [Orlando]	16 May 1927	6/ 509
Butterfield, Lawrence D. [Orlando]	Lamb, Sue Doloris [Orlando]	19 May 1927	6/ 513
Butterfield, Lawrence Delmont	Lamb, Sue	23 Jun 1931	8/ 23
Buttner, James [Winter Park]	Jones, Pauline [Winter Park]	12 Apr 1926	6/ 207
Butts, Charles Shannon	Hickman, Vera Elberta	11 Sep 1928	7/ 187
Butts, Fletcher Castleman	Barton, Nina	17 Dec 1931	8/ 88
Butts, Fred D. [B] [Orlando]	Butts, Marie [Orlando]	3 Mar 1925	5/ 534
Butts, Jim Mack [DeLand]	Bly, Neva Mae [DeLand]	12 Jul 1927	6/ 549
Butts, Owen Merritt	Stough, Juanita Agnes	3 May 1934	8/ 473
Butts, Terrie Howell [W] [Orlando]	Lawson, Dez Lee [Orlando]	3 Jun 1925	5/ 593
Buzzard, Armus Charles [W] [Orlando]	Smith, Agetta Dora [Orlando]	2 Jan 1926	6/ 126
Byanes, Daniel J.	Mann, Evelyn E.	17 Sep 1927	6/ 582
Byington, James Augustus	Mowme, Janice Harlow	15 Sep 1927	6/ 581
Byland, George Alonzo	Walker, Mildred Pauline	3 Jun 1932	8/ 166
Byrd, Dan W.	Beatty, Mary	22 Feb 1930	7/ 418
Byrd, Henry	Jackson, Kattie Belle	27 Mar 1931	7/ 572
Byrd, John Malcolm [Maitland]	Connor, Lucy Belle [Maitland]	19 Oct 1926	6/ 357
Byrd, Johnny [Orlando]	Wilson, Beatrice [Orlando]	28 Jun 1926	6/ 251
Byrd, Jonnie Calloway	Woodard, Mettie Adeline	30 Jun 1932	8/ 181
Byrd, Noah E. [W] [Arcadia]	Daniels, Ilah Cuni [Maitland]	28 Jun 1925	6/ 8

Byrd, Roy Edgar	Quates, Lettie Geraldine	23 Dec 1932	8/ 232
Byrd, Theodore	Anderson, Ruth	26 May 1928	7/ 121
Byron, Horace [Winter Garden]	Quigley, Leona [Winter Garden]	29 Apr 1927	6/ 507

C

Cade, Ben [Orlando]	Heard, Clara Julia [Orlando]	30 Oct 1926	6/ 370
Cadman, Philip Biddle	Huffer, Ellen Rowena	1 Jun 1931	8/ 15
Cadwell, Walter Harsen	Brinson, Mary Frances	7 Apr 1934	8/ 461
Caesar, Lem Julius	Lampkins, Alma	3 Mar 1931	7/ 563
Cahill, John Robert	Grelow, Florence Ruth	8 Sep 1927	6/ 578
Cahill, William Joseph	Grainge, Elsie	27 Jun 1930	7/ 475
Cail, Gentry	Berry, Belle	25 Oct 1930	7/ 513
Cain, Willie Eston	Jones, Mary Remer	21 Dec 1932	8/ 234
Calden, Edward	Peterson, Annie Belle	6 Jul 1930	7/ 476
Caldwell, Elmer Earl	Madden, Mabel Elizabeth	25 Jun 1928	7/ 149
Caldwell, Hubert Robert	Sightler, Nell	4 Feb 1928	7/ 59
Caldwell, James	Robinson, Leola	8 Jun 1933	8/ 311
Caldwell, John Clark	Moore, Edythe Wilma	5 Jul 1930	7/ 479
Calhoun, Hugh Foster	Pellam, Rachel	1 Jul 1934	8/ 505
Calhoun, Luther Daniel	Wise, Marie Julia	23 Mar 1933	8/ 275
Calhoun, Victor Love	Sweat, Lola Jeanette	19 Oct 1929	7/ 359
Calkins, Clifford Benton [W] [St Cloud]	Backes, Emma Louise [St Cloud]	26 Jun 1925	6/ 4
Calkins, Stanley Willis	Bargeron, Helen Clyde	8 Apr 1933	8/ 281
Call, Caleb Onesimus	Mixon, Mollie	26 Apr 1930	7/ 445
Callaway, Thomas Harold	Newman, Edna Earle	1 May 1933	8/ 293
Callin, John Norman	Harpster, Ruth Fraes	29 Jul 1933	8/ 330
Calvin, William John	Cox, Florence Elizabeth	7 Jan 1934	8/ 405
Cameron, Richard James	Henderson, Ruth Catherine	18 Jun 1931	8/ 20
Camp, Frances Hill	Hampton, Marilee Lockhart	26 Apr 1930	7/ 445
Camp, Fred R. [W] [Atlanta, GA]	Tunderberk, Ethel [Columbus, GA]	23 Dec 1925	6/ 115
Campbell, Barney	Geathers, Janie Belle	9 Sep 1933	8/ 341
Campbell, Charles [Jacksonville]	Richter, Florence (Brooklyn, NY)	14 Jan 1927	6/ 437
Campbell, Charles William, Jr [W] [Huntington WV]	Bronson, Lillian R. [Orlando]	18 Jan 1926	6/ 140
Campbell, James Arthur	Peek, Elsie	20 Feb 1929	7/ 250
Campbell, James Arthur, Jr [W] [Orlando]	Smith, Dessie Owens [Orlando]	31 Dec 1925	6/ 126
Campbell, Paul Melville	Wheeler, Florence Isabelle	7 Jun 1931	8/ 15
Campbell, Paul Oliver [Middlesboro, KY]	Morrison, Elizabeth Pearl [Clemont]	18 Jul 1927	6/ 553
Campbell, Reuben [B] [Orlando]	Cunningham, Rachael [Orlando]	31 Dec 1925	6/ 123
Campbell, Solly [Ocoee]	Smith, Rosie [Ocoee]	15 Mar 1927	6/ 473
Campbell, William Robert	Staiger, Edith D.	17 Sep 1927	6/ 582
Campos, Frank Oreiro	King, Gladys Vera	3 Feb 1934	8/ 422
Canady, Arthur	Streetman, Nell	12 May 1932	8/ 154
Candle, Jesse Carl [Orlando]	Twell, Clara Gladys [Orlando]	1 Jan 1927	6/ 432
Cannada, Henry Allen [Bithlo]	Crosby, Lillie Belle [Bithlo]	2 Jul 1926	6/ 284
Cannon, Edwin Eugene	Farley, Jane Gray	17 May 1934	8/ 478
Cannon, Joseph Sumter	Weir, Vivian Adele	14 Jun 1928	7/ 160
Cannon, William Henry [Florence SC]	Fseulo, Marie [Sanford]	29 Aug 1925	6/ 40
Canova, Lewis H. [Lisbon]	Gandy, Leo Ola [Umatilla]	7 Jun 1927	6/ 526

Cantrell, Perle	Googe, Violet Ethel	29 Jan 1928	7/ 55
Capell, William Henry	Inabit, Elva Clara	10 Feb 1934	8/ 425
Carathers, Adrain Fleming	Grier, Ruth Rea	28 Feb 1928	7/ 73
Carder, William Allen [Fairvilla]	Browning, Lorena [Fairvilla]	2 Jan 1926	6/ 107
Carey, Leland M.	Overton, Ruth	7 Jun 1928	7/ 135
Cargill, Jackson A.	Parrott, Lucy Jane	19 May 1933	8/ 307
Cariola, Michael	Anonsen, Thelma	25 Oct 1930	7/ 514
Carlock, Earl Thornton	Theus, Eloise	2 Sep 1927	6/ 576
Carlton, Clifford	McKern, Elizabeth	28 Apr 1932	8/ 151
Carlton, Lester R.	Fulton, Ida Gertude	30 Jun 1928	7/ 155
Carmichael, Alwyn E.	Smith, Mildred	15 Nov 1929	7/ 369
Carmichael, Dewey Alger	Uhl, Helen Annie	23 Dec 1928	7/ 221
Carmichael, George	King, Sarah Belle	21 Dec 1928	7/ 218
Carmichael, Hewall S.	Pettigrew, Elizabeth	6 Mar 1929	7/ 257
Carmichael, Starling Douglas	Hutchinson, Lucy Elizabeth	17 Apr 1931	7/ 586
Carney, Thomas Frances	Boehler, Alice Friida	10 Mar 1932	8/ 126
Carpenter, Charlie	Dority, Gertrude	23 Dec 1933	8/ 389
Carpenter, George Braxton	Chastang, Lula	6 Apr 1932	8/ 137
Carpenter, Jacob Franklin	Adamson, Ruth Iola	6 Feb 1932	8/ 113
Carpenter, Samuel Preston	Bray, Emelyn Coketine	15 Jun 1933	8/ 315
Carpenter, Sidney S.	Woodard, Bessie Marie	24 Dec 1932	8/ 233
Carpenter, Willard Oscar	Dunn, Grace Hutton	18 Mar 1933	8/ 272
Carr, Walter	Callier, Lugunia	28 Apr 1931	7/ 587
Carrie, Keith LaCount	Vinson, Gladys Marie	13 Mar 1930	7/ 426
Carrin, William Bailey	Wilson, Evelyn Beatrice	5 Aug 1933	8/ 332
Carringan, Richard	Emrich, Delphine	5 Sep 1926	6/ 331
Carrington, Richard	Williams, Willie Mae	29 Sep 1930	7/ 500
Carroll, Eddie Everett	Carroll, Rosa Belle	2 Feb 1932	8/ 112
Carroll, Herman	Lanier, Carrie Belle	22 Jul 1933	8/ 328
Carroll, Hurdis Milton	Witt, Wadie Mae	10 Nov 1931	8/ 73
Carroll, James [Orlando]	Donaldson, Emma [Orlando]	29 Oct 1925	6/ 72
Carroll, John Robert [W] [Lockhart]	Youngblood, Nina Mae [Lockhart]	3 Jan 1925	5/ 506
Carson, Alexander Joseph [Orlando]	Patrick, Sarah Frances [Orlando]	23 Oct 1926	6/ 361
Carson, Alphonse Michael [Orlando]	Husband, Grace Louise [Oakland]	22 Aug 1925	6/ 37
Carson, Homer	Dixon, Mary	12 Nov 1927	7/ 16
Carson, John [W] [Orlando]	Carlson, Annie [Orlando]	15 Aug 1925	6/ 34
Carson, Virgil	Shorts, Carrie	31 Mar 1928	7/ 90
Carswell, John Wright	Putnam, Elizabeth	11 Jun 1929	7/ 309
Carter, Archie [W] [Orlando]	Exen, Sarah [Orlando]	16 May 1925	5/ 574
Carter, Broward Glenn	Taylor, Addie Myrtle	16 Jun 1932	8/ 170
Carter, Carl Dean	Shaffer, Contance Helen	29 Sep 1930	7/ 501
Carter, Elige	Daniels, Ella	10 Feb 1932	8/ 114
Carter, Ernest Rice	Lively, Mary Larie	23 Dec 1933	8/ 393
Carter, James Franklin, Jr.	Watford, Lillian	17 Apr 1930	7/ 444
Carter, Jesse Malcolm	Benton, Alkpha	13 Sep 1929	7/ 345
Carter, Jessie [Orlando]	DuVae, Sarah [Orlando]	21 Jun 1926	6/ 279
Carter, Milton C.	Nichols, Della Dealie	3 Mar 1934	8/ 440
Carter, Norwood	McMillan, Margaret	3 Feb 1934	8/ 431
Carter, Randolph [Albany, GA]	Moore, Madge [Orlando]	7 Jul 1926	6/ 289
Carter, William Oscar	Chastain, Blanche	13 Jun 1928	7/ 138
Carver, Jim [W] [Goldenrod]	Baker, Opal [Goldenrod]	28 Mar 1925	5/ 547
Carvin, Arthur Lee	Coleman, Willie Mae	8 Feb 1930	7/ 411

Case, John F	Brown, Mattie	22 Mar 1928	7/ 85
Case, Raymond Nathan [Port Orange}	Hazlett, Nina Ethel [Port Orange]	8 Mar 1926	6/ 175
Cash, Eddie Leo [W] [Clermont]	Fertic, Linnie Alma [Bithlo]	30 May 1925	5/ 584
Cason, Charlie David	Baker, Mamie	2 Mar 1931	7/ 566
Cason, Eugene Wilbur	Ivy, Mae	25 Aug 1928	7/ 176
Cason, Harry Tarbutton [W] [Ocoee]	Thomas, Helen Annette [Orlando]	21 Feb 1925	5/ 538
Cassady, Charles David [W] [Orlando]	Mabbatt, Ethel Marian [Plattsburg, MO]	24 Dec 1925	6/ 125
Casteel, Roscoe	Waters, Bertha Mae	24 Feb 1934	8/ 436
Castile, Lonnie	McAdams, Myrtle	6 Jan 1934	8/ 403
Castile, Virch [B] [Orlando]	Flemings, Mary Virginia [Orlando]	21 Feb 1925	5/ 528
Cates, Claude C.	Holder, Mary	19 Nov 1929	7/ 373
Catledge, Wallie Lawrence	Williams, Athlove Grace	15 Apr 1930	7/ 439
Causin, Samuel	Murphy, Winifred	4 Mar 1931	7/ 565
Cauthen, Judson Alexander, Jr.	Cockeroft, Inez	22 Jun 1929	7/ 328
Caverly, Robert L. [Orlando]	Lehmann, Emma [Orlando] [Lehann on lic]	25 Sep 1925	6/ 59
Caverly, Victor Hund [Orlando]	Rankin, Mildred Ardelle	4 Sep 1926	6/ 337
Cawthon, John Wm [DeLand]	Shelor, Floy Earle [Orlando]	10 Apr 1926	6/ 204
Cawthorn, Bill Hill [Orlando]	Mullins, Eva Elizabeth [Atlanta,GA]	8 Jun 1927	6/ 527
Cecil, Harvey Ward	Gwaltney, Kate	6 Apr 1932	8/ 138
Chaffin, William Theodore [Orlando]	Rippy, Mattie Jane [Orlando]	10 Aug 1927	6/ 562
Chamberlain, Howard Huestis	Bartlett, Elsie Otillia	20 Jul 1931	8/ 34
Chambers, Ernest	Pouncey, Esther	7 Mar 1931	7/ 566
Chambers, Forrest David [Orlando]	Ihrig, Hester Jane [Orlando]	19 Jun 1927	6/ 539
Chambers, Ingram Earl [Orlando]	Marvin, Alice [Orlando]	1 Dec 1926	6/ 396
Chambers, John Lee [Jacksonville]	Small, Mary [Orlando]	8 Jun 1926	6/ 261
Chambers, Levi [B] [Orlando]	Blackman, Janie May [Orlando]	4 Jan 1926	6/ 127
Chambers, Robert [Orlando]	Olivey, Sarah [Orlando]	30 Oct 1926	6/ 370
Champion, William Heyward	Downey, Edith	15 Aug 1931	8/ 42
Champneys, Wallace Topp	Holland, Louisa	1 Mar 1930	7/ 422
Chance, Ray Foye [W] [Orlando]	Long, Viola Rose [Orlando]	31 Dec 1925	6/ 126
Chancy, Joe	Morris, Thelma	27 Jan 1934	8/ 418
Chandler, Albert	Allen, Courmillera	17 May 1931	8/ 9
Chandler, Willliam A.	Chandler, Mary Ethel	14 May 1929	7/ 304
Chaney, General [Altamont Springs]	Blanton, Myrtle [Orlando]	5 Mar 1927	6/ 469
Chapin, Oliver W. [Orlando]	Dolive, Gweneth F. [Orlando]	30 May 1926	6/ 260
Chapman, Bert Edgar	Radford, Rosamunde	2 Apr 1928	7/ 92
Chapman, Chas. Wm. [Monticello]	Britton, Grace [Orlando]	8 May 1926	6/ 232
Chapman, Clarence L. [B] [Orlando]	Culver, Nannie Bell [Orlando]	23 May 1925	5/ 581
Chapman, John William	Benson, Adgie Loween	19 Mar 1932	8/ 129
Chapman, Luther Cecil	Reynolds, Ethel	25 Oct 1932	8/ 207
Chapman, Walter	Griffin, Rub	11 Feb 1928	7/ 63
Charleston, Handy [Winter Park]	Canady, Leila [Winter Park]	27 Feb 1926	6/ 165
Charlow, Weston Charles [Orlando] [Coffee Springs, AL]	Parker, Ruth Dorrington	30 Oct 1926	6/ 376
Charlton, John	Welch, Beatrice Eunice	30 Dec 1931	8/ 97
Charters, Melvin Roy	Longnecker, Anna	14 Nov 1927	7/ 12
Chase, Clarence Bartlett	Porter, Estella E.	28 Apr 1934	8/ 471
Chase, Lloyd	Dease, Essie	20 Jan 1934	8/ 415
Chastain, L. B.	Starling, Doris	10 Dec 1933	8/ 388
Chastaine, Badger	Lancaster, Edwine Adams	22 Jan 1932	8/ 109

Cheevis, R. C. [B] [Orlando]	Scott, Ruth [Orlando]	9 Dec 1925	6/ 105
Cherry, Bocker T. [Orlando]	Williams, Josie [Orlando]	3 Jul 1926	6/ 304
Cherry, Hyatt Varondale [Windermere]	Roadhouse, Mildred [Leesburg]	1 May 1927	6/ 500
Cherry, Louis	Corbett, May	2 Feb 1929	7/ 239
Cherry, Walter	Clayton, Alma	14 Aug 1928	7/ 172
Chesser, LeRoy Roscoe	Hagan, Viola	15 Sep 1929	7/ 352
Childers, John W. [W]	McLeod, Leila Irene	10 Jan 1925	5/ 512
Childers, Thomas Jefferson [W] [Winter Garden]	Prince, Vivian [Winter Garden]	4 Apr 1925	5/ 552
Childs, Albert	Helms, Jennie	30 Jun 1934	8/ 503
Childs, James	Baker, Leola	6 Apr 1931	7/ 574
Chiles, James Colley	Lege, Uranie	26 May 1934	8/ 482
Chisem, William Henry	James, Loretha	9 Aug 1930	7/ 486
Chisholm, Joseph	Jones, Zonetta	28 Nov 1931	8/ 80
Chisolm, Walter	Betties, Lucile	28 Feb 1931	7/ 561
Chisom, Sam	Pinesett, Ada	10 Jul 1933	8/ 322
Christensen, Louis Godfrey	Heisey, Martha Romaine	11 Jun 1932	8/ 173
Christie, Lovearn LeRoy [Lockhart]	DeMille, Hazel [Lockhart]	18 Nov 1926	6/ 386
Christman, Milton Valentine	Dance, Orville Mae	10 Apr 1934	8/ 460
Christmas, Robert [B] [New Orleans, LA]	Hamiter, Janie [Orlando]	24 Jun 1925	6/ 4
Christopher, Fred Leland [W] [Plant City]	Carter, Jewell [Sanford]	2 Apr 1925	5/ 551
Christopher, Wade Albert	Von Dauber, Hazel	22 Jun 1928	7/ 146
Chubb, Kenmore Waters	Martin, Bessie Naomi	12 Apr 1932	8/ 141
Ciffers, James [B] [Orlando] [gives address]	Alexander, Lena [Orlando] (gives address)	21 Dec 1925	6/ 108
Clady, Frank	Richardson, Tallie Lou	5 Sep 1932	8/ 191
Claitty, Isaac [Sanford]	Spann, Eloise [Sanford]	4 Apr 1927	6/ 486
Clapham, George Arnold	McFarland, Ruth Mahala	30 Apr 1928	7/ 111
Clapp, Donald George	Marcott, Mabel Rose	30 Apr 1934	8/ 471
Clapp, Eldridge Andrews [Orlando]	Warren, Ethel Laura [Winter Park]	1 Nov 1926	6/ 380
Clark, Clyde Howard [Maitland]	Posey, Bessie Lou [Maitland]	11 Mar 1927	6/ 475
Clark, Damon	Taplin, Willie	13 Dec 1929	7/ 384
Clark, Daniel William	Fender, Elizabeth Ellen	4 Mar 1931	7/ 564
Clark, Elmer Stuart	Clark, Elinor Maurhoff	21 Nov 1933	8/ 372
Clark, Ernest [Orlando]	Birdsong, Alma [Orlando]	27 May 1927	6/ 516
Clark, Frank [Orlando]	Holder, Cora [Orlando]	12 Apr 1926	6/ 208
Clark, George	Washington, Janie	13 Apr 1931	7/ 579
Clark, George [Orlando]	Robinson, Louise [Orlando]	31 Mar 1926	6/ 195
Clark, Jim	Smith, Fern Lee	8 May 1933	8/ 290
Clark, John Clyde	Belcher, Annie Pearle	27 Jul 1929	7/ 326
Clark, John H. [W] [Clarksville]	Moore, Edith Wilma [Orlando]	1 Mar 1925	5/ 534
Clark, John Morton	Dudley, Minnie Stimpson	2 Jun 1928	7/ 124
Clark, John Wesley	Taylor, Vianna	3 Oct 1931	8/ 55
Clark, Lee Watson	Gallet, Daisy	26 Mar 1928	7/ 88
Clark, Robert	Jones, Everlean	5 Nov 1927	7/ 6
Clark, Robert [Orlando]	Hall, Alberta [Orlando]	26 Sep 1925	6/ 52
Clark, Robert Jesse	Smith, Agnes Voncile	28 Apr 1932	8/ 148
Clark, Roxey John [Miami]	Clark, Pearl Matilda [Orlando]	6 May 1926	6/ 228
Clark, Rufus [Orlando]	Enoch, Maggie [Orlando]	1 Nov 1926	6/ 371
Clark, Walter Henry [Orlando]	Daniels, Emma Louise [Orlando]	28 Apr 1926	6/ 238
Clark, William Clyde	Malloy, Janie Belle	23 May 1929	7/ 297
Clark, William Holloway	Gage, Norma Ames	9 Nov 1929	7/ 369
Claudy, Robert Leslie	Green, Adeline	21 Apr 1928	7/ 100

Claxton, Felton	Scott, Janette	13 Nov 1929	7/ 369
Clay, George Robert	Watford, Lottis	25 Jul 1931	8/ 37
Clayborne, Johnnie Henry	Pierce, Beulah	9 Nov 1931	8/ 72
Claypool, Harry Eugene	Wilson, Anna Ester	2 Jun 1932	8/ 167
Clayton, Archie	Johnson, Ella Mae	28 Jan 1928	7/ 53
Clayton, Arthur James [Windermere]	Brierlely, Florrie Vivian [Windermere]	l Jun 1926	6/ 254
Clayton, Shingler William [Orlando]	Kirby, Ruby Lou [Orlando]	19 Feb 1927	6/ 462
Clayton, Willis Henry [West Palm Beach]	Marshall, Francise Josette [Anderson, SC]	4 May 1927	6/ 502
Clemens, Willie	Bass, Hazel	23 Apr 1928	7/ 102
Clements, Theodore [B] [Orlando]	Wilson, Ruby [Orlando]	26 Jan 1925	5/ 516
Clements, W. Lawrence	Rayburn, Elma Navada	14 Jun 1928	7/ 141
Clemons, Steve	Jewett, Missouri	25 Jul 1932	8/ 180
Cleveland, Hollis [Winter Park]	Hughey, Eliza [Winter Park]	2 Jun 1926	6/ 255
Clevenger, Harry Ross	Eberwein, Olive	16 Apr 1931	7/ 582
Clifton, Elmer Hugh [Orlando]	Hall, Mary Eulalia [Orlando]	3 Jul 1926	6/ 289
Cline, James Elmer	Quirk, Bessie	3 Sep 1932	8/ 190
Cloud, Holman Ratliff [Orlando]	Ammerman, Mabel Clare [Orlando]	15 Jun 1926	6/ 281
Clouser, Maurice W.	Ellison, Emma Jean	19 Mar 1932	8/ 129
Cloutier, Louis Phillip Albert	Youngus, Laura Ann	25 Jan 1931	7/ 547
Clow, James W.	Keene, Edna	6 Jul 1928	7/ 159
Clute, John Henry [W] [Orlando]	Blake, Lena [Orlando]	4 Feb 1925	5/ 524
Clutts, Floyd Pleasant	Rosanthal, Gladys Elizabeth	18 Jan 1930	7/ 401
Clyatt, James Robert	Rehberg, Vera	16 Apr 1932	8/ 147
Clyatt, Major [B] [Orlando]	Salley, Eliza [Orlando]	6 Feb 1926	6/ 150
Coar, Allison	Stephens, Rosiell	22 Mar 1932	8/ 130
Cobb, Calvin H.	Wynn, Mary	31 May 1929	7/ 300
Cobb, Clarence H. R.	Breaden, Ellen Nora	12 Mar 1929	7/ 277
Cobb, Emsley R.,Jr.	Parker, Elizabeth	3 Aug 1929	7/ 328
Cobb, Marshall	Polhill, Ophelia	13 Jan 1934	8/ 400
Cobb, Marshall [B] [Orlando]	Ridley, Marie [Orlando]	27 Jan 1926	6/ 143
Cocke, William Alexander	Farrar, Alice Augusta	8 Oct 1931	8/ 57
Cockran, John L.	Holley, Lena	15 Sep 1927	6/ 580
Code, Jake	Williams, Rozie	17 Nov 1932	8/ 217
Cody, James Isaac [W] [Winter Garden]	Quates, Katie Lee [Winter Garden]	15 Jan 1925	5/ 513
Cody, Willis J. [Babson Park]	Ashley, Thelma J. [Babson Park]	25 May 1926	6/ 257
Coe, Edwin Dalos [Clearwater]	Tellakson, Kyn Beatrice	30 Jun 1926	6/ 299
Coffey, Victor Osborne [Chicago, IL]	Hillsabeck, Mary Ellen [Holdredge, NE]	17 Jun 1926	6/ 272
Coffman, Roy Turnley	Lankford, Aline	16 Jan 1931	7/ 543
Cohen, Nathan	Jackson, Queen	25 Nov 1929	7/ 377
Cohn, Sidney Aycock [Baltimore, MD]	Forst, Dorothy [Orlando]	3 May 1927	6/ 501
Cohnway, James	Whitfield, Willie Mae	26 Oct 1929	7/ 365
Coker, Wiley	Colston, Rachel	16 Nov 1933	8/ 367
Colado, Gavino Frederico	Dickson, Jeannette Watts	7 Nov 1931	8/ 73
Colden, Edward [Orlando]	Oxford, Julie Mae [Orlando]	l May 1926	6/ 223
Colden, Freddie	Smith, Anna Lee	18 Aug 1930	7/ 489
Coldwell, Clifford Arthur [Orlando]	Walton, Minnie May [Pittsburgh, PA]	29 Sep 1925	6/ 57
Cole, Charlie	Daniels, Irene	16 Apr 1932	8/ 143
Cole, Frank R. [W] [Orlando]	Stonnell, Dorothy S. [Orlando]	12 Dec 1925	6/ 105
Cole, Harper Madison	Britt, Effie	22 Feb 1930	7/ 418
Cole, William Harrison	Bailey, Julia Dowell	7 Feb 1932	8/ 113

Coleman, Elijah [B] [Orlando]	Armstead, Ella [Orlando]	10 Jan 1925	5/ 511
Coleman, Reuben	Smith, Geneva	26 Jan 1929	7/ 235
Coleman, Sam [Oakland]	Cook, Gertrude [Oakland]	17 May 1926	6/ 238
Collard, Ernest Ray	Collard, Susan Ruth	8 Apr 1931	7/ 576
Collier, Busby Jennings	Ayers, Corinne Hamilton	15 Sep 1931	8/ 51
Collier, George	Smith, Nellie	7 Mar 1929	7/ 260
Collier, Jesse Allen [W] [Winter Park]	Long, Theda [Winter Park]	7 Apr 1925	5/ 569
Collins, Albert	James, Alberta	6 Jun 1932	8/ 167
Collins, Bailey Reeves [W] [Wichita Falls, TX]	Mitchell, Pauline [Orlando]	16 May 1925	5/ 577
Collins, Beauren	Stevens, Violet Ardean	19 Feb 1933	8/ 261
Collins, Bennie [Winter Park]	Prescott, Oreh [Winter Park]	17 Oct 1925	6/ 66
Collins, Charlie	Lovett, Lilla	15 Aug 1929	7/ 333
Collins, Crenshaw C. [W] [Davenport]	Caruthers, Marjorie [Orlando]	14 Mar 1925	5/ 542
Collins, David	Rowland, Willie Maxciene	12 Jun 1933	8/ 313
Collins, Frank [Orlando]	Brown, Robbie [Orlando]	21 Sep 1926	6/ 341
Collins, Garfield	Young, Clyde	22 May 1933	8/ 302
Collins, Nolen Grey	Hall, Carrie Belle	26 Dec 1933	8/ 395
Collins, Norman [Orlando]	Harris, Dorothy Lee [Orlando]	16 Mar 1927	6/ 478
Collins, Ornan Lamont	Campbell, Lucy Anita	25 Sep 1927	6/ 584
Collins, Thomas	Jackson, Lucinda	8 Aug 1931	8/ 40
Collins, Vernon	Young, Doris Aileen	30 May 1933	8/ 309
Collins, Walter	Johns, Janie Elizabeth	31 Oct 1931	8/ 70
Collins, Walter Joseph	Young, Luisa Emilia	17 Jul 1931	8/ 100
Collins, Willie	Baker, Maude	30 Jan 1933	8/ 253
Colson, William	Johnson, Eva Mae	19 Dec 1931	8/ 89
Colter, Daniel [Orlando]	York, Anna [Orlando]	2 Apr 1927	6/ 485
Coltraine, Johnnie Alexander	Waehaus, Margaret	12 Oct 1931	8/ 58
Colyer, Vincent Benjamin [B] [Orlando]	Draft, Frances Wilhelinina [Orlando]	31 May 1925	5/ 599
Combs, Willie [Orlando]	Roberts, Maggie L.	6 Dec 1926	6/ 401
Commodore, Robert	Brown, Ester	5 Jan 1933	8/ 238
Condon, Arthur	Shadburn, Mary Elizabeth	20 Dec 1933	8/ 387
Cone, William Oscar	Cook, Sarah LaMearle	30 Jun 1931	8/ 26
Conger, Edward Joseph	Harrison, Evelyn Louise	2 Mar 1928	7/ 73
Conley, Richard Saulter	Weidenfeller, Leah	13 Jan 1934	8/ 420
Connell, Billie B.	McCormick, Irene	23 Oct 1932	8/ 210
Connell, Carper	Crane, Ada	15 Oct 1929	7/ 358
Connell, Ernest John	Baker, Nellie Evans	20 Apr 1934	8/ 465
Connell, John Howard	Jones, Almedia	23 Jun 1934	8/ 499
Connell, Wilbur Frank	Reddick, Willie Louise	16 May 1931	8/ 5
Connell, William Hugh [W] [Winter Garden]	Ayers, Irene [Winter Garden]	14 Jun 1925	5/ 589
Conner, Crawford Thomas	Caldwell, Elizabeth	21 Mar 1934	8/ 448
Conner, John	Pringle, Rubie Lee	23 Dec 1927	7/ 38
Conrad, Paul S.	Dawson, Madeleine M.	15 May 1929	7/ 296
Conroy, Frank Philip	Martin, Mildred Louise	12 Mar 1933	8/ 270
Conroy, George Albert	Sproles, Wenona	3 Feb 1934	8/ 422
Constantine, John [Gainesville]	Entz, Ida M. [Gainesville]	22 Jul 1926	6/ 277
Cook, Benjamin Franklin	English, Leota Mae	9 Aug 1934	8 520
Cook, Donald Martin	Anders, Charlotte Louise	13 Nov 1933	8/ 366
Cook, Hamilton H. [Orlando]	Williams, Leila [Orlando]	5 Apr 1926	6/ 202
Cook, John Milton	Powell, Kate Alderman	9 Jan 1933	8/ 242
Cook, Marcus Alonzo, Jr [Orlando]	DeFoor, Dulcie [Orlando]	9 Jun 1926	6/ 264
Cook, Nathaniel	Greyer, Susie	28 Nov 1930	7/ 526

Cook, William	Williams, Mittle	6 Dec 1931	8/ 85
Cooke, Lee Hampton	Carter, Annie Rether	21 Jan 1931	7/ 546
Cooker, Archibald John	Pearce, Ethel Maude	11 Apr 1928	7/ 95
Cooks, Appie [Orlando]	Williams, Aletha [St. Petersburg]	27 Sep 1926	6/ 343
Coonley, Dwight	Dyer, Carolina	20 Jan 1931	7/ 546
Cooper, Clifford Haden [Orlando]	Parron, Beatrice Bea [Orlando]	6 Jul 1926	6/ 287
Cooper, Emery	Tossie, Gladys	21 Nov 1931	8/ 76
Cooper, Fred Edmund	Cone, Allene	12 Jul 1930	7/ 478
Cooper, Guss	Galloway, Elnora	16 Jul 1928	7/ 161
Cooper, John Henry	Moye, Eloise	22 Nov 1931	8/ 79
Cooper, Levi [Winter Garden]	Horton, Mattie Mae [Winter Garden]	4 Apr 1926	6/ 209
Cooper, Raymond Edgar [Orlando]	Harris, Thelma Marie [Orlando]	27 Oct 1926	6/ 365
Cooper, Willis Norton	Willis, Mateel	2 Jul 1928	7/ 155
Copeland, John	Bach, Agnes Hewitt	5 Dec 1933	8/ 380
Coram, Marvin Keese	Bruce, Vivian Nell	21 Jul 1929	7/ 324
Coram, Raymond	McKay, Johnnie	30 Jun 1928	7/ 153
Corbett, Charles Bum	Young, Maggie Lee	8 Jun 1931	8/ 14
Corbett, Lonnie	Demps, Margaret	17 Apr 1930	7/ 440
Corbett, William Brooks [Orlando]	Weid, Martha Paula [Orlando]	14 Dec 1926	6/ 414
Corbett, Willie	Murray, Henrietta	29 Mar 1929	7/ 266
Corbin, Clayton [Orlando]	Vann, Ollie [Orlando]	22 Jan 1927	6/ 442
Cording, James William	McCall, Ernestine	17 Mar 1928	7/ 83
Corkhill, William Lawrence [Orlando]	McKenney, Kate Ivey [Orlando]	2 Jul 1927	6/ 564
Corley, Carver David [Orlando]	Kierman, Natalie [Orlando]	26 Dec 1926	6/ 419
Cornalzer, Hosea Wilbert	Sanders, Rose	1 Feb 1929	7/ 241
Corning, Robert Nelson	Stevens, Elaine	26 May 1928	7/ 104
Cornman, Robert Royal	Brunk, Elizabeth	6 May 1931	7/ 594
Cortez, Don Emanuel	Moran, Sarah	9 Mar 1929	7/ 262
Corzelius, James Clark, Jr.	Giles, Wyldine A.	29 Jun 1929	7/ 320
Cosby, Wesleye	Allen, Wilhelmina	25 Jan 1934	8/ 417
Coston, Harold Stanton	McDaniel, Lucy	26 Jul 1930	7/ 482
Cottingham, Fred [Dayton, OH]	Benson, Mary [Orlando]	24 Mar 1927	6/ 481
Cotton, Peter	Bryant, Florence	20 Jun 1928	7/ 152
Counts, Reuben	Hearing, Ruth	16 Jun 1932	8/ 171
Counts, Reuben	Whittington, Thelma Bernice	4 Oct 1933	8/ 348
Couture, Arthur Joseph [Winter Park]	Mathieu, Lorenza Dora [Winter Park]	14 Jun 1926	6/ 270
Covington, Henry Thomas [Orlando]	Clark, Rosa [Gainesville]	29 Jun 1926	6/ 287
Cowart, Felix	Eaton, Isabel Irene	22 Dec 1928	7/ 225
Cowart, W. E.	Davis, Verna	23 Nov 1933	8/ 373
Cowdrey, Chester Claire	Arnold, Emilie Elizabeth	11 Sep 1931	8/ 49
Cowdrick, Jessie Stanton	Ries, Lois Katheryn	16 Aug 1931	8/ 41
Cowell, Edward Huntington [Orlando]	Hutchins, Dorothy Marie [Orlando]	10 Feb 1927	6/ 456
Cowley, Harry F.	Allen, G. Gaynelle	29 Sep 1929	7/ 351
Cox, Clarence Eldredge	Lyle, Susie Mae	3 Sep 1929	7/ 339
Cox, Floyd	Murray, Dora	24 Sep 1930	7/ 499
Cox, James Douglas	Carreker, Vera Virginia	15 Mar 1934	8/ 446
Cox, Paul LeRoy	Chambers, Hazel LaVerne	14 Feb 1934	8/ 430
Coyle, Patrick Joseph [New Smyrna]	Lowitz, Nancy [New Smyrna]	5 Feb 1926	6/ 148
Crabtree, Granville Hayward [Longwood]	Wynne, Gladys Bell [Sanford]	18 Oct 1926	6/ 356
Crabtree, William Bunyan	Haseman, Elizabeth Marie	11 Jan 1930	7/ 398

Cradle, Junior Cleveland	Crosby, Nannie Henry	15 Oct 1931	8/ 60
Craig, Hubert Eldridge	White, Ida Margaret	1 Sep 1928	7/ 179
Craig, Orin E.	Barrineau, Mattie Lou	27 Jan 1933	8/ 250
Craig, William Addison	Garner, Velma Elizabeth	20 Oct 1928	7/ 200
Cramer, Theodore Everett	Greer, Lella Maurine	25 Jul 1932	8/ 180
Crane, Charles B.	Paul, Marian Elizabeth	27 Aug 1931	8/ 44
Crane, Frank E.	Duke, Iva	18 Jun 1929	7/ 311
Crane, Frank Morrow	Rankin, Louise Kelly	16 Jul 1933	8/ 330
Crane, James Arthur	Simmons, Mary Ethel	25 Jan 1930	7/ 405
Crane, James Arthur	LaPoint, Rose Ora	13 Oct 1927	6/ 593
Cranfill, Thomas A.	Bowen, Sylvia	12 May 1928	7/ 112
Craw, Leonard Marvin [W] [Lockhart]	Watts, Annie Edith [Orlando]	20 Aug 1925	6/ 36
Crawford, Calvert Lawton [Palatka]	Dawda, Amanda Eudora	5 Feb 1927	6/ 452
Crawford, Dayton Hampton	Marshall, Veola Irene	26 Jul 1934	8/ 515
Crawford, Douglas	Williams, Etta Mae	2 Nov 1931	8/ 69
Crawford, Earl John [Orlando]	Lee, Ruth Donifine [Orlando]	1 Jul 1926	6/ 277
Crawford, Eddie	Collier, Gertrude	8 Jun 1931	8/ 14
Crawford, Ernest Owen [Winter Garden]	Meredith, Lois Marie [Winter Garden]	14 Jul 1926	6/ 301
Crawford, George Walter	McBride, Agnes Queen	19 Nov 1932	8/ 222
Crawford, Hoke Smith	Waring, Margaret Virginia	4 Mar 1934	8/ 442
Crawford, John Henry	Tippen, Irma Brougher	8 Apr 1928	7/ 94
Crawford, Oliver Martin	McQuagge, Oleta	20 Nov 1930	7/ 522
Crawford, Raymond	Schmitt, Arty Lue	12 Jan 1931	7/ 541
Crawford, Warren L.	Jones, Hattie Robertson	16 May 1933	8/ 299
Crawford, Whipple Redfen [Winter Park]	McIntyre, Ethel [Chatanooga, TN]	11 Nov 1926	6/ 382
Creech, George Roy	Gary, Ruby Margaret	29 Jun 1931	8/ 25
Crews, William Perry	Woodle, Mell	9 Sep 1929	7/ 343
Crissey, Jay C.	Stansland, Ida Virginia	19 Jun 1930	7/ 473
Crittenden, Charles H. [Pinecastle]	Wallace, Lottie E. [Pinecastle]	7 Aug 1927	6/ 562
Crittenden, James Henry	Anderson, Lidie May	25 Nov 1932	8/ 220
Crittenden, William S.	May, Georgia	1 Apr 1929	7/ 278
Crittenden, William Stanley	Curtis, Lois Bernice	10 Jan 1931	7/ 541
Croell, James [B] [Orlando]	Brown, Mamie [B]	19 Jan 1926	6/ 139
Croley, John Francis	Fleming, Alice Carvassa	3 Nov 1933	8/ 362
Cromer, John Wesley [Orlando]	Wright, Louise [Orlando]	27 Feb 1926	6/ 165
Crompton, Will [W] [Winter Garden]	Adkin, Pearl [Winter Garden]	16 Jan 1926	6/ 135
Croome, James Henry [Apopka]	Dahlke, Lelia Alberta [Apopka]	24 Oct 1925	6/ 70
Crooms, Joll [B] [Orlando]	Jones, Dora [Wildwood]	13 Jun 1925	5/ 591
Crosby, Charles Herbert [W] [Lake Mary]	Jeilison, Susan Ora [Lake Mary]	27 Nov 1925	6/ 92
Crosky, Abraham [B] [Oakland]	Read, Jiny [Oakland] [Ziny on appl.]	7 Nov 1925	6/ 77
Cross, Hushell [B] [Orlando]	Holmes, Annie [Orlando]	7 Dec 1925	6/ 95
Crout, Herman Hardy	Davis, Minnie Ann	16 Apr 1932	8/ 144
Crowder, Harvey Raymond [Orlando]	Wimberley, Nannie Louise [Orlando]	18 Jul 1926	6/ 297
Crowder, James Charles [Winter Garden]	Borgard, Merle [Winter Garden]	4 Dec 1926	6/ 402
Crowder, John Stanley	Hubler, Beulah	6 Dec 1929	7/ 383
Cruells, James	Johnson, Jennie	12 Mar 1928	7/ 79
Crum, Cornelious B.	Campfield, Lauria A.	1 Dec 1928	7/ 215
Crusow, Henry [Apopka]	Gilmore, Eliza [Apopka]	9 Mar 1926	6/ 171
Cucurel, William Barney [Orlando]	Byrd, Evelyn [Orlando] [Bucurel on return]	3 May 1926	6/ 228
Culbertson, Roy Robert [Orlando]	Roach, Dorathy Eleanor [Orlando]	26 Jul 1926	6/ 310
Culbreth, John Franklin	Wilson, Euphamia	17 Sep 1931	8/ 51

Culler, William Herbert [W] [Orlando]	Trask, Enid Marie [Apopka]	29 May 1925	5/ 589
Cullum, Merwyn Louis	Moors, Beatrice Foster	14 Feb 1930	7/ 415
Culp, John Patton	Rudd, Eva Mae	7 Jul 1928	7/ 158
Culpepper, Ernest	Little, Hazel Lovell	15 Jun 1931	8/ 22
Cummer, Oswald Monroe	Morehouse, Lillian Blanche	9 Apr 1931	7/ 577
Cumming, Wm, Gray [W] [Barre, VT]	Martin, Cora Emma [Barre, VT]	5 Jan 1925	5/ 509
Cummings, Scrail Israel	Murphy, Sarah	19 Dec 1928	7/ 227
Cummins, H. E. [Orlando]	Kirkley, Minnie [Orlando]	4 Sep 1926	6/ 329
Cunningham, Benjamin Hutton	Bowles, Letitia Juanita	20 Oct 1927	7/ 1
Cunningham, Jeff	Smith, Ethel Mae	24 Dec 1932	8/ 232
Cunningham, John Workman	Cunningham, Percy Moore	17 Dec 1931	8/ 88
Cunningham, Richard	Jackson, Willie Mae	30 Jan 1933	8/ 251
Curcio, Maurice	Bianco, Mary	5 Feb 1928	7/ 59
Currie, Clarence R. [W] [Daytona]	Allen, Clutha Margaret [Orlando]	26 Jan 1925	5/ 517
Curry, Henry	Lloyd, Carrie Lee	8 Feb 1932	8/ 115
Curtis, William	Smith, Julia	5 Nov 1931	8/ 72
Curtis, William Frank	Thomas, Margrine Alice	15 Dec 1930	7/ 530
Cutts, Cakter	Griggs, Millie	3 Sep 1932	8/ 193
Cutts, Raymond	Purse, Cary	18 Apr 1932	8/ 146
Cyler, Dub	Steen, Mary Lee	17 Aug 1929	7/ 334

D

Dade, William Alexander	Smith, Ester Lanier	1 Jun 1934	8/ 492
Daffron, Lindon D. [W] [Orlando]	Taylor, Emma [Orlando]	27 Nov 1925	6/ 93
Dafoe, Worth J. [Bowling Green, KY]	Cook, Virginia Louise [Orlando]	23Nov 1925	6/ 75
Daggett, Augustine Harrington	Hinsley, Maria Roslett	17 Dec 1927	7/ 27
Daggett, William Franklin [Clermont]	Taylor, Maud [Wilmette, IL]	24 Jan 1927	6/ 444
Dahn, Leo H. [Sanford]	Hunt, Mary Martha	3 Oct 1926	6/ 347
Dale, John Harrison	Mitchell, Margaret	17 Nov 1932	8/ 218
Dale, Philip	Grant, Ina R.	9 Sep 1927	6/ 580
Dale, Walter Edward	Hollen, Pearl	2 Apr 1934	8/ 456
Dallas, Herman [Orlando]	Sweet, Nordica [Bartow]	17 Nov 1926	6/ 385
Dallas, Walter Lohman [Winter Park]	Saunders, Alma Lillian [St.Cloud]	16 Mar 1927	6/ 477
Dalton, Arthur James [Orlando]	Harvey, Hazel Viola [Orlando]	1 Sep 1926	6/ 327
Dalton, Jack Inglis [Orlando]	O'Malley, Francis Edna	1 Sep 1926	6/ 327
Damascus, R. S.	Helms, Daisy	16 Jan 1931	7/ 543
Damps, James	Wells, Mary	31 Jul 1929	7/ 329
Daniel, Charlie [Orlando]	Peterson, Buruer [Orlando]	27 Feb 1926	6/ 166
Daniel, Everett	Weaver, Freda	26 Oct 1928	7/ 199
Daniel, Mack Coy	Holloway, Agnes Luella	6 May 1931	7/ 595
Daniel, Walter [B] [Eatonville]	Mosely, Ada May [Woodbridge]	4 May 1925	5/ 567
Daniel, William Jackson	Atwater, Lillian	7 Jul 1934	8/ 506
Daniels, Harold Kennan	Klug, M. Ruth	26 Sep 1933	8/ 346
Daniels, Isaac	Hall, Clare Belle	6 Jun 1928	7/ 129
Daniels, Major	Washington, Nettie	5 Apr 1934	8/ 454
Daniels, Raymond	Davis, Margaret	14 Oct 1928	7/ 196
Danmark, Clifford	Harris, Ruth	27 Jan 1930	7/ 406
Dann, Thomas Causey [Ocoee]	Drew, Eva Lois [Ocoee]	20 Aug 1926	6/ 319
Danner, George Henry [Orlando]	Robinson, Carrie Lous [Orlando]	18 Sep 1926	6/ 340

Danner, Willie [Orlando]	Taylor, Ora [Orlando]	17 May 1926	6/ 237
Darby, Arthur	Bell, Annie	25 Feb 1934	8/ 436
Darby, Leroy	Williams, Geneva	2 Jan 1929	7/ 228
Darden, Justin Clyde	Downs, Ruth	3 Mar 1934	8/ 439
Darity, Henry	Summerell, Letha	5 Sep 1931	8/ 47
Darity, Martin Hilton	Webb, Emily Pearl	16 Jul 1933	8/ 326
Darling, Horace Velpeau [Orlando]	Latimer, Vera Pearl [Orlando]	19 Aug 1926	6/ 316
Dasher, Richard Haynes [Valdosta, GA]	Cooper, Lillian Elizabeth	2 Jan 1927	6/ 425
Daugherty, Herbert Albert	Cannon, Clorine Herbert	21 Jul 1928	7/ 166
Daughertz, Willard William	Beuer, Augusta Louise	14 Jul 1928	7/ 162
Daughtry, Edgar Charles	Ahik, Ruby Lee	1 Apr 1934	8/ 454
Dausby, Bradley Lanier	Coleman, Mary Sawyer	29 Jul 1928	7/ 170
Davenport, Henry Haskell [Dalleair, FL]	Bates, Dora Whittemore [Tampa]	3 Jul 1926	6/ 286
Daves, Griffin	Davis, Eva Majorie	16 Apr 1933	8/ 285
Davidson, Ernest Levern	Hartley, Bessie Blanche	15 Oct 1927	6/ 593
Davidson, Leslie Eugene [Orlando]	Smith, Dorothy [Orlando]	13 Jun 1927	6/ 536
Davidson, Lock	Davis, Gloria Roberta	12 Apr 1928	7/ 97
Davie, Ralph Williams [Orlando]	Smith, Isadore	4 Nov 1926	6/ 377
Davies, Stuart Johnstone [Daytona]	Newman, Ellen Elizabeth [Orlando]	1 Oct 1925	6/ 56
Davis, Alphonso	Ward, Lillian	6 Jan 1930	7/ 395
Davis, Ambros Else [Leesburg]	Laird, Pansy Arlevie [Winter Park]	28 Oct 1926	6/ 368
Davis, Audie Heasey	Koonce, Sallie Lee	17 Jun 1934	8/ 497
Davis, Boston [Orlando]	Clark, Bertha Lee [Orlando]	15 Feb 1927	6/ 457
Davis, C. J.	Thomas, Leola	9 May 1931	7/ 596
Davis, C. S.	Fields, Essie Mae	19 May 1928	7/ 123
Davis, Cecil Rice	Humphries, Helen Irene	17 Feb 1931	7/ 559
Davis, Charlie L.	Soles, Lura M.	17 Dec 1928	7/ 216
Davis, Clifford Albert [W] [Ocoee]	Bekemeyer, Anna Louise [Winter Garden]	3 Jul 1925	6/ 11
Davis, Daniel Oscar	Ruemmele, Lavon	18 Oct 1931	8/ 61
Davis, Dock Nicholeson	Dorman, Effie	7 May 1930	7/ 449
Davis, Ed	Cook, Ette May	14 Apr 1930	7/ 438
Davis, Gilbert K.	Newman, Ruby Blanche	10 Nov 1932	8/ 215
Davis, Harley	More, Mae Fred	7 May 1930	7/ 449
Davis, Harry Dixon	Echols, Carolyn Elizabeth	8 Mar 1933	8/ 268
Davis, James	Ellis, Katie	6 Jan 1934	8/ 402
Davis, James Linton	Greer, Ruby	6 Jan 1932	8/ 101
Davis, Jesse D.	Miller, Annie May	27 Jan 1930	7/ 406
Davis, Joe J.	Smith, Victoria Marie	23 Feb 1928	7/ 151
Davis, John	Walters, Lillie Mae	21 Sep 1927	6/ 583
Davis, John Henry, Jr.	Adcock, Emma Caroline	2 Jun 1931	8/ 18
Davis, Junior	Canady, Thelma	3 Oct 1931	8/ 57
Davis, Kishman [Apopka]	Thomas, Minnie Lee [Apopka]	28 Mar 1927	6/ 483
Davis, Lawrence [Orlando]	Watson, Pearl [Orlando]	5 Jun 1926	6/ 258
Davis, Lee [Winter Garden]	Webb, Estelle [Winter Garden]	24 Sep 1925	6/ 49
Davis, Lewis Woodley [W] [Orlando]	Simth, Mattie [Orlando]	19 Jan 1926	6/ 137
Davis, Loy Hobson	Butler, Lulu Mae	21 Feb 1934	8/ 434
Davis, Mack	Oliver, Annie Belle	10 Sep 1932	8/ 194
Davis, Maurice [Orlando]	Thomas, Addie Lee [Orlando]	23 Oct 1926	6/ 361
Davis, Meredith Everett [W] [Pitman NJ]	Dooley, Mabel Lee [Orlando]	5 Jun 1925	5/ 596
Davis, Nathan [Oakland]	McClair, Essie [Oakland]	17 Oct 1925	6/ 66
Davis, Richard Lucas	Jones, Katie	24 Mar 1930	7/ 431
Davis, Robert Everette	Adair, Billie	11 Jan 1932	8/ 108

Davis, Roma Charlie [Apopka]	Rowan, Margaret Mae [Apopka]	23 Jan 1927	6/ 445
Davis, Roy Elmer	Whipple, Pearl	16 Feb 1931	7/ 556
Davis, Russell	Williams, Sarah	10 Nov 1930	7/ 519
Davis, Russell T. [W] [Orlando]	Michael, Eva Grace [Orlando]	29 May 1925	5/ 600
Davis, Samuel	Jefferson, Lillie Ruth	3 Feb 1934	8/ 422
Davis, Samuel [W] [Clewiston]	Marshall, Maud [Clewiston]	7 Jan 1926	6/ 129
Davis, Thomas	Gunn, Annie Lou	23 Apr 1934	8/ 480
Davis, Thomas Jefferson [Mineola]	Mallard, Mary Goss [Mineola]	19 Jun 1926	6/ 274
Davis, Wallace Edwin [W] [Orlando]	Waddell, Frances Marian [Winter Park]	9 Jan 1926	6/ 134
Davis, Wesely E.	Bowen, Willie Lee	19 Aug 1934	8/ 524
Davis, Whitley	Gaines, Pearlie May	9 Feb 1929	7/ 243
Davis, Will	Roberts, Hattie	28 Dec 1931	8/ 97
Davis, William Fisher [Orlando]	Dickey, Carrie May [Orlando]	14 Apr 1926	6/ 213
Davis, William Horace	Perry, Vera Inez	11 Apr 1927	6/ 490
Davis, Willie	Sams, Essie Mae	24 Dec 1928	7/ 219
Davis, Willie [Winter Park]	McGee, Bertha [Winter Park]	2 Oct 1926	6/ 345
Davis, Zack	Dorsey, Rosa Mae	10 Dec 1932	8/ 228
Davison, Charles Wandell	Imler, Margaret Alberta	25 May 1931	7/ 593
Dawkins, Milton [B] [Union, SC]	Allen, Rosa [Orlando]	19 Dec 1925	6/ 105
Dawley, Everett	Mallory, Edna	24 Oct 1930	7/ 512
Dawson, Clemon	Praylor, Susie Mae	8 Oct 1929	7/ 356
Dawson, Leon	Harris, Lula Mae	2 Oct 1933	8/ 352
Dawson, Riley	Tillman, Ernestine	7 Jan 1928	7/ 41
Day, George M.	Thiem, Catherine M.	26 Jan 1928	7/ 52
Day, Nathan B.	Berlin, Hannah	9 Jul 1928	7/ 158
Dealing, Edwin Emerson	Wyman, Ethel Louise	25 Aug 1930	7/ 490
Dean, Gideon [Orlando]	Hunter, Jessie May [Orlando]	4 Sep 1926	6/ 330
Dean, Henry Corbett [W] [Orlando]	Baily, Mary Fanida [Orlando]	21 Jul 1925	6/ 21
Dean, Samuel Archer	Yow, Buford Bernice	28 Jan 1928	7/ 54
Dean, Thomas Irvine [Orlando]	Cole, Vera May [Greenwood, SC]	27 Dec 1926	6/ 433
Deane, William Ernest	Hearn, Louise Frances	30 Jun 1933	8/ 319
DeBell, Robert Hudson [Orlando]	Mayo, Elizabeth [Orlando]	18 Nov 1926	6/ 394
Decker, Clifford Allen	Tillis, Sophie Louise	30 Jan 1928	7/ 58
Deere, Alton [City Point]	Bynes, Leola [City Point]	18 Jun 1927	6/ 537
Delano, Herman S.	McFerron, Christine	22 Oct 1929	7/ 361
DeLawrence, Joseph James [Orlando]	Brown, Lucile [Orlando]	27 Sep 1926	6/ 343
Dellinger, Paul Franklyn	Rowe, Pauline Burnham	11 Jan 1933	8/ 243
Deluca, Gennaro Paola	Andrews, Viola Ruth	16 Sep 1931	8/ 50
Demps, Ed [Orlando]	Robinson, Mamie [Orlando]	22 May 1927	6/ 515
Demps, Francis Axwell	Townsend, Althea	2 Mar 1933	8/ 266
Demps, Fred	Williams, Nega	19 Feb 1929	7/ 248
Demps, Nerot [Orlando]	Smith, Rachael [Orlando]	29 Mar 1926	6/ 193
Demps, William	Demps, Janie	25 Dec 1928	7/ 220
Denham, Oren	Gunn, Wilmer	26 Aug 1933	8/ 337
Denmark, Winston	Jackson, Janie	1 Apr 1929	7/ 269
Dennard, James [B] [Orlando]	Watson, Elsie [Orlando]	7 Nov 1925	6/ 77
Dennis, John [Orlando]	Commadore, Mamie [Orlando]	29 Mar 1926	6/ 193
Denny, Benj. Creamer [W] [Carbur?]	Dunwell, Florence Louise [Philadelphia, PA]	23 Feb 1925	5/ 530
Denson, David	Sutton, Sarah	16 Jun 1928	7/ 142
Denson, Willie [B] [Daytona]	Ridley, Nancy [Orlando]	15 Jul 1925	6/ 17

Dent, Emtilla	Bowman, Clara	24 Sep 1928	7/ 186
Depoole, Leon	Rolland, Laura Catherine	1 Apr 1932	8/ 136
Depue, Carl Emerson	Patterson, Florence L'neta	6 Jun 1931	8/ 13
Dernoeden, Peter	Matthews, Mause Isabel	25 Nov 1933	8/ 374
Derthick, Harold Guy	Krause, Elsie Joan	25 Aug 1930	7/ 491
Deshields, Clay	Williams, Lillie	9 Aug 1930	7/ 487
Dessal, John [Orlando]	Lane, Julia	3 Nov 1926	6/ 372
Dettmer, Frederick George	Joiner, Mary Louise	18 Jul 1931	8/ 36
Devore, William Elbert	Flynn, Sybil Esther	22 Jun 1933	8/ 318
Dewberry, Jessie	Riley, Josephine	24 Oct 1927	6/ 597
Dewend, Fred R. [W] [Sarasota]	Allsbrow, Bessie [Moline, IL]	9 Jan 1926	6/ 131
Deyampert, Thomas Bell	Lenard, Beulah	20 Jun 1931	8/ 21
Dial, Leland Jackson	LaPoint, Velma Marie	12 Feb 1931	8/ 37
Dickerson, Emery [Winter Garden]	Ray, Vivian [Winter Garden]	19 May 1926	6/ 241
Dickerson, Sherman [Orlando]	Smith, Rosa Lee [Orlando]	4 Apr 1926	6/ 199
Dickerson, Val	Poole, Ethel Belle	25 Feb 1928	7/ 70
Dickey, James Edward Jr [Atlanta GA]	Cochran, Mary Josephine	8 Feb 1926	6/ 151
Dickson, Arthur [B] [Winter Park]	Brewton, Bernice [Orlando]	6 Nov 1925	6/ 79
Dickson, Francis James [W] [Sarasota]	Price, Lona Beryl [Orlando]	26 Dec 1925	6/ 115
Dickson, Frank Leroy	Minor, Lessie Mae	29 Jan 1933	8/ 252
Dickson, John [B] [Orlando]	Cunningham, Ruth Hazel [Orlando]	12 Mar 1925	5/ 568
Dickson, Raymond George	Hall, Martha Ruth	3 Sep 1932	8/ 193
Dieffenwierth, James Ernest	Harton, Josephine Elizabeth	21 Sep 1933	8/ 347
Dierring, Raymond	Leiter, Vera Alice	7 Apr 1934	8/ 461
Dietrick, Frank [Orlando]	Row, Effie Mae [San Diego, CA]	23 Oct 1926	6/ 398
Dill, Joseph	Mumford, Willie Belle	22 Apr 1932	8/ 148
Dinda, Michael James	Walaskay, Annie	21 Oct 1931	8/ 66
Dingle, Elliott	Donelson, Laura	4 Aug 1929	7/ 332
Dingle, John	Culpepper, Laura K.	1 Jul 1928	7/ 154
Dinkins, Grady [Orlando]	Poole, Ethel [Orlando]	24 Jul 1926	6/ 275
Dinkins, Harry	Brown, Mary Frances	30 May 1932	8/ 162
Dinkins, Kade	Bradley, Marie	2 Apr 1932	8/ 136
Dinnick, Norman Howard	Cossey, Francis Mary	31 Dec 1927	7/ 39
Disbrow, George Henry	Booth, Mary Ethel	3 Mar 1934	8/ 441
Ditman, Alonzo Richard	Cooper, Mamie Oliva	29 Apr 1931	7/ 587
Dixon, Alton James [Apopka]	Dees, R. V. [Apopka]	7 Aug 1926	6/ 311
Dixon, Charley [Sanford]	Winn, Mary Elizabeth [St Petersburg]	15 Feb 1926	6/ 154
Dixon, Orange	Morris, Essie	26 Dec 1929	7/ 389
Dobbins, Belvin Jackson, Jr [Orlando]	Kasper, Sophia Louise [Orlando]	5 Jun 1926	6/ 262
Dobbs, Luther	Barksdale, Sallie	24 Mar 1928	7/ 87
Doby, John Henry	Anderson, Lizzie Mae	8 Apr 1934	8/ 471
Dodd, John Henry	Doty, Elizabeth	26 Nov 1930	7/ 525
Dodd, William Henry, Jr. [Orlando]	Tuggle, Margaret [Orlando]	22 Mar 1926	6/ 190
Doherty, Louis W.	Spence, Mary C.	15 Feb 1931	7/ 557
Doherty, William James [Evanston,IL]	Benson, Betty Olivia [Chicago, IL]	2 Feb 1927	6/ 449
Donahue, Albert Purvis	Bowers, Nettie Myrtle	18 Feb 1931	7/ 557
Donahue, Louis Robert	Cook, Lillie Elizabeth	22 Aug 1933	8/ 336
Donaldson, George	Parker, Lucille	12 Nov 1930	7/ 519
Donaldson, Ira Vallie	Bill, Jamie Maude	17 Apr 1928	7/ 103
Donaldson, James Columbus	Harbin, Louise	8 Jul 1930	7/ 478
Dorsey, Cleve [B] [Orlando]	Murray, Mattie [Orlando]	29 Jun 1925	6/ 7
Dougall, Ray [Oviedo]	Shurman, Lillian [Oviedo]	2 Sep 1926	6/ 328

Dougherty, Bruce Mosser	Sellers, Emilie	4 Jun 1931	8/ 16
Douglas, Edward	McKinzie, Anna Lee	6 May 1929	7/ 290
Douglas, Fredric Reeves [Whitman, MA]	Bowker, Ethel Weston [Brockton, MA]	12 Nov 1926	6/ 382
Douglas, Joe [B] [Oakland]	Mitchell, Mary [Oakland]	6 Jul 1925	6/ 13
Douglas, Prince	Russell, Lillian	16 Jun 1930	7/ 468
Douglass, George Grant [Quincy, MA]	Watrons, Etta Sarah [Marathon, NY]	28 Apr 1927	6/ 498
Dow, Frederick Irving	Corbin, Mary W.	13 Sep 1930	7/ 498
Dowd, Lloyd Michael	Provost, Norma	25 Nov 1931	8/ 82
Dowdy, Edward Earl	Roberts, Frances Louise	11 Feb 1933	8/ 257
Dowdy, Walter Marion	Bennett, Annie Lee	15 Jan 1929	7/ 231
Dowling, Curtis Finley	Slone, Bernice Evelyn	5 Mar 1932	8/ 123
Dowling, Ned Jefferson	O'Berry, Ruth Evelyn	21 Jul 1934	8/ 512
Dowling, Oliver Perry	Torrence, Mildred Isabelle	9 Sep 1933	8/ 340
Downing, Donnie McCrea [Orlando]	Dease, Annie Craford [Orlando]	2 Nov 1925	6/ 75
Doyle, Daniel [Orlando]	Ramsdell, Cecile [Orlando]	27 Nov 1926	6/ 392
Drake, Clyde William	Rouse, Myrtle	10 Jun 1928	7/ 136
Drake, Dale [W] [Orlando]	Heath, Cora Ellen [Orlando]	12 May 1925	5/ 576
Drake, Frank [B] [Thomaston, GA]	Russell, Ella Mae [White Plains, GA]	13 Feb 1925	5/ 526
Drake, Frank I. [W] [Mankato, KS]	Roney, Beulah	19 Mar 1925	5/ 545
Drame, Wright [W] [Orlando]	McCarthy, Ethel [Orlando]	8 Feb 1926	6/ 151
Drawdy, Joseph Levi [Pinecastle]	Braddock, Martha Rae [Pinecastle]	3 Jul 1926	6/ 302
Drexler, Paul Benjamin	Ahik, Pansy Anita	11 Nov 1929	7/ 368
Driggers, William Lewis [Sorrento]	Flether, Martha [Ocoee]	12 Oct 1925	6/ 61
Driskell, James Andrew	Rogers, Francis Jan	12 Mar 1929	7/ 262
Droege, August Julius	Wilkening, Rose Emma	2 Jul 1930	7/ 476
Drummer, Richard Thomas	Welch, Beatrice	28 Dec 1929	7/ 390
Duane, John Patrick [Sarasota]	Stansell, Mittis [Winter Garden]	3 Sep 1926	6/ 328
DuBose, Charlie [B] [Orlando]	Toney, Evangeline [Orlando]	16 Nov 1925	6/ 84
Duckworth, Manley Campbell	Howes, Louise Bowen	4 Feb 1933	8/ 254
Dudley, Harold Daniel	French, Greta Emeline	14 Aug 1933	8/ 334
Dudley, James [B] [Orlando]	Dawson, Beulah [Orlando]	14 Jul 1925	6/ 16
Dudley, Louie Lamore	Young, Alice May	31 Jan 1928	7/ 64
Duffy, Joseph A.	Curry, Lela M.	21 Jun 1928	7/ 150
Duggar, Nathaniel J.	Patris, Thelma G.	15 Nov 1927	7/ 14
Duhart, Dempsey	Plight, Geneva	6 Dec 1928	7/ 213
Duhart, George [Orlando]	Jenkins, Thelma [Orlando]	19 Mar 1927	6/ 478
Duhart, George Frank	Alexander, Lena Lorena	25 Dec 1933	8/ 390
Dukart, Champaine [Orlando]	Douglass, Hazel [Orlando]	25 Jun 1927	6/ 544
Duke, Joseph	Batchelor, Queen Rose	11 Apr 1931	7/ 578
Duke, Olon Cecil	Harper, Mary Zulah	24 Dec 1931	8/ 94
Duke, William Marian	Hurst, Allie Henrietta	24 Oct 1931	8/ 64
Dukes, Daniel Webster	Green, Polly Olivia	24 Dec 1930	7/ 537
Dumars, Hayward Renton	Walker, Elinor Selbourne	11 Mar 1931	7/ 569
Dumm, Joseph Stout	Rehse, Ruth	10 Jun 1931	8/ 17
Dumph, Alfred Edward	Smith, Annie Mae	25 Jun 1934	8/ 507
Dunaway, W. E.	Schue, Ivey	10 Dec 1929	7/ 385
Dunbar, Roy [Orlando]	Brown, Pinkie [Orlando]	14 Jan 1927	6/ 437
Duncan, Buell Gard [Orlando]	Parks, Elizabeth [Orlando]	16 Jul 1926	6/ 296
Duncan, Carman Ercell	Folds, Zelma Christine	6 Jan 1934	8/ 408
Duncan, Horace Harold	Hartman, Phoeba Juanita	24 Jun 1928	7/ 147

Duncan, Jessie	Walker, Ethel	26 Aug 1929	7/ 336
Duncan, John Raymond	Smith, Mamie	14 May 1930	7/ 454
Duncan, John Reynolds	Fiedler, Gertrude Grace	11 Oct 1930	7/ 507
Dungan, Donald Edison	Hinson, Evelyn	10 Oct 1929	7/ 358
Dunham, Willie	Jones, Louise	24 Apr 1933	8/ 286
Dunkin, Wil [Orlando]	Edwards, Mary [Orlando]	5 Oct 1926	6/ 348
Dunlap, William Wallace	Hanner, Annie Louise	15 Sep 1928	7/ 184
Dunlop, Hugh Johnston	Jackson, Eleanor Louise	22 Jul 1930	7/ 482
Dunn, Charles Jr.	Branan, Mattie Mae	1 Jun 1931	8/ 12
DuPre, Sidney William [Orlando]	Henry, Elizabeth [Orlando]	27 Apr 1926	6/ 221
DuRant, Archie China [Orlando]	Jones, Wilma Frances [Orlando]	23 Jun 1926	6/ 291
Durden, Estus [W] [Eustis]	Shayler, Wanda [DeLand]	15 Mar 1925	5/ 540
Durden, William Raymond [W] [Orlando]	Foster, Helen Estelle [Orlando]	10 Dec 1925	6/ 98
Durham, Albert	Tisby, Stella	19 Jan 1929	7/ 234
Durham, Richard	Bell, Addie Magnolia	13 Aug 1932	8/ 183
Dushane, Edward Earl [Sanford]	Tabor, Carmen [Sanford]	26 Aug 1925	6/ 39
Dyal, Jacob	Lamb, Alberta	19 Dec 1931	8/ 90
Dyall, Cecil	Hull, Maggie	16 Jan 1931	7/ 544
Dye, James [Orlando]	McGee, Susie [Orlando]	3 Apr 1926	6/ 196
Dykeman, James F. [Lake Wales]	McInnes, Lena [Lisle, IL]	12 May 1927	6/ 534
Dykeman, James Forster	Edwards, Lillian	5 Jun 1930	7/ 463
Dykes, Marvin	Wesley, Thelma J.	17 Jan 1929	7/ 232
Dyson, George	Kimble, Annie Bell	27 Sep 1932	8/ 199

E

Eads, Clarence	Capers, Lula	9 Jan 1928	7/ 41
Eady, Robert Lee [W] [Malabar]	Shupe, Ellen [Eatonton, GA]	3 Jun 1925	5/ 599
Eagin, Thomas J.	Pomeroy, Francis	23 Nov 1927	7/ 32
Eagleson, William Boal [B] [Wyncotte, PA]	Sturges, Helen Margaret [Orlando]	23 Feb 1925	5/ 532
Ealey, George Washington	Moultry, Arie	22 Mar 1930	7/ 430
Earhart, James Osborn [Dayton, PA]	Tally, Burtis [Luin, MS}	7 Oct 1926	6/ 349
Easley, Lewis	Williams, Evelyn	24 Feb 1929	7/ 256
Eastman, Rufus John	Tanner, Beatrice Allena	5 Jul 1932	8/ 176
Eberhart, Joseph Jackson	Boerster, Bertha Nella Ruth	22 Jun 1929	7/ 316
Echard, Chas. Elmer Randall [Mt Lake Park, MD]	Hutchins, Ruby Mae [Hobart, OK]	28 Feb 1926	6/ 196
Eckreth, Edward Earl	Stopher, Anna Josephine	16 Mar 1930	7/ 428
Eddenfield, William Phairy	Tuton, Harriettee Florence	29 Sep 1927	6/ 588
Eddie, Henry	Batchlor, Mildred	12 May 1930	7/ 453
Eddy, Roy Nathan	Rivenbark, Melba Madelle	21 Oct 1932	8/ 206
Edenfield, Jessie M. [Zellwood]	Goolsby, Pearl [Zellwood]	18 Oct 1925	6/ 69
Edgram, Fred Samuel [Orlando]	Wyatt, Dorothy Knans [Orlando]	13 Aug 1926	6/ 308
Edris, Charles Henry	Skaggs, Frances Allama	26 Mar 1930	7/ 432
Edris, Edwin Nichol	Parker, Geraldine Elizabeth	28 Nov 1931	8/ 86
Edwards, Alonzo [Orlando]	Robinson, Willie Mae	9 Apr 1927	6/ 489
Edwards, Charles [B] [Sorrento]	Thompson, Norma Ray [Plymouth]	27 Jun 1925	6/ 5
Edwards, David Stewart [W] [Zellwood]	Baker, Dorothy Marie [Orlando]	25 Nov 1925	6/ 103
Edwards, George C.	Joiner, Ambrett Laverne	8 Jun 1933	8/ 311
Edwards, Hassie Walker	Jackson, Mabel	13 Nov 1928	7/ 208
Edwards, Jas.(B) [Orlando]	Williams, Rosetta [Orlando]	18 Jul 1925	6/ 18
Edwards, Joe Nathan	Ray, Edith	15 Jan 1931	7/ 542

Edwards, Rufus	McIntosh, Anna	19 Oct 1931	8/ 61
Edwards, Warren Spencer [Ashville, NC]	Metcalf, Bessie Landreth [Ashville, NC]	19 Oct 1926	6/ 357
Edwards, Willie	Jackson, Hattie Mae	21 Oct 1929	7/ 360
Egan, Joseph Thomas	Rock, Francis L.	12 Oct 1928	7/ 241
Einstein, Harry Victor	Hickson, Eleanor Lenora	13 May 1931	8/ 2
Eiselstein, W. D.	Fisk, Susan N.	26 Dec 1928	7/ 223
Ekkelboon, Frederick Meeus	Wind, Jantje	27 Mar 1934	8/ 449
Elam, James [B] [Orlando]	Ginyard, Versele [Orlando]	1 Feb 1925	5/ 520
Elam, Nick	Powell, Ruby	10 May 1930	7/ 451
Eldridge, Everett	Hodge, Anna	31 Jan 1931	7/ 550
Eliby, David	Carrington, Anna	29 Oct 1929	7/ 362
Elkins, Fred [Orlando]	Martin, Lola [Orlando]	28 Oct 1926	6/ 368
Eller, James Harley	Keen, Lillie Lucille	30 Oct 1927	7/ 4
Ellerson, Nelson Leroy	Lane, Gayarine	24 Dec 1927	7/ 30
Ellick, Matt [Orlando]	Moss, Carrie [Orlando]	5 Mar 1927	6/ 469
Elliott, Charles Clifford	Ware, Florence Eleanor	31 Mar 1928	7/ 93
Elliott, Eugene [Orlando]	Cornell, Drucilla [Abba, GA]	31 Dec 1926	6/ 424
Elliott, John [B] [Taft]	Jones, Annie [Taft]	19 Jan 1925	5/ 514
Elliott, William	Snowden, Verona	18 May 1932	8/ 157
Ellis, A. W. [Orlando]	Jansen, Elsie [Orlando]	17 Jun 1926	6/ 270
Ellis, Allen Monroe	Sims, Carmen	13 Nov 1927	7/ 14
Ellis, Conrade Howell	Lewis, Pearl Estelle	9 May 1932	8/ 152
Ellis, Fred LaFayette [W] [Orlando]	Leighty, Mary Viola [Orlando]	11 Dec 1925	6/ 98
Ellis, Lehman Lewis	Skipper, Alma	22 Jan 1928	7/ 51
Ellison, Denver Landsay	Patton, Alice Betty	28 Nov 1928	7/ 209
Ellison, J. W.	Lawrence, Ida	3 Dec 1928	7/ 211
Ellison, J. W.	Goolsby, Dewey	26 Jul 1934	8/ 514
Ellison, Robert	Bradford, Ina	18 Feb 1933	8/ 259
Ellison, Victor D.	Hawthorne, Nellie	26 Dec 1928	7/ 223
Ellsworth, Ralph Waldo	Brown, Maude May	24 Feb 1931	7/ 560
Elmer, John Henry [W] [Orlando]	Thompson, Voncile [Orlando]	20 Jun 1925	6/ 2
Elrod, Leonard	Nicholson, Clara	15 Nov 1929	7/ 370
Elrod, Leonard [Orlando]	Strawn, Gladys Miller [Orlando]	2 May 1926	6/ 229
Elsberry, Homer Grady	Benefield, Clara	5 Mar 1932	8/ 122
Emerick, Charles Russell [Orlando]	Goodwin, Mary Wilder [Orlando]	17 Apr 1927	6/ 493
Emerson, C. V.	Whitshead, Norma	2 May 1930	7/ 451
Emerson, John Francis	Hinson, Bessie Erin	11 Nov 1933	8/ 366
Emmans, David William [W] [Marksboro VT] [Clermont]	Bailey, Edith May 29 Dec 1925		6/ 122
Emmel, Roland [W] [Orlando]	Forrester, Louise [Orlando]	5 Nov 1925	6/ 76
Emrich, William	Wilson, Nellie Frances	11 Oct 1932	8/ 209
Emzie, Joe	Manuel, Hattie	19 May 1928	7/ 115
Engdahl, Harold Allen	Rogers, Alice Josephine	2 Jun 1930	7/ 461
English, Forrest Alexander	Hardy, Harriet Leetta	3 Jul 1933	8/ 321
Ervin, John [B] [Orlando]	Farmer, Julia May [Orlando]	31 Mar 1925	5/ 549
Ervin, Thomas	King, Lillie	29 Mar 1931	7/ 573
Ervine, Charles Douglas	Clark, Anne Doherty	28 Mar 1930	7/ 433
Espedahl, Kaarie	Stark, Susan Elizabeth	14 Jul 1928	7/ 170
Estes, Stuart Rogers [Victor, NY]	Helm, Edith Louise [Manchester. NH]	5 Apr 1926	6/ 198
Estes, William Nicholson	Estes, Dorothy Edna	10 May 1930	7/ 453

Esther, Ernest [B] [Orlando]	Latson, Ida [Orlando]	27 Jun 1925	6/ 5
Etheridge, Walter P.	Harrison, Annie W.	20 Nov 1933	8/ 370
Euell, James [Orlando]	Henderson, Luella [Orlando]	10 Sep 1925	6/ 43
Eunice, Earl G.	Knight, Dorothy Maud	7 Jun 1928	7/ 132
Evans, Amos	Roney, Lillian	22 May 1930	7/ 458
Evans, Frederick Parker	Hanna, Mignon Amanda	7 Jul 1931	8/ 29
Evans, Hamilton Clark [Orlando]	Clark, Katherine Elizabeth [Orlando]	22 Mar 1926	6/ 186
Evans, Herbert Henry	Peterson, Pauline Grace	5 Oct 1933	8/ 349
Evans, J. D., Jr [Lake City]	McCranie, Sallie Mae [Orlando]	5 May 1926	6/ 229
Evans, Loring Palmer [Tampa]	Dukes, Addie Lucille [Bartow, GA]	24 May 1927	6/ 522
Evans, Sam [Orlando]	Harvey, Brazie [Orlando]	30 Oct 1926	6/ 369
Evans, William Lee	Pollard, Leta Ruth	1 May 1928	7/ 107
Evans, William Randolph	Bowen, Edith	11 Aug 1928	7/ 171
Everage, William [Orlando]	Dasher, Lillie Mae [Orlando]	6 Nov 1926	6/ 378
Everette, Grayes Thomas [W] [Apopka]	Baker, Irene [Zellwood]	19 Jun 1925	6/ 2
Everly, Wilbur	Hancock, Viola Elizabeth	17 Apr 1934	8/ 463
Everton, Charles	Thomson, Kate	2 Oct 1927	6/ 592
Exion, Alfred Due	Tillman, Sallie Ree	24 Feb 1934	8/ 437
Ezzard, John T., Jr.	Layton, Charlotte Elizabeth	9 Aug 1929	7/ 332

F

Fair, George Colbourne	Hotaling, Lucile	2 Jul 1933	8/ 321
Fairbank, Bentley Almond	Stark, Elnora Marie	7 Apr 1928	7/ 95
Fairfax, Jessie	Wilburn, Odessa	26 Apr 1930	7/ 443
Faith, Kenneth John [Orlando]	Hier, Kathryn Gena [Orlando]	28 Jun 1926	6/ 285
Fanning, Charlie William	Williams, Evelyn	28 Mar 1933	8/ 277
Farless, Alfred	Smith, Catherine	28 Jun 1934	8/ 501
Farley, Carl Howard	Ingersoll, Dorothy May	2 Mar 1933	8/ 269
Farmer, Robert Lee	Greenburg, Marie Grace	15 Jun 1928	7/ 143
Farrell, Eben Walter	Williams, Mary	1 Nov 1928	7/ 209
Farrington, John Moody [Lovel, ME]	Bower, Helen Beer [Tangerine]	27 Mar 1926	6/ 194
Fashaw, Sampson	Jordan, Annie	19 Oct 1932	8/ 206
Fason, Charlie	Wright, Ollie Mae	29 Apr 1929	7/ 288
Fatula, M. G.	Hockstresser, Florence	18 Aug 1928	7/ 174
Faulk, Joe Brown	Chastain, Jennings Ida	10 Apr 1932	8/ 141
Favors, Richard	Jones, Nettie	10 Feb 1929	7/ 242
Feacher, Anthony [B] [Jacksonville]	Peterson, Estelle [Orlando]	23 Dec 1925	6/ 117
Feainside, Frank Joseph	Perry, Mary Angeline	23 Sep 1930	7/ 501
Fekaney, George	Hage, Waddell	14 Sep 1930	7/ 497
Fekany, Samuel Anthony	Kaba, Rescida	16 Oct 1932	8/ 208
Felder, Eugene [Winter Park]	Laughlin, Mary [Winter Park]	3 Feb 1926	6/ 149
Felder, Willie	Bennett, Mary Agieful	13 Dec 1933	8/ 384
Felipek, Joseph	Tindall, Marjorie Ellen	24 Nov 1927	7/ 18
Fellows, John James	Durdine, Marie Alina	5 Sep 1926	6/ 333
Felton, Alfonso	Brown, Leona	17 Mar 1931	7/ 569
Felton, J. W.	McClendon, Mamie	23 Apr 1933	8/ 287
Felton, P. K.	Morris, Elmira	29 Apr 1930	7/ 444
Fennel, Willie [Orlando]	Hooks, Lucretia [Orlando]	14 Feb 1926	6/ 154
Fenneman, Harry B.	Kirkhof, Lillian M.	23 Jul 1928	7/ 164
Ferguson, Malcolm McAskell	Harrison, Elizabeth Ford	30 Apr 1934	8/ 472
Ferrel, Ira David	Green, Sarah Ethel	2 Apr 1932	8/ 137

Ferris, James Stephen	Curcio, Angeline	10 Apr 1932	8/ 140
Ferris, William Clyde	Faulkner, Florence Elizabeth	3 Nov 1929	7/ 366
Fester, Albert George [Orlando]	Decker, Caroline Hazel [Orlando]	6 Jan 1926	6/ 142
Fetner, Andrew	Smith, Ezelle	14 Apr 1929	7/ 279
Ficken, Hubert Carroll	Grantham, Ellen Faye	11 Jan 1933	8/ 241
Field, Archie P. [Orlando]	Nickerson, Gertrude Johnson	15 Sep 1926	6/ 339
Field, Marton Wesley [Orlando]	Rupp, Lucille [Orlando]	20 Aug 1927	6/ 568
Fields, Daniel Wallace	Smith, Martha Ann	3 Aug 1931	8/ 39
Fields, James	Williams, Lillie	3 May 1933	8/ 289
Fields, Jesse	Quarterman, Essie Mae	17 Oct 1927	6/ 598
Fikes, Leon	Wilder, Sarah	19 Jun 1929	7/ 311
Filosa, Dominick	Semarors, Francis	26 Apr 1928	7/ 104
Fincher, William Carlton	Vose, Margie Lavell	30 Mar 1931	7/ 572
Fink, Albert George [Orlando]	Long, Birdie Mae [Orlando]	4 Jun 1926	6/ 259
Finley, Charles	Holmon, Bertha	3 Mar 1928	7/ 75
Finley, Charley [B] [Orlando]	Blake, Bessie [Orlando]	14 May 1925	5/ 573
Finley, J. B.	Joyner, Viola B.	19 Feb 1931	7/ 558
Finn, Roscoe Samuel [Orlando]	Stewart, Jessie Angela [Orlando]	5 Nov 1926	6/ 381
Finne, Harold A.	Novell, Mildred C.	15 May 1928	7/ 116
Fischer, Edward Ernest	Mach, Mary Ann	13 Jul 1929	7/ 325
Fishback, George Benjamin [Orlando]	Bumby, Florence [Winter Garden]	23 Jun 1927	6/ 545
Fisher, Arch MacMillan	Lamb, Lula Mae	29 Nov 1933	8/ 376
Fisher, Emmett Russell [Winter Park]	Hartshorn, Wanda [Woodsfield, OH]	6 Nov 1926	6/ 375
Fisher, George Harry	Boyd, Margaret Jeanne	9 Nov 1929	7/ 368
Fisher, LeRoy Arthur [Providence, RI]	Belanger, Veronica Philomena [Providence, RI]	15 Feb1926	6/ 155
Fisher, Matthew Yates	Ivey, Mary Bell	25 Apr 1928	7/ 102
Fisher, Rollie Alexander	Foote, Nina Malba	10 Mar 1932	8/ 138
Fisher, Walter E.	Farless, Ruby	9 Feb 1930	7/ 413
Fitzgerald, Albert Edward	Willits, Alice	30 Aug 1933	8/ 338
Fitzgerald, James William	Anderson, Mary Glover	13 Nov 1932	8/ 217
Flanagan, Edward Norman	Ricketson, Sarah Louise	27 Feb 1933	8/ 262
Flanders, Frank [B] [Orlando]	Mills, Lucile M. [Orlando]	31 Jan 1925	5/ 520
Fleming, Dalton	Woodley, Emma Juanita	26 May 1934	8/ 481
Fleming, John Lee	Wright, Florence Emma	18 Dec 1933	8/ 392
Fleming, Seaf	Hay, Jessie	5 May 1929	7/ 292
Fleming, William Ray [Miami]	Crutchfield, Grace [Pinecastle]	24 Jan 1926	6/ 145
Fleming, William Roy	Irvin, Mary	3 May 1934	8/ 472
Flessner, Anthony	Morris, Maude Isabelle	12 Jul 1928	7/ 159
Flett, Robert Haines [W] [Tampa]	Williams, Gladys Edith [Wyoming, NJ]	2 Apr 1925	5/ 551
Flick, Edwin F. [Orlando]	Kloss, Edna Lucile	11 Sep 1926	6/ 338
Flowers, Donald Carroll [Orlando]	Cook, Mildred Elizabeth [Orlando]	25 Feb 1926	6/ 169
Flowers, Jessie Hugh [W] [Winter Park]	Williams, Jessie Irene [Winter Park]	3 Nov 1925	6/ 74
Flowers, John William	Cross, Myrtle Susie	10 May 1932	8/ 152
Floyd, Charlie	Bomens, Addie	28 Feb 1929	7/ 252
Floyd, Daniel	Edwards, Lucinda	19 Jun 1930	7/ 469
Floyd, Ollie	Harris, Lizzie	17 May 1934	8/ 476
Floyd, Willis	Barnes, Beatrice	17 Jan 1928	7/ 47
Flynn, Oswald Lee [W] [Orlando]	Brundage, Lucia Pauline [Orlando]	30 Oct 1925	6/ 73
Flynn, Van Watson	Weeks, Lois Odell	12 Apr 1931	7/ 579

Flythe, Oscar	Bassford, Jennie May	20 Jan 1932	8/ 105
Fobbs, James Olin	Ambrose, Thelma Roberta	19 Oct 1931	8/ 62
Folds, Richard Ham	Ivey, Mary Elizabeth	23 May 1931	8/ 5
Folk, Benjamin F.	Arrington, Mae E.	13 Oct 1929	7/ 361
Foller, George Dewey [East Orange, NJ]	Andrews, Jessie Mable	1 Apr 1927	6/ 488
Folts, Meade Colbrook	Lilly, Carol Mary	13 Nov 1933	8/ 367
Foote, Robert William	Woodard, Ellen	18 Nov 1933	8/ 370
Ford, Abraham	Hill, Mary Lee	12 Feb 1931	7/ 557
Ford, Albert Hamlin	Taylor, Bessie	22 Mar 1928	7/ 86
Ford, Anderson Berk	Smith, Jessie	8 Jan 1934	8/ 407
Ford, Arthur [Orlando]	Smith, Willie Mae [Orlando]	25 Oct 1926	6/ 364
Ford, Charles	Ford, Priscille	14 Nov 1929	7/ 373
Ford, Claud	Parkam, Mary	22 Dec 1928	7/ 221
Ford, Clifton	Bryant, Corine	10 Jan 1930	7/ 399
Ford, Dan Rabon [B] [Orlando]	Morris, Bella [Orlando]	13 Jan 1926	6/ 133
Ford, Harry Preston	Gilliam, Ruth	30 Aug 1930	7/ 494
Ford, Louis	Cuyler, Ellen	5 Dec 1931	8/ 84
Ford, Oliver	Brown, Beatrice	11 Dec 1932	8/ 227
Ford, Oscar Frederick	Adkins, Ruby Elizabeth	12 Jun 1932	8/ 168
Ford, Otis Bell	Dantley, Lucy Mae	6 Feb 1934	8/ 424
Fordham, James	Williams, Birdie M.	20 Feb 1930	7/ 417
Fore, Nolan	Jacobs, Evelyn Annie	22 Apr 1933	8/ 286
Foreman, Charlie [Orlando]	Hill, Hettie [Orlando]	9 Nov 1926	6/ 378
Foreman, Reuben Daniel	Nolen, Rosa Lee	2 May 1933	8/ 291
Former, Calvin	McNish, Mable	14 Nov 1931	8/ 74
Forrester, Albert [Orlando]	Herring, Mamie [Orlando]	21 Apr 1926	6/ 215
Forster, Clarence	Cutts, Nettie Mae	10 Feb 1934	8/ 426
Fort, Frank	Washington, Polly	3 Oct 1932	8/ 202
Fort, James	Figgin, Cora	23 Feb 1928	7/ 69
Fort, James A.	Brown, Elizabeth	19 Apr 1930	7/ 440
Fortenbach, Julian [W] [E. Rutherford, NJ]	Bagett, Luella [Pinecastle]	12 May 1925	5/ 580
Fortman, Frank Homer	Richey, Ruth Elizabeth	9 Sep 1930	7/ 496
Fortney, John [B] [Winter Park]	Brooks, Isabelle [Winter Park]	20 Jun 1925	5/ 586
Foss, Clarence Claude	O'Steen, Lena Agnes	26 Jul 1931	8/ 35
Foster, Earl Allen	Goodie, Lucile Fayette	19 Mar 1931	7/ 570
Foster, Eddie Lee	Whitlow, Gertrude	5 May 1930	7/ 446
Foster, George A.	Ashmore, Annie Laura	20 Jun 1928	7/ 144
Foster, Ira	Smith, Mabel	3 Aug 1933	8/ 331
Foster, Joselone	Smith, Edith	10 Jan 1928	7/ 48
Fowler, Doss [Wilmer, NC]	Mitchell, Lula	2 Feb 1927	6/ 449
Fowler, Floyd	Porcher, Cora	12 Jul 1927	6/ 552
Fowler, Harold Earl, Jr.	Britt, Sarah Virginia	4 Oct 1929	7/ 355
Fox, Frank Andrew [Manchester, NH]	Choats, Sarah Liza [Manchester, NH]	22 Dec 1926	6/ 415
Fox, Leonard Alfred	Liberoff, Sylvia	1 Jun 1930	7/ 463
Fox, William Martin	Brady, Ruth Violet	21 Dec 1927	7/ 35
Foxworth, Lewis	Jones, Arlie	24 Dec 1928	7/ 219
Foxworth, Lonnie	Little, Lottie	6 May 1930	7/ 448
Foy, Jonas	Warren, Mildred Blackstock	18 May 1932	8/ 158
Francis, Robert	Thompson, Leola	11 Oct 1930	7/ 505
Franklin, Elmer Everett	Gregory, Cora Lee	12 Dec 1931	8/ 87
Franklin, Frank [Winter Garden]	Mitchell, Lollie [Winter Garden]	2 Mar 1926	6/ 167
Franson, Claus	Arthur, Nellie John	14 Apr 1934	8/ 462

Fraser, Guy Blaine	McSweeney, Lenora	10 May 1930	7/ 452
Frawley, Ulysses B. [W] [Orlando]	Hers, Mary [Orlando]	19 Mar 1925	5/ 544
Frazer, Stepney [Apopka]	Brown, Lizzie [Apopka]	16 Feb 1927	6/ 457
Frazier, Joseph L.	Larson, Mary	26 Mar 1931	7/ 571
Frazier, Sollie	McClinton, Maggie	29 Dec 1927	7/ 35
Frederick, Albert	Ray, Annie Lee	25 Oct 1928	7/ 199
Frederick, Jim	Lee, Sarah	3 Nov 1928	7/ 201
Fredericks, F. [W] [Sanford]	Baxter, Mary [Mims]	20 Jul 1925	6/ 25
Frederickson, Carl	Pearson, Christine	3 May 1932	8/ 151
Fredrick, Alvin O. [Cleveland, OH]	Smith, Bernice [Orlando]	2 Sep 1925	6/ 41
Freelove, Alvin Whittier [Orlando]	Dingwell, Ruth McNairn [Portland, ME]	5 Mar 1927	6/ 475
Freeman, Elliot [B] [Orlando]	Lesesne, Mary [Orlando]	22 Jun 1925	6/ 1
Freeman, Francis Clyde	Spivey, Frances Elizabeth	24 Jun 1933	8/ 316
Freeman, George Chester	Franklin, Myrtle Ione	1 Jun 1929	7/ 339
Freeman, James	Smith, Zilla	9 Oct 1929	7/ 356
Freeman, Wade Wolfe	Boyd, Mary Velma	30 Aug 1933	8/ 338
French, Allison Taylor	Carson, Ida Maud	8 Sep 1929	7/ 344
French, John Lynn	Hartley, Elma Etha	17 Aug 1932	8/ 185
Friend, Frederick William [W. Palm Beach]	Stone, Gladys M. [W. Palm Beach]	30 Apr 1927	6/ 510
Friend, Theodore Henry [Orlando]	Comstock, Lucy Daniels [Orlando]	1 May 1926	6/ 227
Frier, Edgar Monroe	Ray, Sybil Pauline	14 Jan 1933	8/ 244
Frint, Thomas [Orlando]	Porter, Mattie Nell [Huntington, WV]	14 Oct 1926	6/ 354
Frison, Carroll Gerard	Alexander, Mildred Inez	10 Feb 1934	8/ 428
Froe, Sybil	Brown, Marjorie	25 Nov 1927	7/ 17
Fronk, Arthur James	Patrick, Thelma Louise	20 May 1933	8/ 302
Frost, Webster Marion [Elberton, GA]	Smith, Theodoria Zeno [Orlando]	19 Feb 1927	6/ 463
Fryer, John [Orlando]	Mauer, Viola	2 Aug 1927	6/ 566
Fugate, Burl Wesley	Wiggins, Ruth Evelyn	24 May 1933	8/ 304
Fulbright, Fred	Pattigrew, Mary Elizabeth	7 Mar 1928	7/ 79
Fuller, Glen Lyman [W] [Jacksonville]	Smith, Flora Arsula [Jacksonville]	18 Aug 1925	6/ 35
Fuller, Henry Dewrel [W] [Winter Garden]	Jones, Laura [Winter Garden]	19 May 1925	5/ 576
Fuller, Horace [Orlando]	Bennett, Arree [Orlando]	24 May 1926	6/ 245
Fuller, John [Orlando]	Flournoy, Laura [Orlando]	22 Nov 1926	6/ 388
Fuller, John [Orlando]	Brooks, Ella [Orlando]	10 Jun 1926	6/ 263
Fuller, John [Orlando]	Jordan, Anna [Orlando]	22 May 1926	6/ 244
Fuller, Leo Herbert	Freeman, Bessie Lee	11 Feb 1928	7/ 63
Fuller, Russell Lewis	Foley, Helen Erskine	19 Oct 1930	7/ 510
Fulmore, Alexander	Mills, Lucile	2 Apr 1929	7/ 271
Fussell, Timothy Jacob	Ennis, Lillie Mae	8 Dec 1928	7/ 212
Futch, Frank	Griner, Dorothy Louise	10 Jun 1931	8/ 16
Futch, Marcus Lee	Melson, Estella May	7 Apr 1928	7/ 93
Futral, William E. [Ft Meyers]	Pruther, Zona H. [Maryville, TN]	2 Oct 1925	6/ 62
Futrell, George Washington [Orlando]	Newton, Lillie Adell [Orlando]	3 Apr 1926	6/ 195
Futrell, Grover Cleveland [W] [Conway]	Martin, Sarah Lunet [Orlando]	24 May 1925	5/ 579

G

Gadaire, Clifford Eugene [W] [Brookfield, MA]	Llewellyn, Doris Grace [Worcester, MA]	21 Feb 1925	5/ 531

Gadeberg, Robert Fischer	Klingberg, Kaura	8 Nov 1931	8/ 73
Gadson, Alonzo	Douglass, Letha	14 Feb 1931	7/ 555
Gage, Verne Ellworth	Schuell, Emma Louise Amelia	21 Dec 1929	7/ 387
Gainer, Ben	Ross, Blanche	17 May 1930	7/ 456
Gaines, Berrien L. [W] [Orlando]	Raulerson, Maggie [Bithlo]	7 Mar 1925	5/ 536
Gaines, Dwight A. [W] [Clermont]	Kirwin, Ruby N. [Clermont]	28 Jan 1925	5/ 517
Gaines, Elijah	Albright, Annie Mae	26 Sep 1932	8/ 199
Galbraith, Renwick Dodds [W] [Orlando]	Huheey, Sarah Alice [Orlando]	23 Jun 1925	6/ 6
Gallagher, Patrick Byron	Dibble, Dorothy	27 Dec 1929	7/ 390
Galloway, Leroy [Orlando] (gives address]	Patrick, Fannie [Tampa] (gives address]	26 Dec 1925	6/ 116
Gamble, Albert P.	Blair, Mildred	9 Jul 1928	7/ 160
Gamble, Theodore [B] [Orlando]	Butts, Mattie [Orlando]	20 Jun 1925	5/ 586
Gamble, William	Dyke, Elizabeth	29 May 1928	7/ 131
Gambrill, Roland Gladyn	Jones, Eloise Ozella	21 Feb 1928	7/ 68
Gandy, Walter [Orlando]	Roberson, Corine [Orlando]	3 Sep 1926	6/ 329
Garcia, Manuel	White, Lizzie	2 Apr 1930	7/ 434
Gardenhire, Fred Jetmore [W] [Orlando]	Abbott, Caryl Bird [Orlando]	12 Jun 1925	5/ 593
Gardner, Henry Elbert [Ft. Pierce]	Phillipp, Willie Vera	25 May 1927	6/ 515
Gardner, Henry George	Rowell, Veedie Othalia	29 Aug 1928	7/ 177
Gardner, Martin Luther	Freeman, Mary	2 Mar 1929	7/ 255
Garfield, James Jenkins [Orlando]	Acky, Mary Liza [Orlando]	4 Mar 1926	6/ 168
Garman, A. G. [Orlando]	Hicks, Betty [Orlando]	5 Mar 1927	6/ 470
Garman, William	Marshall, Elizabeth	30 Jan 1934	8/ 420
Garnett, George	Gilbert, Rebecca	18 Apr 1932	8/ 143
Garret, John [Orlando]	Werlene, Lucille [Orlando]	25 Sep 1925	6/ 52
Garrett, Artie [Eustis]	Driggars, Estelle [Eustis]	20 Mar 1926	6/ 182
Garrett, Herman	Alben, Willie Rae	10 Aug 1930	7/ 488
Garrett, Palmer [Orlando]	Jones, Julia [Orlando]	18 May 1927	6/ 511
Garrison, Solomon Geesner [Pekin, IN]	Daugherty, Mildred [Pittsburg, PA]	22 Feb 1927	6/ 468
Garvin, Lucius [Ocoee]	Coriker, Georgia [Ocoee]	13 Feb 1926	6/ 154
Garvin, Rufus Wilson	Hull, Edna Veda	29 Dec 1933	8/ 404
Garvin, Willie	Borders, Estella	29 May 1928	7/ 121
Gary, A. Z. [Orlando]	Owens, Maud [Orlando]	20 Jun 1927	6/ 538
Gary, Jack	Mathis, Rosa	6 Jan 1934	8/ 401
Gary, James [Orlando]	Prince, Neetie May	6 Jul 1927	6/ 545
Gary, Wheeler [B] [Orlando]	Gordon, Catherine [Orlando]	15 Aug 1925	6/ 32
Gaskin, Shelby Gunn	Donnell, Shirley	22 Mar 1932	8/ 132
Gaskins, Willie	McGuire, Leanna	25 Dec 1933	8/ 394
Gasslin, Louis Emerson, Jr.	Fuller, Dorothy	27 Oct 1933	8/ 357
Gaston, William [B] [Orlando]	Thompson, Ethel Mae [Orlando]	5 Mar 1925	5/ 537
Gatlin, Lewis Jackson	Bronson, Margaret Elinor	13 Mar 1932	8/ 127
Gaulding, Norman Miller	Hawks, Bessie Sanders	8 Feb 1930	7/ 412
Gaulman, James Marion	Phillips, Leola	24 Jul 1933	8/ 328
Gavin, James W.	Finch, Allie N.	21 Jun 1928	7/ 149
Gavin, Theodore [Orlando]	Colden, Daisy [Orlando]	19 Sep 1925	6/ 47
Gay, James Lewis, Jr.	Price, Helen Dae	28 Oct 1933	8/ 357
Gay, Joseph	Draffin, Mae	16 Jan 1928	7/ 45
Gemeinhardt, Otto Henry	Touchstone, Sadye Elizabeth	9 Feb 1934	8/ 428
Gemeinhardt, William August [Orlando]	Buick, Louise Barbara [Orlando]	2 Dec 1926	6/ 398
Genrett, Rosevelt	Hedgman, Izora	21 Jan 1934	8/ 415
Gentile, Luther Joe	Bailey, Imogene	16 Dec 1927	7/ 26
George, Eugene	Gambrell, Clara	17 Jan 1928	7/ 46

Geraci, Domenick	Gentile, Lena Mary	28 Jun 1931	8/ 25
Gibbs, James C.	Griffith, Katherine Hunter	21 Mar 1932	8/ 132
Gibson, Bunyon Alton	Watford, Lois	1 Sep 1929	7/ 340
Gibson, Edward Lane	Matthews, Lucille Alma	19 Nov 1931	8/ 84
Gibson, Norman William [Orlando]	Campbell, Mabel Elizabeth [Orlando]	10 Apr 1926	6/ 204
Gibson, Reese Erritt	Brinson, Laura Mae	25 Nov 1932	8/ 220
Giddens, Charles Buford	McDonald, Mamie	3 Apr 1932	8/ 139
Gilbert, Ad. S. [DeLand]	Sanderson, Emily [Kissimmee]	6 Feb 1927	6/ 459
Gilbert, Charles Turner [Orlando]	Jersey, Josephine Theresa [Pinecastle]	5 Jun 1926	6/ 261
Gilbert, Josh [Orlando]	Bankston, Katie May [Orlando]	16 Jul 1927	6/ 551
Gilbert, Marvin L. [Sanford]	Runge, Gertrude [Sanford]	15 Sep 1925	6/ 46
Gilham, Taylor [B] [Orlando]	Weaver, Mattie [Orlando]	9 Jan 1925	5/ 510
Gilleon, John Bert	Dease, Annie Laura	30 Jan 1932	8/ 111
Gilles, James	James, Lettie	16 Oct 1930	7/ 509
Gilliam, Garrette Irving [Clarcona]	Richardson, Elva Mae [Plymouth]	14 May 1927	6/ 506
Gilliam, William Napier	Anderson, Lillian	16 Apr 1931	7/ 584
Gilliard, J. D. [Winter Garden	Carter, Lila [Winter Garden]	27 Sep 1926	6/ 344
Gillies, Theodore Edward [Orlando]	Clark, Juanita Margaret [Miami]	10 Nov 1926	6/ 379
Gillison, Ike [Orlando]	Mays, Carrie [Orlando]	12 Jul 1927	6/ 549
Gilman, R. B. [W] [Orlando]	Power, Maud Lee [Florence, AL]	8 Jul 1925	6/ 11
Gilmore, Henry	Jackson, Rosland	10 Nov 1930	7/ 518
Gilmore, Irvin Erastus	Green, Laurie Lillian	28 Apr 1932	8/ 149
Gilyard, Elishe	Chislom, Emma Lane	13 Jun 1931	8/ 18
Gironard, Adelard	Teneyck, Daisy M.	4 Jul 1933	8/ 322
Givens, Joseph Royce [Wichita, KS]	Kibler, Mary Francis [Winter Park]	26 Jan 1926	6/ 145
Givens, Tom [B] [Orlando]	Girley, Lula [Orlando]	10 May 1925	5/ 571
Gladden, Michael [Apopka]	Means, Edith Arleen	13 Sep 1926	6/ 338
Gladis, John Joseph	Zeller, Mary Courtney	6 Jun 1931	8/ 14
Glass, George J. [B] [Orlando]	Pasture, Emma [Ocala]	12 Apr 1925	5/ 559
Glass, Nelson Sanford	Roberts, Jane LaRue	14 May 1932	8/ 161
Glass, Robert Heman	Welch, Katherine Hollis	27 May 1933	8/ 308
Glass, Wilbert Julian	Rudd, Rochelle	3 Sep 1932	8/ 190
Gleaner, Raymond Chester [Trenton, NJ]	Eistell, Elan Owen [Aromgellia, KY]	4 Jun 1927	6/ 526
Glenn, Hill James [W] [Sanford]	Myers, Ruth Irene [Sanford]	28 Jul 1925	6/ 30
Glenson, Don Mattherson	Warner, Mary Edna	12 May 1928	7/ 113
Glisson, Benjamin Frank [Orlando]	Milton, Erma [Orlando]	16 Dec 1926	6/ 408
Glouser, Zack [Winter Haven]	Kikts, Gertrude [Winter Haven]	8 Nov 1926	6/ 379
Glover, Arthur Leland	Bronson, Kathryn Louise	27 Dec 1927	7/ 32
Glover, Cornelius [Oakland]	Revels, Susie [Oakland]	11 Jun 1927	6/ 530
Glover, Martin [Orlando]	Johnson, Lillian [Orlando]	6 Jun 1927	6/ 525
Glover, Thomas Armstrong	Smith, Flora Mae	1 Mar 1929	7/ 254
Glover, Willie	Dantzler, Viola	17 Feb 1934	8/ 433
Glymph, James	Walker, Cordie	4 Nov 1929	7/ 367
Glynn, Willis James	Parker, Julia	16 Apr 1934	8/ 467
Godard, Albert J.	Alverson, Mary Lee	1 Oct 1927	6/ 589
Godbee, Albert B.	Farmer, Iva	5 Apr 1930	7/ 436
Godbold, Roy	Shaw, Flora Mae	18 Oct 1930	7/ 512
Godwin, Isaac Spencer	Humphrey, Cleo Edna	2 Aug 1934	8/ 518
Goethe, Edward Eemeys	Johnson, Celia Faye	18 May 1929	7/ 314
Goette, William Louis [Eustis]	Harris, Nannie Davis [Winter Park]	10 Jun 1926	6/ 266

Goff, Edwin Preston	Powers, Lois	10 Nov 1929	7/ 371
Goforth, Ralph Suggs [Orlando]	Smith, Marie Anna Statia [Orlando]	16 Aug 1927	6/ 566
Goin, Frank H.	Peckham, Claudine	2 Sep 1928	7/ 179
Golden, Albert Edward [Orlando]	Hendry, Gladys Elizabeth [Orlando]	22 Apr 1926	6/ 215
Goldman, Bosey	Anthony, Annie Lee	5 May 1928	7/ 109
Goldsmith, James G.	Bell, Irene	5 Apr 1933	8/ 280
Goldwire, Mose [B] [Orlando]	Mitchell, Gertrude [Orlando]	5 Jan 1925	5/ 507
Golphin, Lee [Orlando]	Lace, Irene [Orlando]	4 May 1926	6/ 227
Good, John Wilson, Jr. [Orlando]	Hession, Mary Acilia [Orlando]	19 May 1927	6/ 521
Gooden, Sol	Lemon, Genia Mae	8 Oct 1928	7/ 191
Goodenough, Major [Plymouth]	Jerome, Ida [Plymouth]	10 Nov 1926	6/ 380
Goodman, Edward Frong [W] [Orlando]	Grover, Susie Katherine [Tampa]	15 Aug 1925	6/ 32
Goodram, Marion Hubert	Crawford, Virginia	4 Apr 1931	7/ 580
Goodrich, Julian Steele	Cadwell, Lucy Udell	24 Dec 1930	7/ 535
Goodson, Sam D.	Pope, Ethel	9 Dec 1927	7/ 22
Goodwin, Henry [Ocoee]	Hilliard, Lillie [Ocoee]	23 Nov 1926	6/ 389
Goolsby, F. E. [Apopka]	Linton, Susan [Mt Dora]	15 Oct 1925	6/ 64
Gordan, James	Pasco, Eva	30 Jun 1930	7/ 474
Gordon, Burton Crowl	Polzer, Emma Rezia	31 Aug 1933	8/ 339
Gordon, Cloyce Franklin	Jeffcoat, Opal Louise	6 Jul 1934	8/ 516
Gordon, Son [Orlando]	Slone, Euts [Orlando]	18 Apr 1927	6/ 493
Gordon, William Russell	Barke, Essie	18 Apr 1929	7/ 280
Gore, Arthur Wood	Rankin, Bessie Edna	4 May 1930	7/ 447
Gore, Gordan	Waters, Daisy	13 Oct 1928	7/ 193
Gormican, Eugene Patrick	Kahle, Bertha Margaret	4 Apr 1930	7/ 435
Gossett, John Robert [Orlando]	Rex, Irene Elizabeth [Orlando]	2 Mar 1926	6/ 172
Goto, M.	Suzuki, Masano	6 Jan 1930	7/ 395
Gould, Louis Henry [W] [Orlando]	Smith, Louisa [Orlando]	28 Jun 1926	6/ 150
Gould, Robert Walden	Jones, Margaret Olive	29 Jun 1934	8/ 502
Graddy, Isaiah	Smith, Mattie	26 May 1934	8/ 481
Graesbeck, Edward Willis [Orla Vista]	Godfrey, Mabelle [Fontana, WI]	30 Dec 1926	6/ 426
Graham, Charles Lanyton, Dr [Orlando]	Deahan, Sarah [Orlando]	4 Apr 1926	6/ 205
Graham, Dowling C. [Kissimmee]	Willis, Jessie Lee [Kissimmee]	17 Apr 1926	6/ 315
Graham, George H. [B] [Lake Wales]	Mays, Lula W. [Orlando] (gives address)	28 Nov 1925	6/ 111
Graham, Henry Osterling	Darden, Vera	23 Apr 1934	8/ 465
Graham, Herbert L.	Young, Clara Mae	20 Apr 1932	8/ 145
Graham, Jake [Winter Park]	Neeley, Mamie [Winter Park]	7 Apr 1926	6/ 201
Graham, James Mack [Winter Garden]	Smith, Amy [Lisbon]	17 May 1927	6/ 510
Graham, Pierce Lacy	Doucette, Fidel Evelyn	30 May 1933	8/ 307
Graham, Stanley James [Orlando]	Richards, Ethel Belle [Detroit, MI]	5 Jun 1926	6/ 260
Graham, Walter [Louisville KY]	Gibson, Clothille [Newberia, LA]	18 Mar 1926	6/ 181
Grammer, J. P. [Orlando]	Priest, Margaret	28 Jun 1926	6/ 316
Grandboushe, Alfred E.	Santo, Mabel	22 May 1929	7/ 297
Granger, Elisha Morton, Jr.	Rodwell, Luella Kessler	24 Jan 1928	7/ 52
Grant, Berry	Butler, Gertrude Beatrice	20 Aug 1934	8/ 524
Grant, Clarence Kirven	Lynes, Madeline Jackson	6 Jul 1933	8/ 322
Grant, Ellis	Monroe, Rosa Lee	10 Nov 1933	8/ 362
Grant, Floyd [B] [Orlando]	Bell, Bessie [Orlando]	26 Jan 1925	5/ 517
Grant, Isaac [Jacksonville]	Burney, Elouise [Jacksonville]	27 Oct 1926	6/ 365
Grant, King	Thomas, Carrie	20 Mar 1930	7/ 429
Grant, Prince	Daniels, Henrietta	16 Aug 1932	8/ 184
Grant, Robert Hunter [Kissimmee]	Makinson, Dorothy [Kissimmee]	12 Feb 1926	6/ 169

Grantham, George [Cocoa]	Brown, Georgia [Jessup, GA]	24 Sep 1925	6/ 49
Grantlin, Walter Lee	Matthews, Olivia Linton	10 Feb 1934	8/ 433
Grass, Fred R. [Orlando]	Rivers, Clifford [Sanford]	20 Aug 1927	6/ 568
Graves, George Frederick [Kankakee, IL]	Gray, Marian [Philadelphia]	5 Jun 1926	6/ 264
Graves, Leonard A.	Woods, Pauline	17 Dec 1927	7/ 29
Graves, Thomas Aulstrin	Durdee, Gladys	24 Feb 1929	7/ 254
Gray, Claude Luke	Huheey, Edith	1 Jun 1928	7/ 126
Gray, Frank Dorsey	Taylor, Winifield Mary	25 Jul 1928	7/ 165
Gray, Harry Raymond [Orlando]	Jones, Eleanor S. [Utica, NY]	25 Mar 1926	6/ 190
Gray, Jesse [Orlando]	Whitaker, Annie Belle [Orlando]	8 Feb 1926	6/ 153
Gray, Osie Charles	Williams, Carrie Belle	17 Jul 1933	8/ 326
Gray, Sidney Garth, Jr.	Howell, Elwyn	1 Jun 1931	8/ 11
Green Johnnie	Robinson, Gussie	17 Feb 1934	8/ 431
Green, Ennis	Howard, Elma	5 Aug 1928	7/ 169
Green, Ernest	Colman, Annie Mae	2 Jun 1934	8/ 485
Green, Frank	Martin, Gertrude	15 Nov 1930	7/ 521
Green, George	Smith, Viola	4 Jan 1934	8/ 399
Green, George McEwen [Tampa]	Crooms, Alfreda Juanita	26 Jun 1926	6/ 318
Green, Ivan [Orlando]	Birdsong, Daisy Lu [Orlando]	2 May 1926	6/ 244
Green, J. B. [Orlando]	Peterson, Harriet [Orlando]	7 Jun 1926	6/ 259
Green, James	Kelley, Lorrene	19 May 1931	8/ 4
Green, Jesse Redden [Orlando]	Turner, Mary Julia [Orlando]	4 Nov 1926	6/ 373
Green, Jessie [Orlando]	Eiley, Arie [Orlando]	5 Mar 1927	6/ 470
Green, John Boyt	Fairfield, Genevieve Beatrice	4 Oct 1930	7/ 503
Green, Johnny	Rearse, Florence	25 Dec 1927	7/ 41
Green, Lawrence Earl	Jenkins, Maude Ala	22 Apr 1931	7/ 585
Green, Lloyd	Green, Bertha	14 May 1930	7/ 453
Green, Lonnie	Tyson, Ella Louise	10 Sep 1932	8/ 194
Green, Lonzie [B] [Orlando]	Collins, Irene [Orlando]	26 Mar 1925	5/ 552
Green, Milton E.	Duff, Lois	8 Sep 1928	7/ 182
Green, Reverend A. [Orlando]	Avery, Viola [Orlando]	11 Jul 1925	6/ 14
Green, Will [Winter Garden]	Calvin, Pauline [Winter Garden]	4 Oct 1926	6/ 345
Green, William Owen	Booker, Lottie Mae	29 Sep 1932	8/ 203
Green, William T.	Hudson, Ella Mae	19 Nov 1928	7/ 205
Green, William Theodore [Orlando]	Thomas, Serena May [Orlando]	1 May 1926	6/ 224
Green, Willie [B] [Orlando]	Schofield, Sweetie Georgia [Orlando]	24 Nov 1925	6/ 91
Greene, Claude [W] [Orlando] (Green on return)	Ware, Delia [Orlando]	24 Dec 1925	6/ 128
Greene, Harry Stanley	McMair, Nancy Jane	23 May 1934	8/ 483
Greene, Raymond Wood [Winter Park]	Freeman, Wilhelmina Drake [Winter Park]	5 Jun 1926	6/ 26
Greene, Sol Victor [Orlando]	Thomas, Olive Phoebe [Orange City]	20 Oct 1926	6/ 360
Greenhalgh, Carl Davis	Traugh, Mary Elvada	24 Apr 1934	8/ 469
Greenwood, Melvin [Kissimmee]	Willeford, Emma [Pinecastle]	18 May 1927	6/ 512
Greer, Harold Lynn	Boyd, Marie Savannah	3 Sep 1932	8/ 190
Greer, Hubert [Winter Garden]	Wilkes, Florence [Winter Garden]	9 Oct 1926	6/ 347
Greer, James Washington	Darden, Nettie	18 Oct 1930	7/ 509
Grenier, Ernest Fleetwood	Martin, Kate	21 Jun 1928	7/ 147
Grice, Whaley [Orlando]	Boone, Ruth [Orlando]	18 Jun 1927	6/ 550
Grier, John Newton [Windermere]	Jaquith, Grace Cummings [Windermere]	28 Jun 1927	6/ 563
Griffin, Andrew S. [Holopaw]	Finley, Gussie [Orlando]	18 May 1926	6/ 240

Griffin, Benjamin Arthur	Jones, Bernice Ellinor	11 Jul 1931	8/ 31
Griffin, Benjamin Luther [W] [Ocoee]	Caster, Lovina [Ocoee]	11 Jan 1925	5/ 512
Griffin, Eidde	Lawton, Norah	18 Aug 1932	8/ 185
Griffin, John P. [Little River]	Partin, Maud T. [Maitland]	19 Sep 1925	6/ 49
Griffin, Joseph [W] [Orlando]	Allen, Lillian [Orlando]	21 Jul 1925	6/ 29
Griffin, Luther William	Fisher, Frances	27 Nov 1932	8/ 224
Griffin, Tommie	Smith, Gracie	28 Apr 1928	7/ 106
Griffin, Willis [Orlando]	Marshall, Ula [Orlando]	8 Nov 1926	6/ 377
Griffith, Gaylord [Orlando]	Toole, Carrie Louise [Orlando]	24 Apr 1926	6/ 219
Griffith, Lyle George [Miami]	McClean, Jeanne Venita [Peoria, IL]	28 May 1926	6/ 249
Griffith, Rupert Bain	Blakely, Mildredge Elizabeth	20 Jan 1930	7/ 404
Griffiths, Elmer Leo	Davis, Sarah	17 Oct 1927	6/ 594
Griggs, Gerell	Jones, Ruth Mae	9 Apr 1928	7/ 94
Grimes, Clarence B.	Silas, Juanita Mildred	13 Sep 1933	8/ 340
Grimes, Esley	Robinson, Charlotte	27 Sep 1930	7/ 500
Grimes, Wesley	Foster, Evelyn	21 Jun 1928	7/ 145
Griner, John Wesley	Cotter, Iva Lou	10 Jul 1933	8/ 327
Grinnell, George [W] [Northville, MI]	Huck, Gladys M. [Three Mile Bay, NY]	10 Jan 1925	5/ 511
Grisson, Louis Wiley	Macy, Margaret Jane	23 Apr 1931	7/ 585
Grizzle, Andrew	Williams, Jennie Eaver	12 Aug 1930	7/ 488
Groenberg, Martin Jacob [Orlando]	McCready, Alice Virginia [Orlando]	2 Jan 1927	6/ 443
Gromlich, Malon	Howarth, Hannah Jane	17 Sep 1933	8/ 342
Grono, George Lemuel	Callender, Wilhelmina Caroline	29 Apr 1933	8/ 288
Groome, George Monroe	Smith, Mary Elizabeth	10 Jun 1933	8/ 312
Grooms, Charles Humphrey	Deaton, Virginia	24 Oct 1930	7/ 512
Gross, Fred	Marshall, Sallie	26 May 1932	8/ 161
Grossman, Johnnie William	Andrews, Mabel	1 Jan 1931	7/ 539
Grosvenor, Carroll	Shroufe, Hilda Irene	4 Jan 1934	8/ 406
Grubbs, Dan [Orlando]	McNair, Lottie [Orlando]	5 Aug 1927	6/ 558
Gudger, James Roy	Grantham, Quennie Ann	27 Jan 1934	8/ 418
Guerin, Camille	Mariani, Adele C.	5 Feb 1930	7/ 413
Guinyard, David	Day, Doris	3 Nov 1932	8/ 213
Guinyard, Eugene	Campbell, Grace	14 Apr 1931	7/ 580
Gulusha, Robert A. [W] [Kettle Creek MI]	Holdren, Lucy Mae [Orlando]	19 Jan 1926	6/ 138
Gunn, Dock [Winter Garden]	Brown, Mamie [Winter Garden]	26 Sep 1925	6/ 51
Gunn, Edward B. [Orlando]	Jordan, Susan P. [Orlando]	16 Jul 1927	6/ 564
Gunn, John	Smith, Carrie	2 Apr 1928	7/ 91
Gustafson, Harry Edward [Orlando]	Patrick, Myrtle Irene [Orlando]	30 Jun 1926	6/ 284
Gustafson, John Hjalner	Gustafson, Clara	18 Jul 1934	8/ 512
Guy, Irvin [Dayton, OH]	Jones, Lettie [Orlando]	23 Jul 1927	6/ 555
Guy, James Earl	Smith, Mildred Ethel	20 Mar 1933	8/ 272
Guyitt, Frederick John	Deverall, Kathryn Elizabeth	25 Dec 1930	7/ 539

H

Haas, Frank Henry Jr.	Cookinham, Marion Ester	22 Sep 1932	8/ 199
Haberson, Lonnie	Stringer, Leona	30 Dec 1933	8/ 401
Hadden, Cecil	Sloat, Jeannette	12 Jan 1928	7/ 46
Haddes, Christopher Columbus	Coates, Elizabeth Jackson	2 Nov 1927	7/ 5
Hagan, Charles A. [B] [Sanford]	Thomas, Katherine D. [Sanford]	8 Jul 1925	6/ 12
Hagan, Otto Woodford	Wilson, Ethel Irene	6 Jan 1934	8/ 400

Hagan, Rinzo [Winter Garden]	Gunn, Adeline [Winter Garden]	6 Jan 1927	6/ 430
Hagan, Robert Lester	Decker, Virginia Jo	16 Oct 1931	8/ 63
Hagen, Richard	Lilley, Edith May	1 Jun 1929	7/ 303
Hagerman, Orlo Kenneth	Wright, Eula Belle	28 Jan 1932	8/ 110
Hagstrom, Raiford Gustaf	Anson, Marion Agnes	10 Mar 1934	8/ 447
Hailey, Willie	Manuel, Pinkie	24 May 1928	7/ 119
Hailey, Willie Rufus	Mays, Eloise Elizabeth	13 Jun 1931	8/ 20
Haim, Albert Louis [W] [Ocoee]	Oliver, Josie Minnie Lee [Ocoee]	25 Feb 1925	5/ 531
Haines, Webber Bly	Billingham, Lou Janet	1 Jan 1931	7/ 536
Hale, Timothy [Orlando]	Britten, Lucile [Orlando]	4 Jan 1927	6/ 429
Hall, Allen James	Norton, Ida Roberts	2 May 1931	7/ 591
Hall, Charles Virgil	Newbold, Catherine Marie	20 Apr 1930	7/ 441
Hall, Elisha	Blackman, Nola Mae	18 Nov 1930	7/ 521
Hall, Foy G. [W] [Umatilla]	Kennedy, Mildred [Sorrento]	3 Jul 1925	6/ 9
Hall, Gilyard	Cuyler, Isabelle	27 Feb 1932	8/ 119
Hall, Harold Hale	Waters, Daisy Lee	29 Jun 1934	8/ 502
Hall, Jack	Hall, Lula	23 Nov 1929	7/ 375
Hall, Jesse James	Tyson, Lottie	21 Sep 1929	7/ 348
Hall, John Clovis	Wheatley, Vivian Nellie	3 Oct 1931	8/ 56
Hall, Johnnie	Luster, Effie	1 Apr 1929	7/ 269
Hall, Leighton	Dockery, Pearl	7 Aug 1928	7/ 180
Hall, Malcolm W. [W] [Orlando] [Harvey on return]	Culver, Alice Leathern [Orlando]	23 May 1925	5/ 581
Hall, Orris [Orlando]	Eck, Vivian [Orlando]	31 Dec 1926	6/ 439
Hall, Oscar	Hart, Bertha	9 Mar 1929	7/ 258
Hall, Oscar [Bunker Hill, FL]	Love, Rosa [Bunker Hill]	20 Sep 1926	6/ 340
Hall, R. Murray	Peurifoy, Mildred	20 Jun 1928	7/ 143
Hall, Robert	Alderman, Allie	22 Dec 1928	7/ 226
Hall, Sam	Jerrigan, Vanilla Omarvise	11 Apr 1928	7/ 103
Hall, Sandy Dork	Tyson, Mattie Lee	10 Jan 1931	7/ 540
Hall, Stanley Raymond	Stowe, Edith Ramona	2 Jun 1932	8/ 164
Hall, Timothy [Orlando]	Cook, Ira Lee [Orlando]	4 Sep 1926	6/ 330
Hall, Willie [B] [Taft]	Williams, Beatrice [Taft]	14 Jul 1925	6/ 17
Hallback, Othor [B] [Orlando]	Rogers, Flossie [Orlando]	11 Jul 1925	6/ 14
Hallden, Henry	Brown, Alberta	30 Nov 1927	7/ 19
Hallett, Clements [Altamont Springs]	Bolter, Muriel [Winter Park]	5 Jan 1927	6/ 430
Halley, Calmer Butworth	Hendershot, Edith Ida	6 Jun 1931	8/ 17
Halliday, Henry H. [W] [Avon Park]	Wright, Novella [Orlando]	1 Feb 1925	5/ 524
Hallon, Kelly	Rouse, Pearl Diamond	14 Jul 1929	7/ 323
Hamarach, Roy Landra [Miami]	Hampton, Gladys Davis [Buckhead, GA]	5 Jun 1926	6/ 268
Hamill, Edwin Thomas	Prevatt, Verlie Mae	20 Dec 1932	8/ 230
Hamilton, John	Jefferson, Fannie	5 Mar 1931	7/ 567
Hamilton, John Henry [Orlando]	Ashby, Mattie [Orlando]	16 Aug 1926	6/ 305
Hamilton, Walter Harold [W] [Columbus, OH]	Bray, Gladys Medora [Winter Garden]	31 Dec 1925	6/ 125
Hamman, Ruben Earl [Orlando]	Albritton, Mona Viola	26 Aug 1926	6/ 321
Hammond, Dean Albert	Arendt, Margaret Katheryn	25 Dec 1930	7/ 533
Hammond, George Victor	Jolly, Julia Bernice	31 Aug 1926	6/ 326
Hammond, Philo Lincoln	Dreggers, Laura M.	16 Jul 1933	8/ 325
Hammond, Ralph	Ronske, Rose Virginia	27 Jul 1929	7/ 327
Hammond, William Lester [Winter Garden]	Walker, Alloria [Winter Garden]	30 Mar 1927	6/ 484

Hampton, Nelson [Oakland]	Butler, Emma Lee [Oakland]	4 Oct 1925	6/ 57
Hancock, Edwin Howard	Day, Martha Louise	25 Nov 1933	8/ 377
Hancock, Haiden Henry [Orlando]	Nye, Gladys Fay	7 Jul 1926	6/ 299
Hancock, Olin Morrison	Durant, Dorothy Elizabeth	20 Jul 1931	8/ 35
Handy, Richard DeLeon [B] [Sanford]	Hamilton, Willie Mae [DeLand]	3 Feb 1926	6/ 147
Hanes, Darwin Haleston [Pinecastle]	Carmichael, Mary Edna [Orlando]	19 Aug 1927	6/ 569
Hanesworth, John W.	Crenshaw, Oma	26 Jan 1929	7/ 235
Hankerson, Charlie [Orlando]	Hollingsworth, Beatrice [Orlando]	27 Aug 1925	6/ 40
Hankins, James Garland	Moseley, Kathryn Field	29 May 1931	8/ 12
Hann, Harry Vernon [Haines City]	Harland, Marie [Haines City]	26 Jul 1926	6/ 275
Hannah, Harry Burgwyn [Windermere]	Barber, Adeline [Windermere]	18 Dec 1926	6/ 412
Hannah, Orlando Eolin	Churchill, Leona Estille	27 Dec 1927	7/ 60
Hannah, Samuel Alexander [Lake Wales]	Lahr, Ruth Ida [Lake Wales]	26 May 1926	6/ 247
Hanner, Joseph Cobb	Teed, Ida Grace	4 Mar 1934	8/ 440
Hanrion, Herbert Frances [Ft. Pierce]	Bell, Mary Evelyn [Pensacola]	2 Jul 1927	6/ 542
Hans, John Edward [Cumberland, MD]	Cunningham, Pearl Kathleen [Cumberland, MD]	5 Jan 1927	6/ 431
Hansel, Bert Oscar	Hansel, Vera	24 Dec 1933	8/ 391
Hanshoe, Paul Dwight [W] [Evansville, IN]	Finke, Florence May [Evansville, IN]	28 Feb 1925	5/ 533
Hanson, Dale	Browning, Cathleen	23 Jun 1934	8/ 498
Hanson, Robert Edward	Blanton, Agnes Kathryn	26 Oct 1932	8/ 210
Hardeman, John Vines [Miami]	Austin, Gertrude Elinor [Miami]	10 May 1926	6/ 234
Hardeman, William Gardiner	Mathews, Edna Louise	30 Jun 1928	7/ 153
Hardemon, John	Nottingham, Margaret	11 Dec 1927	7/ 23
Harden, Richard Tyrus	Harris, Veda	22 Jun 1929	7/ 313
Harding, Arthur Ellsworth	Corbett, Viola Mable	25 Jan 1933	8/ 249
Harding, Richard Henry	Wolf, Loretta Clara	23 Dec 1931	8/ 92
Hardy, Clarence Christopher	Wells, Novella	14 Oct 1929	7/ 358
Hardy, James Thomas [Sanford]	Starr, Victor [Sanford]	1 Jun 1926	6/ 293
Hardy, Lucian Wayland [Bradenton]	McMurry, Ned Wesley [Summerfield]	17 Apr 1926	6/ 213
Hardy, Rassie Robert [Orlando]	Pemberton, Thelma Ruth	16 Oct 1926	6/ 357
Hardy, William Herschel [Orlando]	Dean, Mary Gladys [Orlando]	24 Apr 1927	6/ 498
Harger, Leverett Clark [Detroit, MI]	Owens, Ida F. [Johnston, PA]	29 Apr 1927	6/ 508
Hargis, Charles B.	Johnson, Tiny	21 Jun 1932	8/ 173
Harkey, William Harvey	Campbell, Esther	31 Dec 1927	7/ 36
Harley, Walter John	Heath, Minnie Lee	18 Jun 1929	7/ 312
Harllee, Orren Farr	Davis, Lillian Ester	21 Aug 1932	8/ 187
Harlow, Lawrence Pierce [Davenport]	Appleby, Lena [Boston, MA]	3 Jul 1926	6/ 292
Harmon, George Grant [W] [Evanston, IL]	Thomas, Laura Estelle [Newberry]	24 Jul 1925	6/ 23
Harp, Henry Wanklin	Dorety, Susan Gertrude	4 Jun 1930	7/ 397
Harper, Joe Sewell	Morgan, Blanche Missouri	18 May 1928	7/ 113
Harper, John	Harris, Willie	22 Feb 1928	7/ 68
Harper, John Thomas [Winter Park]	Hinkle, Loa Edna [Winter Park]	12 Apr 1927	6/ 492
Harrall, Thomas William	Frint, Edith Mildred	6 Sep 1930	7/ 494
Harrell, Clinton Leo	Godfrey, Waudie Mae	14 Mar 1931	7/ 567
Harrell, Edgar LeRoy	Pace, Lucille	19 May 1929	7/ 296
Harrelson, Olen Tommy	Waters, Dubby	8 Jul 1933	8/ 323
Harrigan, John Joseph	Bennett, Martha Mildred	12 Jan 1932	8/ 103
Harris, Alex	Scott, Virginia	5 Dec 1932	8/ 225
Harris, E. B. [B] [Orlando] [gives address]	Taylor, Leo [Orlando] [gives address]	21 Nov 1925	6/ 87
Harris, Edwin Ross	Alford, Elizabeth Eugenia	19 Sep 1933	8/ 343
Harris, Frank	Lee, McCarthy	11 Nov 1928	7/ 202

Harris, George	Hilyard, Annie Mae	9 Aug 1930	7/ 485
Harris, George Washington [Orlando]	Lane, Mary Eliza [Orlando]	3 Mar 1926	6/ 167
Harris, Hayward M.	Batten, Claudia A.	3 Aug 1929	7/ 329
Harris, Hollis [W] [Tampa]	Hicks, Madie [Orlando]	3 Jan 1925	5/ 505
Harris, Hollis [Orlando]	Beebe, Dorothy [Orlando]	30 Mar 1927	6/ 488
Harris, Howard	Jones, Gladys	17 May 1928	7/ 114
Harris, Irvin Osis	Helms, Rosie	16 Apr 1934	8/ 463
Harris, James	Thomas, Katina	18 Feb 1929	7/ 245
Harris, Jas. Horace [Orlando]	Page, Mildred Ruth [Orlando]	14 Apr 1926	6/ 211
Harris, John Jack [Orlando]	Adern, Rachel Lee	1 Sep 1926	6/ 333
Harris, Major	Woodard, Lillie	9 Mar 1933	8/ 267
Harris, Masten Leak	Peacock, Romie Lee	18 Feb 1933	8/ 260
Harris, Robert Bascom	Young, Laura Johnson	16 Oct 1930	7/ 508
Harris, Robert Ennis	Thomas, Louise Harriett	21 Dec 1931	8/ 91
Harris, Tom	Link, Farrie Hattie Lee	15 Oct 1932	8/ 210
Harris, Verdie E. [Winter Park]	Thomas, Alvina [Orlando]	9 Aug 1927	6/ 561
Harris, Wesley	Harmon, Rosa	7 Sep 1926	7/ 127
Harris, William [B] [Taft]	Grimes, Lillie Mae [Taft]	7 Aug 1925	6/ 33
Harris, William Henry Clay	Crane, Iva Duke	9 Jul 1934	8/ 508
Harrison, Benjamin [Orlando]	Birdson, Pearlie [Orlando]	5 Feb 1927	6/ 458
Harrison, Henry St. Aubert [Orlando]	Middleton, Mathilda Louise	13 Jul 1926	6/ 304
Harrison, Herbert Harris [Orlando]	Brueser, Bettie Marie [Orlando]	28 Feb 1927	6/ 468
Harrison, James	Brockington, Elizabeth	21 Oct 1933	8/ 353
Harrison, Oscar Martin	Steele, Allie Mae	29 Dec 1928	7/ 224
Harrison, Percy Jordan	Harvey, Sylvia Aleen	24 May 1928	7/ 120
Harrison, Raymond Franklin [Petersburg, VA]	Monroe, Nezzie Lee [Orlando]	13 Jan 1927	6/ 437
Harrison, Richard Hobson	Boddy, Reba Mae	14 Apr 1933	8/ 282
Harrold, Eddie	Mickens, Savannah	27 Oct 1928	7/ 199
Hart, George Washington	Rawls, Violet Odella	28 Mar 1934	8/ 451
Hart, George Washington [Orlando]	Howard, Ruby M. [Orlando]	3 Apr 1927	6/ 492
Hart, James Gordon	Lane, Dorothy Elizabeth	3 Feb 1929	7/ 240
Hart, Maurice Henry	Hunter, Elva Marie	22 Dec 1928	7/ 191
Hart, Phillip Carrington	Drake, Malvana	11 Feb 1930	7/ 413
Hart, Rueben [Leesburg]	Taylor, Lucy [Orlando]	28 Jun 1926	6/ 251
Hart, Thomas [Orlando]	Randall, Annie [Orlando]	8 Aug 1927	6/ 560
Hartsfield, James [B] [Orlando]	O'Neal, Frankie [Orlando]	19 Jan 1925	5/ 514
Hartsfield, James [Orlando]	Baker, Mary [Orlando]	23 Feb 1926	6/ 163
Harvard, Reginald Fall	Smart, Naomi	31 May 1930	7/ 462
Harvey, Charlie	Belving, Mary	15 Jan 1931	7/ 542
Harvey, George Evans	Largent, Thelma Christine	2 Jul 1934	8/ 507
Harvey, Hanard Andrew	Woodley, Katie	29 Mar 1933	8/ 279
Harvey, James Victor	Merrian, Gussie Merrill	15 Jan 1931	7/ 542
Harvey, Joe [B] [Orlando]	Robinson, Lucile [Orlando]	12 Jan 1926	6/ 132
Harvey, John Dennison [Jacksonville]	Monser, Ethel Bell [Orlando]	8 Sep 1925	6/ 44
Harvey, Myron J. [W] [Orlando]	Reese, Dorothy A. [Orlando]	8 Nov 1925	6/ 81
Harvey, Will [Orlando]	Josey, Vina [Orlando]	7 Aug 1926	6/ 313
Harvey, Will H.	Peterson, Marie	9 Feb 1930	7/ 411
Harvey, Zibie Newton	Crux, Alice Taylor	18 Aug 1930	7/ 492
Haskins, Elmer Sherman	Denham, Elizabeth	2 May 1929	7/ 287
Hastings, Charles Bernard [New York NY]	Hazen, Ruth [Orlando]	15 May 1926	6/ 239

Hatfield, Harry Edward [W] [Ft Meyers]	Lamons, Evie [Ft Meyers]	24 Dec 1925	6/ 114
Haug, Oscar	Sprague, Esther	29 Feb 1928	7/ 74
Haughton, Clifford Betsworth [Orlando]	Slemons, Dorothy [Orlando]	8 Oct 1925	6/ 60
Hauser, Carl Emil	Warren, Alice Louise	29 Sep 1932	8/ 201
Haven, Ray, Jr.	Dunson, Madaline	26 Nov 1930	7/ 523
Haviser, Victor Hugo	Kelley, Mary Ellen	8 Aug 1933	8/ 333
Hawkins, Anderson Denver	Warren, Bessie	10 Sep 1930	7/ 495
Hawkins, Carl Ray	Hixon, Virginia Marvene	27 Nov 1931	8/ 81
Hawkins, Elisha	Young, Louise	5 Mar 1929	7/ 257
Hawks, Curtis Alexander	Carter, Annice Juanita	23 Mar 1930	7/ 431
Hawley, Edwin Clarence	Hodges, Margaret Loretta	9 Feb 1933	8/ 255
Hawthorne, Leland Gordan	Robards, Lula Mae	19 Jul 1928	7/ 162
Hay, Henry Allston	Burdick, Gertrude Marion	17 Jun 1930	7/ 469
Haydock, Stanley Vincent [W] [New York NY]	Seel, Maude Victoria [Los Angeles, CA]	20 Feb 1925	5/ 530
Hayes, Curtis [Apopka]	Carpenter, Hester [Apopka]	9 May 1927	6/ 504
Hayes, Felton	Walls, Elsie	8 Jan 1933	8/ 239
Hayes, George Wilson [Chicago, IL]	Brooks, Katherine Rosanne [McKeesport, PA]	24 Mar 1926	6/ 189
Hayes, Gulmer [Winter Garden]	Scott, Corine [Winter Garden]	17 Nov 1926	6/ 384
Hayes, Gus	Clark, Edna	26 Nov 1928	7/ 207
Hayes, Jasper	Hall, Virginia	16 Jan 1932	8/ 104
Hayes, Joseph Joshua [Delray]	Laney, Irma [Adel, GA]	11 Jun 1927	6/ 535
Hayes, Loy Elma	Kerns, Goldie Mae	20 Apr 1933	8/ 286
Haymon, Joe	Cunningham, Josiebell	30 Aug 1930	7/ 493
Haynen, William James [Lake Wales]	Campbell, Sarah Gertrude	13 Aug 1927	6/ 572
Haynes, Charlie H. [B] [Winter Garden]	Williams, Flora [Winter Garden]	21 Mar 1925	5/ 545
Haynes, German	Beauford, Minnie Lee	10 Mar 1934	8/ 443
Haynes, Isham [B] [Orlando]	Roberson, Ruth [Orlando]	14 Mar 1925	5/ 540
Haynes, Jacob Olif	Denham, Lessie	29 May 1929	7/ 299
Haynie, Herman	Arnold, Margaret	26 Oct 1931	8/ 65
Hays, Joe [B] [Orlando]	Hills, Lubenia [Orlando]	1 Jan 1925	5/ 515
Hayward, Joe [B] [Orlando]	Holmes, Tinsie Bell [Orlando]	22 May 1925	5/ 577
Hayward, Richard	Drummond, Earlene	4 Jun 1932	8/ 165
Hayworth, Walter Hugh	Syfret, Mary Ligon	27 Dec 1927	7/ 34
Hazel, Arthur	Nipper, Elizabeth	28 Jan 1933	8/ 250
Hazel, Bennie [Winter Park]	Lemon, Viola [Winter Park]	2 Jun 1926	6/ 254
Hearn, Albert	Carter, Mystice	11 Jul 1929	7/ 321
Heck, Verlin Venoy	Holliday, Mabel Clarice	8 May 1933	8/ 294
Hedgapeth, John	Eady, Polly	27 Jan 1930	7/ 407
Heinberg, J. H. [Orlando]	Lewis, Elsie [Orlando]	22 Jan 1927	6/ 442
Heinoldt, Theodore [Orlando]	Hoffman, Helen [Orlando]	30 Mar 1926	6/ 194
Heisey, George Henry	Bandy, Virginia Lee	23 Feb 1929	7/ 251
Heldmyer, Fred [Orlando]	Davis, Mary Louise	21 Dec 1926	6/ 418
Helmer, Richard Adolph [Orlando]	Samuels, Eloise Jackson [Orlando]	16 May 1927	6/ 521
Helms, Harper	Galloway, Ruby	31 May 1929	7/ 305
Helms, John M.	Firkins, Jane L.	29 Jan 1929	7/ 233
Helms, John S,.Jr. (Dr.)	Pippin, Louise	10 Aug 1929	7/ 333
Helms, Malcolm Theron	Eady, Gladys Genevieve	20 Jun 1929	7/ 315
Helms, William Bryan	Luther, Ruth Louise	30 Jul 1932	8/ 181
Henderson, Carey	Brooks, Mary	2 Jun 1928	7/ 126
Henderson, Charles Samuel [Sanford]	Sellers, Virginia Mae [Sanford]	22 Nov 1926	6/ 388
Henderson, Charlie [Orlando]	Waters, Rosa [Orlando]	21 Mar 1927	6/ 478

Henderson, Charlie [Orlando]	Burnett, Geneva [Orlando]	7 Mar 1926	6/ 182
Henderson, Chester Arthur	Johnson, Helen Belle	17 Dec 1932	8/ 237
Henderson, George W.	Wilson, Lillie	16 Apr 1930	7/ 439
Henderson, Harold	Long, Johnie Doris	17 Jan 1933	8/ 247
Henderson, Louis Chester	Hardeman, Mary	30 Jul 1934	8/ 517
Henderson, Walter Noel	Harrison, Evie Lorene	24 Aug 1933	8/ 336
Hendricks, Anderson [Orlando]	Wilson, Fleta [Orlando]	27 Nov 1926	6/ 392
Hendrickson, George Richard [Astor]	Johnson, Nannie Lee [Astor]	2 Oct 1925	6/ 55
Hendrix, Raymond Luther	Payne, Olive Bernice	5 Mar 1934	8/ 441
Hendrix, Rufus E.	Bland, Versa	15 May 1930	7/ 456
Hendry, Ewart	Stafford, Fayne Ida	23 Feb 1929	7/ 251
Hendy, C. P.	Asey, E. Myrtle	23 Oct 1928	7/ 198
Henney, Charles	Whidden, Rose	1 May 1930	7/ 455
Henry, Charles C. [Melbourne]	Dodson, Helen [Alexandria, VA]	2 May 1927	6/ 499
Henry, David	Kennedy, Jessie	13 Aug 1928	7/ 172
Henry, David Wiley, Jr.	Scherick, Bessie Mae	29 Apr 1930	7/ 444
Henry, Gene James	Pugh, Helen Dodd	31 May 1934	8/ 485
Henry, George [B] [Orlando]	Dowdell, Nora [Orlando]	17 Jan 1926	6/ 136
Henry, Ike	Bailey, Josephine	27 Apr 1934	8/ 470
Henry, Jessie	Paige, Martha	13 Jan 1934	8/ 410
Henry, John [Winter Park]	Thomas, Hoyt [Eatonville]	25 Mar 1926	6/ 192
Henry, Mercer Jackson	Hall, Clara Louise	30 Jun 1934	8/ 505
Henry, Peyton J. [W] [New York, NY]	Solesbee, Nina V. [Charlotte, NC]	8 Mar 1925	5/ 537
Henry, Samuel	Williams, Lucile	16 Jun 1929	7/ 310
Henry, William [Winter Garden]	Reed, Essie [Winter Garden]	30 Apr 1927	6/ 499
Herd, Tom [Orlando]	Johnson, Estelle [Orlando]	4 Dec 1926	6/ 399
Herndon, Julius Mathew [Ocoee]	Peavey, Laura [Ocoee]	3 May 1926	6/ 225
Herrick, Clarence French [W] [Orlando]	Dixon, Eugenia Addie [Waukegan, IL]	11 Apr 1925	5/ 560
Herring, Asben McCurry	Givens, Quida Queen	3 Mar 1934	8/ 440
Herring, Louis Carlton	Kirst, Dorothy Jane	17 May 1931	8/ 5
Herriott, Joseph [B] [Oakland]	Brunson, Evelina [Oakland]	7 Feb 1925	5/ 523
Hertz, Jerome [W] [New York, NY]	Stein, Tillie [Orlando]	8 Nov 1925	6/ 81
Hess, Lawrence	Lowe, Edith	17 Dec 1928	7/ 216
Hewitt, Charles Eli	Shepherd, Anne Carnegie	25 Mar 1931	7/ 584
Hiatt, Clifford R.	Gregory, Gladys	14 Jun 1928	7/ 144
Hicks, Allen [Clermont]	Carter, Neta [Tulsa, OK]	10 Dec 1926	6/ 405
Hicks, Authur [Orlando]	Creek, Evelyn	14 Aug 1926	6/ 305
Hicks, Charlie	Wallace, Sophia	1 Nov 1927	7/ 4
Hicks, Ervin	Murray, Ruth	14 Jul 1934	8/ 509
Hicks, J. Stuart	Montague, Margaret	19 Nov 1929	7/ 373
Hicks, James Robert [Miami]	Lutz, Dora [Miami]	21 Dec 1926	6/ 413
Hicks, Will [B] [Orlando]	Stokes, Elizabeth [Orlando]	8 Apr 1925	5/ 555
Hickson, Luther	Lewis, Emily	24 Mar 1928	7/ 86
Hiers, Bryant Dickinson, Jr.	Smith, Janet Anne	16 Nov 1930	7/ 521
Higginbotham, Roger McDonald [Orlando]	Turner, Dora Belle [Orlando]	15 Apr 1926	6/ 212
Higginbotham, William Clyde	Sullivan, Ethyl	20 Jun 1928	7/ 143
Higgins, Raymond George	Lind, Elizabeth	16 Jul 1932	8/ 179
Hightower, David	Thompson, Ulyses	17 Mar 1928	7/ 81
Higley, David Milton	Keene, Ethel Mae	2 Jun 1931	8/ 11
Hill, David [Orlando]	Smith, Estella [Orlando]	19 Jun 1926	6/ 274

Hill, Lesley Savagg (Dr) [W] [Orlando]	Schweikart, Freda Louise [Orlando]	19 Dec 1925	6/ 106
Hill, George	Thompson, Annie Bell	5 May 1928	7/ 109
Hill, Homer Hicks [Orlando]	Merriman, Annie Marie	29 Jun 1927	6/ 541
Hill, Isaac James	Sulatychi, Beatrice Marie	6 Sep 1932	8/ 192
Hill, James Harold [W] [Maitland]	Greer, Inez [Winter Park]	3 Apr 1925	5/ 553
Hill, Judge H.	Bettis, Annie Belle	21 Jan 1928	7/ 49
Hill, Nathaniel	Stephen, Susie May	6 Apr 1929	7/ 273
Hill, Russell Burdett [Orlando]	Wiggins, Aline Lucy [Orlando]	29 Jun 1927	6/ 544
Hill, Shack [B] [Orlando]	Rogers, Annie Mae [Orlando]	15 Jul 1925	6/ 17
Hill, Sibbrin	Long, A. J.	5 Apr 1928	7/ 95
Hill, Stanley C. [Orlando]	Johnson, Violet M. [Peoria, IL]	5 Nov 1926	6/ 375
Hill, Starling Marion	Philpott, Lorena Jane	7 May 1933	8/ 298
Hill, Walter Herbert, Jr. [San Antonio, TX]	Sligh, Sarah Wheeler [Orlando]	11 Jun 1927	6/ 565
Hill, William	Mingo, Laura	18 Feb 1929	7/ 246
Hillyard, Adam Porter	Hash, Laura	17 Nov 1930	7/ 522
Hinchey, Robert Wayne [DeLand]	Coles, Hettie Glen [Orlando]	12 Feb 1927	6/ 455
Hines, Arnold Verlyn	Pitt, Clara Victorine	27 Jul 1929	7/ 326
Hines, Walter Palmer [New York, NY] [lic. 24 Dec 1925; recorded 11 May 1926]	King, Louise [Plattsburg, MO]	24 Dec 1925	6/ 233
Hinman, Fred W. [New Smyrna]	Greer, Nancy [New Smyrna]	5 Jun 1926	6/ 267
Hinson, Arnett	Woodard, Addie	12 Oct 1929	7/ 357
Hinson, Joe	Jones, Catherine	15 Dec 1930	7/ 529
Hinson, Sylvanus [Sanford]	Crosby, Edna [Haines City]	5 Jan 1927	6/ 429
Hinson, Vance Lamar [W] [Orlando]	Richardson, Romaine [Taft]	2 May 1925	5/ 568
Hiscock, William Dana	Martin, Ann	18 Feb 1934	8/ 433
Hixon, Curtis [Tampa]	Yantis, Lila [Lake Stearns]	2 Jul 1927	6/ 546
Hixon, George W.	Van Sickle, Eva B.	19 Sep 1928	7/ 184
Hoagland, Jasper Newton [Orlando]	Earl, Dollie K. [Orlando]	11 Sep 1925	6/ 55
Hobbs, Hosea [B] [Orlando]	Johnson, Daisy [Orlando]	2 Feb 1925	5/ 519
Hobby, Luther Beasley	Osteen, Clyde Chevis	10 Mar 1934	8/ 444
Hockett, Roland Selby [Orlando]	Jackson, Florence Josephine [Orlando]	31 Jul 1927	6/ 557
Hodge, Rufus [Lockhart]	Mims, Martha [Apopka]	13 Jun 1927	6/ 533
Hodges, Clifford Christopher	Giles, Estelle	5 Feb 1929	7/ 244
Hodges, Edward	Kimbo, Mary	19 Mar 1928	7/ 82
Hodges, Harold	Pope, Annie Mae	17 Sep 1933	8/ 343
Hodges, Otis	Lancaster, Katherine	23 Oct 1927	7/ 3
Hodrick, Frank	McLendon, Rosella	9 Dec 1929	7/ 382
Hoefler, Charles Homer, Jr.	Ray, Zelma Myrtle	20 Jun 1931	8/ 22
Hoefter, Howard T.	Petterson, Eva	1 Apr 1930	7/ 435
Hoequist, Carl Ernest	Hall, Lila Lorraine	3 Jun 1928	7/ 155
Hoequist, Carl Kenneth	Eubank, Eula Cordelia	28 Jul 1934	8/ 517
Hoffman, Edward Joseph	Cahill, Anna Marie	3 Mar 1930	7/ 423
Hoffner, Ted Clair	Norman, Winnie Estelle	15 Oct 1928	7/ 190
Hogan, J. Walker [W] [Melbourne]	Ogden, Pauline [Orlando]	21 Mar 1925	5/ 593
Hogan, Walter Lee	Hylick, Juanita	2 Jul 1934	8/ 504
Hogarth, Edwin A.	Davis, Sintha L.	26 Aug 1929	7/ 336
Hoisley, Les Vinicery	Clayton, Ruby	15 Dec 1927	7/ 29
Holcombe, William Lee	Blair, Mildred	23 Feb 1934	8/ 435
Holdeman, James Lionel	Turley, Mary Ella	13 May 1928	7/ 117
Holden, Perry Lee	Condrey, Genevieve Catherine	2 Dec 1933	8/ 384
Holden, Thomas [B] [Pinehurst]	Woodrow, Mattie [Pinehurst]	25 May 1925	5/ 583
Holderness, Gordon F.	Ward, Annie Dorine	28 Sep 1928	7/ 188

Holiday, Earl D.	Greenvell, Dorothy	31 Jan 1930	7/ 409
Holiday, Jesse Rex	Barton, Ila Yvetta	4 Sep 1930	7/ 497
Holland, Alex Keese	Stallings, Irma Lottie	1 Aug 1930	7/ 483
Holland, George	Brantley, Maria	12 Dec 1927	7/ 23
Hollehan, James	Paulk, Evelyn	5 Dec 1929	7/ 380
Hollinger, John Joseph	Bellinger, Eshie Louise	28 Jul 1934	8/ 520
Hollingsworth, James E. [Orlando]	Liebe, Edris Elizabeth [Orlando]	12 Sep 1925	6/ 44
Hollingsworth, Pat	Pittman, Eddie Mae	15 Oct 1927	6/ 593
Hollingsworth, Wm. Estes [Kissimmee]	Skelton, Etolia [Kissimmee]	16 Feb 1926	6/ 160
Hollins, Tom	West, Mattie	12 Dec 1928	7/ 216
Hollmon, Benjamin Haynes	Jackson, Deloise	8 Feb 1934	8/ 429
Holloman, E. L.	Scott, Lee G.	24 Jul 1934	8/ 514
Holloman, Ed [Winter Park]	Thomas, Rosalie [Winter Park]	10 Jan 1925	5/ 510
Holloway, Ernest	Day, Willie Lee	24 Sep 1928	7/ 187
Holloway, Ernest [Orlando]	Pace, Mattie B. [Orlando]	18 Jul 1927	6/ 553
Holloway, Holcombe Gaston	States, Evelyn Eudora	10 Mar 1934	8/ 447
Holloway, Keith Patrick	Strickland, Nina Lucile	29 Mar 1930	7/ 434
Holloway, Truman Willard [W] [Orlando]	McClellan, Bertha Myrtle [Kissimmee]	23 Jul 1925	6/ 22
Holly, William Benjamin	Jackson, Ester Louise	2 Mar 1932	8/ 122
Holmes, Carson McLendon	Reardon, Edith	21 Jun 1934	8/ 498
Holmes, Charles	Pool, Rosa Lee	18 Jul 1934	8/ 510
Holmes, Emmett O'Neal	Schoolcraft, Edith Mae	3 Mar 1933	8/ 265
Holmes, George Washington	Matthews, Henrietta	16 Dec 1933	8/ 396
Holmes, Joe [Orlando]	Collins, Pearl [Winter Park]	1 Jul 1926	6/ 286
Holoman, Ben	Smith, Idella	5 Jun 1929	7/ 303
Holoman, Roosevelt	Williams, Verah B.	29 Jan 1931	7/ 549
Holsclaw, Ralph William	Lawrence, Virginia Cherry	10 Jul 1930	7/ 481
Holt, Homer D. [W] [Sanford]	McGahaigin, Irene [Sanford]	14 Mar 1925	5/ 542
Holt, J. C. [B] [Winter Park]	Lewis, Eula B. [Winter Park]	20 Jun 1925	5/ 586
Holt, Roger Clerc	Dawson, Grace Wherry	10 Aug 1933	8/ 333
Holton, Grover Barclay [Orlando]	Corley, Byron Olivia [Orlando]	29 May 1927	6/ 536
Honour, George Thomas	Harris, Florabelle	11 Jan 1928	7/ 45
Honour, Joseph Burt [Orlando]	Hitzil, Margaret [Orlando]	1 Jun 1927	6/ 525
Hood, Michael Amos	Carr, Margaret	9 Jul 1931	8/ 30
Hook, Alvin Louis	Brockman, Lillian Florence	20 Jul 1934	8/ 513
Hook, Harold Joseph	Haile, Eva Carroll	25 Feb 1933	8/ 263
Hooker, LeRoy [Orlando]	Branch, Kathlene [Orlando]	18 Nov 1926	6/ 386
Hooks, George [Orlando]	Harvey, Julie [Orlando	31 Jan 1927	6/ 448
Hooks, John	Sanders, Zula	24 Mar 1928	7/ 148
Hooper, Eddie [Orlando]	Hicks, Lula [Orlando]	28 Dec 1926	6/ 422
Hopkins, John S.	Millard, Emma Sue	3 Dec 1933	8/ 380
Horan, Elroy	Demarest, Helen Rachel	11 Apr 1931	7/ 581
Horn, Henry Burris [Bay Ridge]	Taylor, Ludie Leonora [Apopka]	1 May 1925	6/ 43
Hornbeek, Farrell Lee	Nicholson, Lois	26 May 1934	8/ 483
Horne, Buford William	Wallace, Mary Belle	25 Apr 1931	8/ 18
Horne, Clarence Leon	Rewis, Melva Lee	21 Jul 1928	7/ 164
Horner, James Millard	Crawford, Rachel	24 Feb 1934	8/ 435
Hornstein, Louis Albert	Bruce, Mildred Mossman	30 Jun 1933	8/ 319
Horsley, Samuel	Adams, Billie Saunders	24 Feb 1934	8/ 435
Hoskins, James Marvin	Guenthner, Erna Kathryn	15 May 1930	7/ 458

Houghtaling, J. F. [Forest City]	Courter, Edith L. [Forest City]	25 Nov 1926	6/ 396
House, Arthur	Burchett, Alla Maloda	6 Feb 1930	7/ 412
Houston, Freddie	Kirkley, Nannie	12 Dec 1928	7/ 215
Houston, Robert Hunter, Jr [W]	Root, Eleanor Aileen [New York NY]	25 Feb 1925	5/ 533
Hovey, Edward A. [W] [Orlando]	Gwynn, Edith Craycraft [Noblesville, IN]	18 Mar 1925	5/ 544
Howard, Bolding [B] [Miami]	Norman, Birdie [Orlando]	7 Nov 1925	6/ 86
Howard, Erna Atkinson	Clifton, Veda Margueritta	17 Jun 1930	7/ 470
Howard, Ernest [B] [Winter Park]	Jackson, Roberta Inez [Winter Park]	26 Jan 1925	5/ 516
Howard, Henry C.	Read, Minnie E.	23 Jul 1934	8/ 512
Howard, Henry [Orlando]	Devine, Hattie [Orlando]	29 Sep 1925	6/ 53
Howard, Julian Durham	Crenshaw, Virginia Taylor	12 Dec 1933	8/ 384
Howard, Morgan Goodmen	Mink, Veva Leota	2 Nov 1927	7/ 5
Howard, Mose	Williams, Leatha Mae	23 Dec 1933	8/ 390
Howard, Richard Clarence	Andrews, Evelyn LaDell	17 Dec 1933	8/ 387
Howard, Robert Fulton [W] [Orlando]	Fitzgerald, Mary Silver [Orlando]	14 May 1925	5/ 574
Howard, Roy Arthur [Orlando]	McDuffie, Evelyn Caroll	4 Sep 1926	6/ 331
Howard, Sam [Winter Park]	Robinson, Bessie [Winter Park]	24 Dec 1926	6/ 425
Howard, Thomas William [Kissimmee]	Jones, Mabell [Kissimmee]	3 Nov 1926	6/ 373
Howard, Wade	Larking, Marie	26 Feb 1932	8/ 119
Howe, Charles Luke [W] [Orlando]	Lowe, Estelle [Morganstown, WV]	17 Mar 1925	5/ 545
Howell, Charles [Orlando]	Sutherfield, Hazel [Orlando]	7 Jun 1926	6/ 262
Howell, Walter Maurice	Willoughby, Irene Elizabeth	14 Jan 1933	8/ 245
Howell, William Kimbrough	Hill, Ursula Ewart	19 May 1930	7/ 457
Howes, William Crowell	Graham, Vivian Alverta	15 Oct 1932	8/ 206
Howington, Erastus Cyral	Bowen, Thelma Lee	6 Mar 1928	7/ 76
Howison, William Hardy	Webb, Vivian Barbour	19 May 1933	8/ 301
Howze, C. D. [Lithnia]	Smith, Dahlia [Orlando]	21 Nov 1926	6/ 399
Hoxeys, Lee Edward [St. Petersburg]	Jensen, Victoria [Orlando]	21 Aug 1926	6/ 326
Hoxt, Preston S. [W] [Orlando]	Schank, Esther E. [Hightown, NJ]	29 Jun 1925	6/ 6
Hubbard, Edwin Smith [W] [Federal Point]	Bryce, Frances Louise [Sanford]	30 Jun 1925	6/ 8
Hucbsch, Robert E.	Westerman, Rena	4 Feb 1933	8/ 253
Huckel, Heldana Huckel	Hamer, Sallie McCall	7 Feb 1931	7/ 554
Huckins, Guy Woodward	Nolan, Helen Mary	9 Feb 1928	7/ 61
Hudgins, Jesse [Raleigh, NC]	Hall, Avil Sorell [Sanford]	31 May 1927	6/ 518
Hudnall, Mayes	Riley, Clara Belle	29 Dec 1929	7/ 392
Hudson, John [Orlando]	Moses, Ellen [Orlando]	25 Sep 1925	6/ 51
Hudson, Lonnie [Apopka]	Murphy, Ruth [Apopka]	19 Jun 1926	6/ 282
Hudson, Malba	Shaw, Nora Lee	14 Jun 1932	8/ 174
Hudson, Paul David [Charlotte, NC]	Wigfall, Georgie Patrick [Orlando]	27 Apr 1927	6/ 509
Huegele, Herbert Conrad	Fielmore, Jane Florence	4 Apr 1930	7/ 436
Huff, Charles [Indian Harbor, IN]	Kibrige, Anna Kate [Barrington, IL]	5 Aug 1926	6/ 311
Huggins, Charlie White [Tampa]	Corley, Blanche [Tamps]	24 Jun 1926	6/ 291
Huggins, James T. [W] [Orlando]	Kaiser, Louise [Orlando]	17 Nov 1925	6/ 89
Huggins, Jesse Franklin	Jansen, Vera Mae	25 Dec 1932	8/ 234
Huggins, Philip	Hayes, Alvia	28 Jun 1930	7/ 475
Huggins, Robin G. [Orlando] Rubin on lic.	Moore, Ida [Orlando]	24 Aug 1925	6/ 37
Huggins, Will Zack, Jr [W] [Quitman, GA]	Franklin, Zama Marzelle [Orlando]	28 Dec 1925	6/ 137
Hughes, Frank [Orlando]	Waitman, Gertrude [Orlando]	24 Oct 1926	6/ 365
Hughes, Lewis Walter [Orlando]	Purcell, Buris Clifford [Orlando]	2 Jun 1927	6/ 541
Hughes, Thomas [Spartanburg, SC]	Holimon, Beatrice	29 Dec 1926	6/ 426
Hughes, Vern Marshall [Delray]	Eagley, Agnes Edith [Jacksonville]	20 Apr 1926	6/ 215

Hughey, Malcolm Darum	Cain, Maggie Belle	24 Jun 1933	8/ 316
Hughston, Hubert Holmes, Jr.	Adams, Dorothy	11 Oct 1929	7/ 359
Hull, Herman John	Oliver, Guinevere Elaine	30 Oct 1930	7/ 515
Hull, Louico Mitchell	Thompson, Rubie Lynch	7 Apr 1928	7/ 97
Hull, Moyer	Lehman, Norma	27 May 1933	8/ 305
Humlong, Frank Gray	Lambert, Ferande Eugenie	29 Jun 1929	7/ 322
Humphrey, Curtis [Winter Garden]	Johnson, Susie [Winter Garden]	11 Aug 1926	6/ 309
Humphrey, Ernest LeRoy	Hyrne, Margaret Frances	6 May 1930	7/ 448
Humphrey, George	Brooks, Eloise	21 Jan 1933	8/ 249
Humphrey, Henry	Hall, Flossie	9 Feb 1933	8/ 255
Humphrey, James	Jackson, Lucille	17 Jan 1930	7/ 403
Humphrey, James [Winter Garden]	Gibson, Nancy [Winter Garden]	4 Nov 1926	6/ 374
Humphrey, Sonny	Thomas, Claudia	24 May 1928	7/ 118
Humphreys, Mike	Merrill, Mabel	3 Mar 1929	7/ 256
Humphries, Lester C.	Branch, Lula	12 Jun 1928	7/ 144
Hundley, Clifford L. [Orlando]	Mann, Elizabeth H.	29 Jun 1927	6/ 543
Hunt, Albert Brewer	Beattie, Marian Virginia	30 Apr 1930	7/ 446
Hunt, Charles B.	Dates, Sarah Sudie	15 Dec 1927	7/ 29
Hunt, George Herbert [Orlando]	O'Brien, Dorothy Elizabeth [Orlando]	9 Feb 1927	6/ 453
Hunt, Richard S.	Kelly, Elizabeth L.	18 Oct 1928	7/ 197
Hunt/Hurt, Dallas [Orlando]	Brown, Corean [Orlando]	20 Dec 1926	6/ 412
Hunter, Dan	Morris, Elvira	22 May 1928	7/ 117
Hunter, Elijah [Orlando]	Cooks, Mary [Orlando]	23 Dec 1926	6/ 414
Hunter, Harold Headley [Marion, OH]	Hoftshouse, Myrtle Mae [Marion, OH]	22 Oct 1925	6/ 69
Hunter, Herman Charles [W] [Orlando]	Bass, Jennie Elizabeth [Orlando]	16 Jun 1925	5/ 588
Hunter, Ralph Vernon	Hinkle, Loa Edna	4 Jun 1934	8/ 488
Hunter, William Penn	Humphrey, Gladys	5 Jun 1928	7/ 129
Huntley, Willie	Davison, Willie Mae	28 May 1933	8/ 306
Hurkmer, Frank Henry [Orlando]	Allen, Amy Beatrice [Orlando]	11 Apr 1927	6/ 492
Hurst, Harrison [Orlando]	Burnett, Inell [Orlando]	10 Jul 1927	6/ 548
Hurst, James Robert [W] [Ocoee]	Harrell, Katie [Ocoee]	30 May 1925	5/ 600
Hurst, John Franklin [Ocoee]	Smith, Delia [Winter Garden]	7 May 1927	6/ 504
Hurt, Clarence Columbus	Johnson, Lona Opal	14 Jun 1933	8/ 313
Hurton, James Madison	Cowart, Beulah Mae	6 Feb 1933	8/ 254
Hussey, George Aaron	Showers, Lula Belle	22 Aug 1933	8/ 335
Huston, Arthur Eugene [Cropsey, IL]	Smith, Grace Chowning [Orlando]	26 Feb 1927	6/ 467
Huston, Harold Francis	Smith, Rauline Nina	26 Oct 1933	8/ 357
Huston, Robert	Windsor, Gertrude	14 Jun 1930	7/ 466
Hutchins, Joel Thomas	Jones, Janie Haynes	21 Dec 1927	7/ 28
Hutchinson, George	Moore, Estelle	11 Nov 1933	8/ 362
Hutchinson, John Ensol	Jackson, Nellie Barbara	15 Mar 1928	7/ 86
Hutchinson, Philo Allen [Orlando]	Main, Beatrice Evelyn [E. Coninth, VA]	7 Jan 1927	6/ 433
Hutchinson, Walter	Ogden, Callie	1 Apr 1928	7/ 91
Hutsell, Sith [Athens, TN]	Israel, Margaret [Hendersonville, NC]	15 Feb 1927	6/ 460
Huttig, John Noble Penrod [Winter Park]	Randall, Laura Thomson [Winter Park]	16 Feb 1927	6/ 461
Hyde, David Burns Jr.	Wilson, Selina	29 Jun 1932	8/ 177
Hyde, J. L. [Orlando]	Jackson, Francis [Orlando]	11 Oct 1926	6/ 366
Hyde, John Grady	Post, Marien Julia	24 Dec 1933	8/ 395
Hylick, Jack	Allen, Rena	21 Jan 1933	8/ 248

I

Idelson, Isaac	Kohn, Lena	11 Jun 1928	7/ 142
Inabit, Merl Elmo	Caldwell, Laura Katherine	19 May 1934	8/ 478
Ingalls, Charles Jefferson	Peacock, Beulah LaFrentz	11 Aug 1932	8/ 183
Ingham, R. L.	Hayes, Etta	14 Apr 1930	7/ 442
Ingham, Robert Lee	Stevenson, Willie Ada	5 Jul 1928	7/ 156
Ingram, Ernest Lee [B] [Orlando]	Bowden, Annie [Orlando]	8 Dec 1925	6/ 120
Ingram, Hollis Carlyle	Howard, Mary Frances	8 Sep 1929	7/ 343
Ingram, Joseph Nelson	Wilson, Martha Louise	10 Dec 1927	7/ 24
Inman, James	Baker, Lillie	10 Sep 1932	8/ 194
Irrgang, Charles William	Bloodgood, Frances Eleanor	16 Aug 1934	8/ 523
Irvine, Arthur William [Orlando]	Daniels, Doris Vance [Orlando]	28 Jun 1926	6/ 252
Irving, Charlie [Orlando]	Johnson, Lorean [Orlando]	2 Apr 1927	6/ 485
Irving, Shepherd	Lewis, Agnes	6 Apr 1930	7/ 439
Isaac, Will	Brafton, Willie Mae	16 Oct 1928	7/ 194

J

Jackson, Albert [B] [W. Palm Beach]	Ashe, Bluette [Orlando]	11 Jan 1926	6/ 131
Jackson, Amos Everett	Rose, Gertrude Edythe Stuart	15 Aug 1930	7/ 489
Jackson, Andrew	Dismuke, Jossie Bell	4 Oct 1932	8/ 203
Jackson, Arthur [Orlando]	Rodnesky, Ethel R. [Orlando]	13 Jun 1927	6/ 533
Jackson, Carl C. [Orlando]	Dodd, Sybil Anna [Orlando]	14 Jul 1927	6/ 553
Jackson, Charlie Lester	Helms, Lillie	5 May 1934	8/ 473
Jackson, Claude Lee	Houk, Hazel	6 Oct 1930	7/ 504
Jackson, Earl Kenneth	Driskell, Lucille Edith	23 Dec 1927	7/ 30
Jackson, Edward	Marshall, Sallie	20 Jun 1929	7/ 312
Jackson, Frank Rogers	Woodard, Rosene	13 Feb 1932	8/ 116
Jackson, Geanie	Howard, Lula Mae	14 Nov 1933	8/ 365
Jackson, George	Willis, Sallie Mat	30 Jul 1929	7/ 327
Jackson, George [Winter Park]	Hughs, Gertrude [Winter Park]	14 Apr 1926	6/ 208
Jackson, Henry [Orlando]	Johnson, Sophronia [Orlando]	24 Aug 1925	6/ 38
Jackson, J. C.	Davis, Bessie	15 Nov 1929	7/ 379
Jackson, James Edward [W] [Orlando]	Squires, Willie Cox [Orlando]	9 May 1925	5/ 572
Jackson, Jessie Vernon [W] [Plymouth]	Leach, Ruby Mae [Plymouth]	7 Feb 1925	5/ 524
Jackson, John	Motton, Willie Belle	29 Dec 1932	8/ 235
Jackson, Johnnie	Gainous, Thelma Roberta Olivia	2 Apr 1934	8/ 453
Jackson, Jonah J. [Orlando]	Ogletree, Bess [Orlando] [Oglertree on return]	21 Sep 1925	6/ 48
Jackson, Joseph Andrews	Rudisaile, Ellen Marie	26 Dec 1933	8/ 399
Jackson, Joseph Richard [W] [Sanford]	Snead, Mildred [Durham, NC]	12 Apr 1925	5/ 560
Jackson, Julian	Jones, Rachel	26 Dec 1931	8/ 94
Jackson, Leonard [Orlando]	Hawkins, Polonia [Orlando]	5 Sep 1925	6/ 42
Jackson, LeRoy	Barnes, Savannah	31 Oct 1931	8/ 68
Jackson, Lonnis [Clemont]	Mobley, M. [Winter Garden]	2 Jun 1927	6/ 523
Jackson, Louie	Homes, Josifine	18 May 1929	7/ 295
Jackson, Nesby	Gautt, Elizabeth	23 Sep 1929	7/ 349
Jackson, Paul	Rawlins, Maxine	17 Apr 1930	7/ 454
Jackson, Richard	Thomas, Freddie Mae	12 Jul 1929	7/ 321
Jackson, Richard [Orlando]	Dean, Annie [Orlando]	10 Oct 1925	6/ 61
Jackson, Robert Lee	Brown, Rosa	22 Oct 1927	6/ 595

Jackson, Roscoe	Gary, Mattie	18 Jan 1929	7/ 232
Jackson, Spencer	Wesley, Margaret	10 Sep 1928	7/ 182
Jackson, Thomas Michael [Orlando]	Shuby, Anna Ceilia [Orlando]	31 Jan 1927	6/ 464
Jackson, Walter	Campbell, Hattie	28 Jan 1929	7/ 236
Jackson, William [Orlando]	Isom, Clemmie [Orlando]	25 Jun 1927	6/ 529
Jackson, William McMorris [Tampa]	Ledbetter, Nellie [Tampa]	11 Aug 1927	6/ 562
Jackson, Willie [Winter Park]	Morris, Alberta [Winter Park]	15 May 1926	6/ 235
Jacobs, Henry Strobel	Overstreet, Hazel	23 Sep 1933	8/ 344
Jacobs, Lee [Orlando]	Williams, Sissie [Orlando]	17 Apr 1926	6/ 211
Jacobs, Samuel	Baker, Susie	10 Feb 1931	7/ 554
Jacobs, Samuel [Ocala]	Verren, Melissa [Ocala]	28 Sep 1925	6/ 52
Jacobs, Walter Glenn [W] [Orlando]	Hanks, Ethel Minnie [Orlando]	8 Apr 1925	5/ 557
Jacobsen, Christian Melfsen	Lindsey, Jessie	25 Apr 1930	7/ 449
Jaeger, Paul Arthur [Eustis]	Weigand, Lillie Blanche [Eustis]	6 Apr 1926	6/ 199
James, Coleman	Taylor, Emma	19 Jan 1931	7/ 544
James, David Daniel	Johnson, Claudie Mae	10 Jan 1928	7/ 45
James, Emmett	Mitchell, Blanche Lee	7 Jan 1933	8/ 239
James, George [Taft]	Straughter, Leah [Taft]	25 Oct 1926	6/ 364
James, Herman	Madison, Jewell	4 Oct 1930	7/ 502
James, Isaac	Thompson, Bertha	25 Nov 1933	8/ 374
James, Julius	Wright, Mozella	6 Jan 1934	8/ 402
James, Julius [B] [Orlando]	McNeill, Alma [Orlando]	13 Jun 1925	5/ 591
James, Rufus	Williams, Jerushious	13 Jun 1931	8/ 21
James, Sebring	McFadgeon, Beulah Mae	9 May 1931	7/ 596
James, Willie	Reed, Nellie	16 Jan 1928	7/ 46
Jamieson, John	Rouse, Arlener	13 May 1933	8/ 297
Jamison, Samuel [Sanford]	Richardson, Anice [Sanford]	10 May 1910	6/ 585
Jane, Anthony Alexander	Stewart, Margaret Beareice	16 Jun 1934	8/ 496
Jarden, Lindsey	Allen, Mamie	27 Mar 1933	8/ 277
Jarocha, Ladislaus Edward [Scranton, PA]	Pelletier, Marie Jeannie [Berwick, ME]	8 Apr 1926	6/ 203
Jeffcoat, Rhett Wilbur	Hancock, Florence Eugenia	27 Dec 1933	8/ 394
Jeffcoat, Robert [Taft]	Ellis, Bernie Mittie [Taft]	10 Jan 1927	6/ 435
Jefferson, Arthur	Drayton, Ida	9 Jun 1928	7/ 133
Jefferson, Lesture Clarence	Frazier, Valeta	26 Feb 1931	7/ 561
Jefferson, Lonnie	Leonard, Mae	11 Feb 1934	8/ 427
Jefferson, Walter	Robinson, Maddie Lee	7 Aug 1928	7/ 172
Jenkins, Dan	Gadson, Louise	11 Feb 1929	7/ 243
Jenkins, Ernest Samuel	Graw, Lavon Mildred	20 Jul 1933	8/ 327
Jenkins, Henry [B] [Orlando]	Byrd, Sadie [Orlando]	22 Jun 1925	6/ 1
Jenkins, Isaac [Orlando]	Johnson, Aldra [Orlando]	4 Sep 1926	6/ 330
Jenkins, Isriah B. [Sanford]	Brown, Mamie [Sanford]	14 Jul 1909	6/ 586
Jenkins, James B.	Baker, Clare	8 Aug 1929	7/ 330
Jenkins, Oliver [Orlando]	Barber, Eva [Orlando]	16 Apr 1927	6/ 494
Jenkins, Sam	Minerve, Edna	12 Mar 1929	7/ 261
Jenkins, Samuel Daniel	Oliver, Leola	25 Oct 1932	8/ 212
Jenkins, William	Blackman, Dellar	4 Dec 1932	8/ 224
Jenks, Charlie	McGillis, Corrie	9 May 1931	8/ 1
Jenks, William Lawrence [Winter Park]	Roberts, Marie Iones [Winter Park]	1 Sep 1926	6/ 327
Jenlike, Frank [Orlando]	Thompson, Sophia [Orlando]	21 Dec 1926	6/ 418
Jennings, Asa Will	Mackedon, Mary Irene	31 Mar 1934	8/ 452

Jerigan, Roy	Arnold, Alice	22 Dec 1928	7/ 221
Jeringan, Lawrence [Orlando]	Mefford, Cleao [Orlando]	17 Apr 1926	6/ 216
Jernigan, Adis	Kilgore, Mildred	16 Apr 1932	8/ 144
Jernigan, Frank LeRoy	Corbett, Charlton Lucia	24 Nov 1932	8/ 221
Jerrigan, Harry Emanuel [Orlando]	Rabun, Frankie Erine [Orlando]	16 Jun 1927	6/ 546
Jerry, Dallas [Maitland]	Jones, Ida Mae [Eatonville]	7 Mar 1927	6/ 470
Jester, Charlie	Smith, Sucie	30 Mar 1928	7/ 90
Jester, Edwin [Miami]	Griffin, Bernice [Orlando]	29 Jan 1927	6/ 464
Jeter, Rufus Wesley [Orlando]	Miller, Mattie Elizabeth [Orlando]	5 Jan 1927	6/ 430
Jewell, John Davis	Powell, Tula	12 Jan 1934	8/ 412
Jewett, Leland Stanford [Orlando]	Wells, Ruth Irene [Charlemont, MA]	30 Apr 1926	6/ 225
Jinkins, Thomas	Wilson, Georgia	1 Mar 1929	7/ 254
Jochem, Philip Lloyd	Fullingham, Margaret Josephine	15 Mar 1930	7/ 428
Jodrey, Morley Arden	West, Bertha Myrtle	9 Mar 1933	8/ 267
Johns, Clarence Curtis	Evans, Edna Louise	28 Dec 1932	8/ 234
Johns, George F.	Johns, Ella M.	13 May 1932	8/ 156
Johns, Henry	Gillis, Cora	6 Oct 1929	7/ 370
Johns, Irvin [Winter Garden]	Hilliard, Georgia [Ocoee]	5 Aug 1927	6/ 558
Johns, John W.	Troy, Ella Mae	18 May 1928	7/ 114
Johns, Lewis	Timmons, Marie	9 Dec 1933	8/ 382
Johns, Madison A. [Pinecastle]	Gloner, Florence [Pinecastle]	25 May 1925	5/ 597
Johns, Mark	Curry, Thelma	11 Nov 1928	7/ 203
Johns, William [B] [Orlando]	Green, Jewelry [Orlando]	29 Jan 1925	5/ 519
Johnson, Abram	Perry, Elma	4 Aug 1934	8/ 518
Johnson, Albert Morse	Stimpson, Rebecca Emmaline	3 Sep 1933	8/ 341
Johnson, Allen	Brown, Idella	22 Jun 1929	7/ 313
Johnson, Amadee Lawrence [Lake Alfred]	Helms, Ula Alleyia [Orlando]	25 Dec 1926	6/ 421
Johnson, Arthemon	Hill, Mary Jane	18 Feb 1932	8/ 118
Johnson, Arthur	Thorp, Addie Lee	2 Aug 1930	7/ 486
Johnson, Bob [Orlando]	Murray, Mabel [Orlando]	13 Dec 1926	6/ 406
Johnson, Carl [Atlanta, GA]	Reed, Lalor Mildred [Montgomery, AL]	13 Jan 1927	6/ 436
Johnson, Charles [B] [Sanford]	Brown, Lillie [Lake Pickett]	25 May 1925	5/ 578
Johnson, Charles A.	France, Ruth E.	8 Sep 1928	7/ 184
Johnson, Charles Elmer [Winter Park] [lic. 11 May 1926, recorded 14 May 1926]	Sheafer, Mildred Lenore [Winter Park]	11 May 1926	6/ 235
Johnson, Charlie Lewis	Dagler, Clara Kathryn	31 Dec 1927	7/ 38
Johnson, Clarence	Collier, Parilee	1 May 1931	7/ 590
Johnson, Clarence Albert	Woods, Hariett Elizabeth	8 Oct 1933	8/ 349
Johnson, Clarence Vardy [Miami]	Tatum, Beulah Louise [Miami]	223 Jul 1926	6/ 277
Johnson, Clauson	Waggoner, Marie Louise	31 Dec 1927	7/ 38
Johnson, Clauson [W] [Orlando]	Truesdell, Clare Louise [Orlando]	7 Mar 1925	5/ 538
Johnson, Clement W. [Boca Grande]	Stevens, Georgie [Orlando]	11 May 1927	6/ 506
Johnson, Coleman [Orlando]	Smith, Lucinda [Orlando]	26 Jun 1926	6/ 250
Johnson, Counsel [Orlando]	Clemons, Coring [Orlando]	25 Jun 1926	6/ 283
Johnson, Daniel Webster	Reeder, Annie Pearl	23 Dec 1930	7/ 532
Johnson, Dumas	Johnson, Lula	27 Apr 1929	7/ 284
Johnson, Earnest [Albany, GA]	Byrd, Frances [Apopka]	8 Oct 1926	6/ 350
Johnson, Edgar Lee	Willis, Olga Maybelle	24 Dec 1932	8/ 233
Johnson, Edgar William	Bailey, Imogene	28 Jun 1933	8/ 318
Johnson, Edward [Winter Garden]	Harring, Dollie [Winter Garden]	9 Aug 1926	6/ 313
Johnson, Elijah	Willis, Sarah	11 Jun 1928	7/ 136
Johnson, Eliphlet LeRoy	Sullins, Miriam Clyde	8 Feb 1934	8/ 429

Johnson, Ellis [Orlando]	Stephens, Violar [Orlando]	13 Nov 1926	6/ 382
Johnson, Frank [Orlando]	Palate, Francis [Orlando]	26 Jun 1926	6/ 288
Johnson, Frank Alfred [Orlando]	Harrman, Louise Elizabeth [Orlando]	7 Aug 1927	6/ 560
Johnson, George Henry	Hamilton, Flossie Bell	25 Dec 1927	7/ 37
Johnson, George W. [B] [Orlando]	Duhart, Aletha [Orlando]	12 Jul 1925	6/ 21
Johnson, Harrold Marion	Brooks, Mary Erin	24 Jun 1930	7/ 473
Johnson, Henderson	Campbell, Bessie	9 Jun 1928	7/ 133
Johnson, Henry	Simmons, Henrietta	22 Oct 1927	6/ 596
Johnson, Henry	Shackleford, Lena	22 Nov 1930	7/ 523
Johnson, Henry [Daytona]	McDonald, Marcia Elizabeth [Daytona]	13 May 1926	6/ 236
Johnson, Hollis	Hilton, Susie	11 May 1928	7/ 148
Johnson, Jack C.	Williams, Julia	27 Jul 1931	8/ 36
Johnson, James	Bush, Rosa Lee	14 Nov 1927	7/ 11
Johnson, Jesse [B] [Orlando]	Lewis, Cora [Orlando]	15 Jun 1925	5/ 590
Johnson, Jesse Aaron [Orlando]	Brown, Irene Hansell [Pinecastle]	6 Mar 1926	6/ 174
Johnson, Jesse J. [B] [Orlando]	Street, Viola [Orlando]	2 Apr 1925	5/ 552
Johnson, Joe	Davis, Fannie Mae	9 Dec 1929	7/ 383
Johnson, Joe Carlyle	Elleck, Francis	10 Jul 1928	7/ 158
Johnson, John Davis	Fritz, Emma	25 Mar 1932	8/ 138
Johnson, John H. [Orlando]	Howell, Pearlie Bell [Orlando]	3 Jul 1926	6/ 287
Johnson, John William	Eldridge, Annie Evelyn	7 Apr 1932	8/ 169
Johnson, Jonnie	Webb, Cenellar	26 Feb 1934	8/ 436
Johnson, Lawson	Stanley, Margaret	7 Dec 1929	7/ 381
Johnson, Lonney [Orlando]	Mitchell, Mattie [Orlando]	27 Sep 1926	6/ 343
Johnson, Lucius [Orlando]	Gaskin, Queen Esther [Orlando]	19 Apr 1927	6/ 497
Johnson, Maxey Willis	Bassett, Sue Frances	2 Oct 1933	8/ 350
Johnson, Meldon	Wiggins, Fanny Lee	1 Sep 1932	8/ 189
Johnson, Nathaniel [Winter Park]	Paul, Allie Mae [Winter Park]	5 Apr 1926	6/ 197
Johnson, Neal	Jenkins, Clara Mae	23 Mar 1932	8/ 131
Johnson, Paul Stacy	Holton, Effie Mae	2 Jun 1934	8/ 486
Johnson, Robert	Foster, Beatrice	9 May 1934	8/ 475
Johnson, Robert	Meadows, Beatrice	14 Mar 1929	7/ 263
Johnson, Robert James [W] [Cordele, GA]	Watson, Vernice E. [Groveland]	20 Aug 1925	6/ 35
Johnson, Robert Lee	Shepherd, Grace Roberta	25 Jan 1932	8/ 109
Johnson, Robert R.	Wheatley, Elizabeth	25 Sep 1929	7/ 350
Johnson, Roby Jewell	Morris, Marion	6 May 1933	8/ 290
Johnson, Rocels [Orlando]	Williams, Ida [Orlando]	19 Jun 1926	6/ 279
Johnson, Roy	Morgan, Susie	15 Sep 1932	8/ 196
Johnson, Sam [Orlando]	Bland, Isabell [Orlando]	23 Oct 1926	6/ 362
Johnson, Sovay [Auburndale]	Peeples, Annie Maria	13 Jun 1927	6/ 532
Johnson, Sylvester	Smith, Corine	9 Feb 1931	7/ 553
Johnson, Theodore [Plymouth]	Gary, Louise [Orlando]	24 Sep 1925	6/ 54
Johnson, Thomas	Brown, Corinne	24 Mar 1932	8/ 131
Johnson, Tom [Sanford]	Johnson, Bessie [Mrs] (Sanford)	3 Jul 1909	6/ 586
Johnson, Tom [Ocoee]	Kerce, Lona [Ocoee]	5 May 1926	6/ 228
Johnson, Washington [Winter Park]	Samuel, Pearl [Winter Park]	10 Aug 1926	6/ 312
Johnson, Wellington Ezra	Johnson, Carolyn Ann	26 Mar 1934	8/ 450
Johnson, Will	Minis, Daisy	4 Feb 1929	7/ 240
Johnson, William Christian [W] [Dayton, OH]	Artmeir, Alice Myrtle [Chattanooga, TN]	5 Feb 1926	6/ 149
Johnson, Willie	Sampson, Lilla Mae	5 Apr 1934	8/ 455

Johnson, Willie	Jones, Leona	23 Jun 1932	8/ 180
Johnson, Willie	Simons, Viola	3 Oct 1931	8/ 57
Johnson, Willie	Spencer, Hilda Mae	10 Mar 1930	7/ 424
Johnson, Willie	West, Hattie	25 Nov 1929	7/ 376
Johnson, Willie	Nelson, Ella Elizabeth	18 Apr 1932	8/ 143
Johnston, Fred Lee [W] [Orlando]	Douthitt, Pauline [Orlando]	6 Nov 1925	6/ 82
Johnston, Samuel William	Waring, Lucy	30 Sep 1933	8/ 345
Johnston, William Raymond [Ft Meyers]	McDaniel, Winnie [Ft Meyers]	17 Jun 1926	6/ 270
Johus, William Way	Robinson, Mamie	18 Feb 1928	7/ 69
Joiner, C. I. [Orlando]	Daniel, Ruth [Orlando]	7 May 1927	6/ 503
Joiner, Charles Jefferson	Schimpff, Marguerite Leone	20 Dec 1931	8/ 90
Joiner, James B. L.	Chastang, Nettie	9 Mar 1929	7/ 258
Jolos, William [Binghampton, NY]	Weaver, Ida Ellen [Elmire, NY]	2 Jun 1926	6/ 302
Jones, Albert George	Bennett, Mary Anna Lee	27 Jun 1929	7/ 318
Jones, Alex	Cheatam, Sammie Lee	7 Dec 1929	7/ 381
Jones, Belton [Taft]	Austin, Lela [Taft]	27 Nov 1926	6/ 391
Jones, Buster	Ward, Mattie Mae	1 Nov 1933	8/ 360
Jones, Calvin	Groover, Valrea	21 Sep 1931	8/ 52
Jones, Charles L. [B] [Orlando]	Posey, Matilda [Orlando]	3 Feb 1926	6/ 147
Jones, Charlie B.	Porre, Mary	2 Jun 1928	7/ 128
Jones, Charlie Haywood [B] [Orlando]	Mitchell, Gertrude [Orlando]	11 Jan 1926	6/ 131
Jones, Chester [B] [Orlando]	Moran, Charlotte [Orlando]	30 May 1925	5/ 584
Jones, Clarence	Washington, Lillian	28 Oct 1929	7/ 362
Jones, Clifton Floyd	Schori, Thelma	4 Oct 1928	7/ 189
Jones, Conley	James, Marie	12 Dec 1927	7/ 23
Jones, Dan	Manuel, Mattie Mae	14 Dec 1929	7/ 384
Jones, Dave	Black, Mittie	28 Sep 1927	6/ 587
Jones, E. B. [Orlando]	Goldson, Mae [Orlando]	28 Aug 1926	6/ 323
Jones, E. Ulman	Drummond, Evelyn Maud	21 Dec 1929	7/ 386
Jones, Ed Allen	Webb, Alline	26 Jan 1931	7/ 548
Jones, Eddie Neal	Masongale, Cynthia	7 Feb 1932	8/ 113
Jones, Edward	Hollmon, Mattie Louise	13 Mar 1932	8/ 127
Jones, Edwin Pitchford	McCormick, Sara Margaret	1 Nov 1930	7/ 517
Jones, Elias [Winter Park]	Johnson, Nora [Winter Park]	26 Jun 1926	6/ 249
Jones, Elijah	Bennett, Bertha	22 Nov 1928	7/ 206
Jones, Ellis [B] [Eatonville]	Morton, Armetta [Eatonville]	14 Dec 1925	6/ 100
Jones, Elmer Douglas [W] [Donelson TN]	Thomas, Claudia McClendon [Donelson TN]	14 Dec 1925	6/ 101
Jones, Elmer I.	McCall, Lillian Mae	22 Dec 1931	8/ 96
Jones, Ernest	Haynie, Johnny Mae	4 Oct 1930	7/ 502
Jones, Ernest [B] [Orlando]	Harris, May [Orlando]	24 May 1925	5/ 578
Jones, Ernest James	Young, Christina	5 Mar 1928	7/ 75
Jones, Ezra Collins	Rhodes, Helen May	14 Jan 1930	7/ 399
Jones, Fred	Brown, Evelyn	8 Dec 1930	7/ 527
Jones, Frederick Walter	Stanley, Betty	12 Jun 1934	8/ 493
Jones, George	Gilcrease, Blanche	8 Apr 1929	7/ 276
Jones, Harry [Orlando]	Duncan, Martha Lee	20 Jan 1927	6/ 441
Jones, Henry	Smiley, Maggie	12 Nov 1932	8/ 216
Jones, Henry	McCray, Willie Mae	8 Sep 1927	6/ 575
Jones, Henry Alfred	Johnson, Annie	21 Jun 1930	7/ 472
Jones, Herbert [Orlando]	Williams, Sadie [Orlando]	31 Jan 1927	6/ 454
Jones, Isaac	Gibbs, Sarah	29 Oct 1931	8/ 66

Jones, James	Williams, Clara	6 Dec 1930	7/ 528
Jones, James Denison [DeRidder, LA]	Kakas, Mildred B. [Saratoga, IA]	29 Mar 1927	6/ 484
Jones, James Earley [Orlando]	Miller, Ludie [Orlando]	8 May 1927	6/ 512
Jones, Jim [Orlando]	Paul, Kizzie [Orlando]	8 Sep 1926	6/ 332
Jones, Jim Finn	Kilpatrick, Sarah Jane	2 Aug 1928	7/ 168
Jones, John Clifton	Stroud, Elmer	16 Nov 1929	7/ 371
Jones, John L.	Edwards, Laura	3 Jun 1928	7/ 128
Jones, John Richard	Cary, Ethel Missouri	31 Aug 1929	7/ 338
Jones, Joseph William	Miller, Dora	9 May 1929	7/ 292
Jones, Lewis [Sanford]	Johnson, Cora [Sanford]	16 Jul 1927	6/ 552
Jones, Marshall Burns	Watson, Hazel	20 Oct 1933	8/ 354
Jones, Maxie Daniel [Winter Garden]	Scott, Agnes [Winter Garden]	13 Oct 1926	6/ 353
Jones, Melvin	Williams, Amy	15 Oct 1927	6/ 592
Jones, Mose	Callius, Edith	2 Feb 1928	7/ 55
Jones, Odell	Bledace, Christina	25 Apr 1930	7/ 442
Jones, Richard Hamilton	Beuckler, Lucy Virginia	10 Mar 1929	7/ 261
Jones, Samuel	Bronson, Acenith	27 Nov 1929	7/ 380
Jones, Sike Jas. Jr.	Paul, Margaret	18 Feb 1933	8/ 258
Jones, Sim	More, Lucile	27 Jun 1931	8/ 26
Jones, Sim	Sills, Annie Mae	19 May 1930	7/ 457
Jones, Solon Luther	Rizer, Thelma	24 Dec 1932	8/ 241
Jones, Theodore Roosevelt [W] [Orlando]	Beckman, Annie [Orlando]	28 Nov 1925	6/ 95
Jones, Thomas [B] [Orlando]	Williams, Estella [Orlando]	25 Nov 1925	6/ 96
Jones, Wade	Boyd, Daisy	28 Jan 1928	7/ 49
Jones, Walter Carlos [W] [Winter Garden]	Stewart, Irma Effalain [Winter Garden]	19 Feb 1925	5/ 527
Jones, Waymon [Winter Garden]	Bill, Mamie Lou [Winter Garden]	21 Oct 1926	6/ 359
Jones, Will [B] [Orlando]	Pierce, Lulu [Orlando]	19 Nov 1925	6/ 86
Jones, William	Kirkland, Janie	9 Dec 1933	8/ 385
Jones, William Roy	Gardner, Gladys	4 Sep 1927	6/ 574
Jones, William Walter	Richards, Esther	18 Jun 1934	8/ 496
Jones, Willie	Holmes, Nellie Mae	28 Jan 1929	7/ 236
Jones, Willie [B] [Orlando]	Lovick, Eva May [Orlando]	2 Feb 1926	6/ 147
Jordan, Annis [Orlando]	O'Neil, Frankie [Orlando]	8 May 1926	6/ 232
Jordan, Theodore	Ashford, Johnnie May	24 Jan 1933	8/ 249
Jordan, Will	Henderson, Dora	19 Jun 1931	8/ 20
Jordan, Will	Henderson, Dora Tucker	9 Apr 1931	7/ 577
Jordan, Willie Edwin [Orlando]	Williams, Nettie [Detroit, MI]	27 Oct 1926	6/ 372
Jordon, James [W] [Orlando]	Lawson, Hattie [Orlando]	15 Aug 1925	6/ 34
Joseph, Collis Percival	Green, Essie	13 Jul 1928	7/ 161
Joseph, Nathan Ackerman	Liberoff, Eve	6 Jan 1932	8/ 102
Josey, Ambrosia	Williams, Cora Lee	30 Nov 1931	8/ 82
Joslin, Ralph Herbert [Orlando]	Murray, Elizabeth Marjorie [Winter Park]	20 Apr 1927	6/ 495
Joyner, Millard	Lee, Clifford	10 Sep 1927	6/ 581
Juby, Charles William	Johnson, Marie	1 Feb 1928	7/ 61
Judd, Frederick Arthur	Reagan, Marcella	29 Apr 1931	7/ 588
Julian, Calvin Edward [Orlando]	McClarren, Eva Hazel [Windemere]	5 Nov 1926	6/ 377

K

Kaimkle, George [Orlando]	Whitley, Elizabeth [Orlando]	18 Nov 1926	6/ 387
Kaiser, Jessie [Orlando]	Gillion, Eva [Orlando]	18 Jan 1926	6/ 138
Kale, Everette H. [W] [Chicago, IL]	Simpson, Nelle Ellen [DeLand]	14 Feb 1925	5/ 527
Kalet, Roy Ellsworth	Pillow, Maun Ola	3 Jul 1931	8/ 29
Kampen, Hugh	Cooper, Gloria	31 Jul 1930	7/ 484
Karel, Frank, Jr.	P'Pool, Helen Lee	2 Aug 1930	7/ 484
Kasper, Albert G. H. [Orlando]	Durrenberger, Lillie M. [Orlando]	19 May 1926	6/ 247
Kasper, Edward Otto	Christenson, Marguerite Iris	7 Mar 1932	8/ 127
Kasper, Ernest August, Jr (Orlando)	Puck, Ella Marie [Kiss]	12 Nov 1926	6/ 395
Kasper, Harry Edward [W] [Orlando]	Arndt, Elvira [Orlando]	1 Nov 1925	6/ 79
Kasper, John Gilbert	Shelton, Mildred Elizabeth	23 Dec 1933	8/ 396
Kasper, Walter [Orlando]	Tusing, Leatha [Orlando]	20 Mar 1926	6/ 186
Kastner, Emil Joseph	Loughran, Lillian May	5 Apr 1934	8/ 457
Kates, John Jacob	O'Berry, Ruth Evelyn	7 May 1933	8/ 295
Katz, Ben Irving	Sigel, Edythe	10 Aug 1930	7/ 488
Kaufman, George W.	Deaham, Bertha	18 Apr 1931	7/ 584
Kaufmann, George Conrad	Westmeyer, Mildred Arah	29 Mar 1933	8/ 278
Kay, Alexander T.	Williams, Bessie Mae	23 May 1928	7/ 118
Kean, Albert Elmer	Jensen, Mabel Malinda	25 Dec 1930	7/ 540
Keaton, William Hutchinson [W] [Orlando]	Ashley, Naomi D. [Orlando]	15 Aug 1925	6/ 35
Keef, Leard Moore	Scott, Claudine Florina	13 Jul 1929	7/ 322
Keeley, Jim [B] [Orlando]	Cason, Mary [Orlando]	7 Nov 1925	6/ 79
Keen, Godfrey Theodore	Allen, Hazel Helen	24 Dec 1933	8/ 406
Keenan, Dallas John	Daoust, Gilbertine Margaret	24 Dec 1926	7/ 7
Keene, Cecil Edward	Fussell, Frances Leola	22 Feb 1930	7/ 419
Keith, Eugene Peter	Burgess, Corene Lois	20 Apr 1931	7/ 583
Keith, Maxie	Sullivan, Queen	13 Mar 1933	8/ 270
Kelley, Herman Earnest [W] [Ocoee]	Raines, Myrtle Ree [Ocoee]	21 Feb 1925	5/ 529
Kelley, T.G.	Conley, Sadie	6 Jan 1934	8/ 400
Kelley, Willie Lee	Evans, Strawde Belle	17 Oct 1931	8/ 67
Kellim/Kilburn, Harry H. [Sarasota]	Brown, Lucy McKay [Maitland]	2 Jun 1927	6/ 523
Kelly, George Taylor	Smith, Blanch Victoria	15 Nov 1931	8/ 74
Kelly, Harry Kenneth [Winter Park]	Dickinson, Helen Elizabeth [Winter Park]	9 Jun 1925	5/ 594
Kelly, John Martin, Jr.	Graham, Ruth Lillian	27 Dec 1928	7/ 222
Kelsey, William Henry [Oviedo]	Jones, Annie Lee [Oviedo]	21 Mar 1927	6/ 479
Kembro, Chester	Fountain, Maggie	16 Oct 1928	7/ 196
Kemp, Ernest Eugene	Holland, Lillian Lucile	26 Jan 1932	8/ 107
Kemp, Thomas Crawford	Dees, Ella [Apopka]	19 Aug 1926	6/ 318
Kenan, Alexander [B] [Maitland]	Anderson, Martha [Maitland]	15 Jun 1925	5/ 590
Kendrick, Brennen Delro	Overholser, Aleen Marie	4 Nov 1933	8/ 359
Kendrick, William Earl	Payne, Edwina Davis	7 Jun 1934	8/ 490
Kennedy, Cap. [Orlando]	Clark, Georgie [Orlando]	31 Mar 1926	6/ 195
Kennedy, Floyd [B] [Orlando]	Jackson, Jessie [Orlando]	13 Nov 1925	6/ 95
Kennedy, Frank Allen [Orlando]	Wills, Willie Byrd	24 Jan 1927	6/ 447
Kennedy, Henry	Crawford, Mattie Mae	31 May 1930	7/ 461
Kennedy, Marion Joseph	Walker, Alice Rebecca	20 Mar 1931	7/ 572
Kennedy, Richard Pickens	Moore, Margaret Elizabeth	20 Jul 1930	7/ 481
Kennedy, Thomas [Orlando]	Laneece?, Thelma [Orlando]	13 Mar 1926	6/ 177
Kenyon, Julius [Orlando]	Green, Beatrice [Orlando]	28 Apr 1926	6/ 246

[lic 25 Apr 1926; no return or recording; also at 6/ 312]

Kerce, Dave	Hurst, Ruby Irene	28 Oct 1933	8/ 355
Kerns, Clarence Arthur	Lawrence, Roberta	22 Aug 1929	7/ 335
Kerns, William Howard [W] [Winter Park]	Coffin, Lois [W] [Winter Park] [Coffman on return]	13 Jan 1926	6/ 132
Kerr, Clifford Stanley	Poundstone, Clara Louise	28 Mar 1933	8/ 278
Kerr, Elmer Haswell	Segraves, Elmira Grace	26 Mar 1932	8/ 133
Kerr, Joseph Frank [New Smyrna]	Shaw, Addie Mitchell [Winter Garden]	26 Feb 1927	6/ 475
Kerse, Fred	Thompson, India	29 Jun 1934	8/ 502
Kersey, Lester Lee [Orlando]	Vernia, Mary Rebecca [Orlando]	20 Apr 1926	6/ 217
Kester, Milton Robert	Welch, Mary Frances	26 Jun 1929	7/ 315
Ketcham, Charles Leslie	Sandfort, Gladys Ruth	28 Jul 1928	7/ 167
Ketchum, Leonard Corning	Wakeman, Caroline Alice	27 Mar 1931	7/ 573
Key, Arthur Hobson	Coleman, Lydia Ellen	12 Sep 1928	7/ 183
Keyes, Cecil Milton	Bass, Essie Blanche	25 Dec 1929	7/ 392
Keys, Hugh	McAfee, Mattie Gammon	5 Nov 1927	7/ 9
Kibby, Lawrence Hayward [W] [Orlando]	Ward, Florence Hesper [Portland, ME]	23 Mar 1925	5/ 547
Kiddy, Walter J. [W] [Buchanan, WV]	Curtis, Ernestine [Buchanan, WV]	27 Dec 1925	6/ 124
Kiel, Jack	Morris, Sarah Jane	6 Sep 1933	8/ 339
Kilgore, James S. [W] [Ocoee]	Walls, Illa Mae [Ocoee]	30 May 1925	5/ 582
Killen, Richard Beaman	Gardner, Mary Frances	26 Sep 1932	8/ 200
Kilmore, Leslie Mearl	Gus, Louise Angela	6 Mar 1928	7/ 76
Kilpatrick, Aaron Nixon	Foor, Florence Rebecca	25 Jan 1932	8/ 107
Kilpatrick, Allen	King, Odessa	21 Mar 1931	7/ 570
Kilpatrick, Moses	Ginlack, Vera	23 Mar 1929	7/ 266
Kimball, George Sharpe	Tyson, Thelma Huckaby	12 Jun 1930	7/ 467
Kimball, Raymond Fleming	Wright, Mary Rollo	22 May 1931	8/ 6
Kimber, William Ambrose	Watkins, Lillie Mayfield	22 May 1934	8/ 480
Kimbrough, Rubie King	Prather, Addie Mae	11 Jul 1931	8/ 31
Kincaid, Marion Troy	Sellers, Thelma Ernestine	3 Sep 1929	7/ 340
King, Andrew	Smith, May Belle	18 Oct 1933	8/ 355
King, Arthur Murphy	Sanger, Gertrude Anna	16 Sep 1933	8/ 342
King, Charles Edwin	Collins, Azalena Christine	19 Feb 1933	8/ 260
King, Edward Franklin [Detroit, MI]	Cashwell, Claudia [Asheville, NC]	19 May 1926	6/ 240
King, Edward [New York, NY]	Schulmerich, Dorothy [New York, NY]	14 Apr 1926	6/ 209
King, Frank [Orlando]	Burke, Hattie [Orlando]	17 Jun 1927	6/ 537
King, Harry	Chestnut, Lottie	28 May 1928	7/ 120
King, Harry Alphonse	Weston, Lucile	16 Dec 1933	8/ 386
King, J. C. [Orlando]	Ross, Annie Lou [Orlando]	19 Feb 1927	6/ 463
King, James	Rollins, Annie Mae	13 Sep 1929	7/ 345
King, James Lonnie	Pollock, Lelia Juanita	25 Apr 1931	8/ 28
King, James Robert	Rowe, Margaret Elizabeth	20 Jan 1934	8/ 414
King, James Wesley	Livingston, Iris	30 Aug 1933	8/ 337
King, Joe [Winter Garden]	Johnson, Eddie Mae [Winter Garden]	24 Apr 1926	6/ 221
King, Pat Neff [Leesburg]	Merrill, Louise [Mt.Dora]	8 Dec 1926	6/ 411
King, Ralph Obed	Moore, Mary Elizabeth	25 Sep 1933	8/ 344
King, Randolph	William, Hattie	20 Aug 1928	7/ 175
King, Will [B] [Orlando]	Crumley, Ida [Americus GA]	16 Mar 1925	5/ 541
King, William M., Jr [W] [Greensboro, NC]	Auferheide, Irma [Indianapolis, IN]	9 May 1925	5/ 581
King, Willie	Stevens, Lula	16 Nov 1929	7/ 371
Kinney, Melvin Edgar [Oaksville, NY]	Amyx, Cecil [Knoxville TN]	18 May 1926	6/ 238

Kinnon, George Herman	McMakin, Edith Emlyn	17 Jun 1928	7/ 142
Kiphuth, John Herman	Whitaker, Mildred Rebecca	30 Aug 1930	7/ 493
Kiplinger, Lance Edward [Ocala}	Drake, Gladdys [Ocala]	18 Feb 1926	6/ 163
Kirby, George	Nettles, Alpha	23 Dec 1927	7/ 40
Kirby, L. E. [Sanford]	Register, Elsie [Sanford]	2 Oct 1926	6/ 347
Kirkland, George [Sanford]	Howell, Essie [Sanford]	20 Mar 1926	6/ 184
Kirkland, Ruel Axon [W] [Orlando]	Huppel, Meta Marie Elizabeth [Orlando]	12 Feb 1925	5/ 525
Kirkwood, Clois Emanuel [Orlando]	DeGonzolese,Delorese Evelyn [Orlando]	31 May 1926	6/ 255
Kirkwood, Cody Christopher	Sharp, Helen Farris	2 Mar 1929	7/ 256
Kirtin, Eliot L. [Minnceola]	Thomas, Annie May [Winter Garden]	15 Mar 1927	6/ 476
Kirtley, Homer Abraham [Orlando]	Patrick, Marie [Indianapolis, IN]	17 Jun 1926	6/ 272
Kissam, Allen [Orlando]	Lynch, Doris Amelia	25 Jan 1927	6/ 447
Kitchen, John	Floyed, Leatha	28 Dec 1932	8/ 235
Kitchens, Willie B.	Stanley, Ethel	31 Mar 1934	8/ 452
Kitchin, Emmons LaHue	Briggs, Isma Gertrude	26 Oct 1931	8/ 65
Kizer, John Edward	Kizer, Mabel Mary	8 Dec 1932	8/ 227
Kleckley, James [B] [Lockhart]	Clark, Lula [Lockhart]	30 May 1925	5/ 584
Klein, Irving [Orlando]	Weiner, Dora	26 Jun 1927	6/ 541
Klettner, August William	Hutchinson, Marjorie Esther	1 Jun 1934	8/ 491
Klinest, Lester Morris	Roglitz, Frieda Irene	13 Feb 1928	7/ 71
Klink, Edward Anthony	Stoinoff, Marie	14 Feb 1934	8/ 430
Knapp, Jasper Edwin	McNeal, Willie Alma	10 Jan 1930	7/ 398
Knight, Albert	Dawson, Sallie Mae	10 May 1930	7/ 451
Knight, Charlie	Daniel, Minnie Lee	18 Oct 1930	7/ 511
Knight, George William	Torrance, Margaret Allison	28 Apr 1931	7/ 590
Knight, Hugh Edwards	Ray, Ellen Lucile	26 Nov 1931	8/ 79
Knight, John William	Umstott, Maudella	7 Feb 1932	8/ 115
Knight, Leroy	Thomas, Larrill	30 Aug 1928	7/ 178
Knighton, Willie [Orlando]	McKinzie, Ada [Orlando]	8 Mar 1926	6/ 171
Knollenberger, Karl Augustus	Seivert, Helen Freeborn	9 Mar 1933	8/ 268
Knox, Robert	Brown, Fannie	31 Jan 1929	7/ 238
Konickie, Benjamin [Orlando]	Paul, Alice [Orlando]	1 Mar 1927	6/ 468
Koons, George Earl	Lee, Mary Alma	29 Jan 1933	8/ 252
Korfhaze, Harris Rudolph [W] [Orlando]	Warner, Hattie Henrietta [Orlando]	6 Feb 1926	6/ 152
Krebs, Henry, Jr. [Orlando]	Mabley, Leona [Orlando]	6 Dec 1926	6/ 400
Krewingjaus, Edgar John	Rumph, Merle Vernelle	1 Jan 1934	8/ 411
Krieger, Sheldon Peter	Chapman, Elmina Mary	19 Mar 1934	8/ 446
Kuhns, Frank Miller [Orlando]	Harden, Evelyn Mae [Orlando]	14 Mar 1926	6/ 184
Kuhr, Charles Anthony	Siese, Clara Elizabeth	8 Sep 1933	8/ 341
Kummer, Carl Otto, Rev. [W] [Orlando]	McRainey, Mary Ethel [Orlando]	15 Jul 1925	6/ 20
Kurtz, LaRue Moore [Orlando]	Morgan, Laura Blakesly [Orlando]	20 Jun 1926	6/ 281
Kyle, Marcus LeRoy	Widdis, Margaret Lucile	2 Jul 1933	8/ 320
Kyzer, Ernest Ray	Weger, Harriet Katherine	1 Feb 1931	7/ 552

L

Lacry, Sidney	Read, Prinsell	18 Feb 1928	7/ 67
Lahman, Harry	King, Kate	14 Nov 1928	7/ 204
Lalor, Hugh	Williams, Ruba	24 Oct 1927	6/ 597
Lamar, LeRoy [Orlando]	Hall, Sadie Mae [Orlando]	9 Aug 1926	6/ 314
Lamb, Charles Stuart [Winter Garden]	Wilkes, Lula Mae [Winter Garden]	3 Jul 1927	6/ 544
Lamb, Isaac Malcolm [W] [Kissimmee]	Newton, Mollie Ann [Palmer, NE]	6 Jan 1926	6/ 130

Lamb, Joe	Sanford, Loraine	25 Aug 1929	7/ 336
Lamb, Tommie	Daniels, Geneva	17 Feb 1934	8/ 431
Lambkin, Bryant [Orlando]	Parks, Gussie Mae [Orlando]	21 Jan 1927	6/ 441
Lampertins, Paul Warren [Orlando]	Bailey, Ada Alton [Orlando]	13 Jul 1927	6/ 549
Lampkins, Benjamin Franklin	Rollerson, Helen	28 May 1931	8/ 7
Lampkins, James	Richardson, Bessie	28 Feb 1931	7/ 562
Lampp, Julian Dell	Broadwell, Lela	14 Feb 1933	8/ 258
Lamps, Julius [B] [Orlando]	Babb, Roberta [Orlando]	12 Apr 1925	5/ 559
Lancaster, Tom	Ross, Alberta	17 Sep 1933	8/ 342
Lance, Bennie	Moore, Estella	8 Apr 1929	7/ 275
Lance, Eddie LeRoy	King, Agnes Marie	23 Nov 1932	8/ 219
Lance, Harry Wilbur [Dade City]	Gulley, Iva Lorena [Oakland]	14 Oct 1925	6/ 68
Lane, Aleck	Beans, Elma	12 Jan 1933	8/ 243
Lane, James [Sanford]	Shadix, Maude [Sanford]	21 Aug 1925	6/ 36
Lane, John Temple	McNeill, Annie Mildred	24 Dec 1931	8/ 95
Lane, Thomas Jefferson	Bronson, Elizabeth	31 Aug 1929	7/ 337
Laney, Harrison Jean	Lawton, Lillian Elizabeth	6 Jun 1934	8/ 490
Laney, Sam Alexander	McMann, Letha Rosie	20 Oct 1928	7/ 197
Lang, George [Orlando]	Barnwell, Lena [Orlando]	14 Sep 1925	6/ 46
Lang, Ike [Orlando]	Clayton, Sarah [Orlando]	6 Apr 1926	6/ 199
Lang, Thomas Calvin [Eagle Lake]	Brannon, Frances Gay [Ashland, AL]	27 Nov 1926	6/ 401
Lang, William Raymond [Orlando]	Banker, Lillie Mae [Orlando]	17 Jul 1926	6/ 298
Langford, James Otto	Cannada, Alida Pauline	3 Jan 1929	7/ 228
Langford, Thomas I.	McMillan, Vera	22 Oct 1928	7/ 197
Langford, William Carlton	Thompson, Maurice Ola	10 Dec 1929	7/ 383
Langford, William Carlton	Thompson, Mamie	13 Apr 1929	7/ 281
Langiotti, Eddie	Peters, Katie Virginia	31 Mar 1932	8/ 136
Langley, Albert Weasley	Mole, Anna Rebecca	7 Jul 1934	8/ 509
Langston, Carol Howard	Livingston, Dorothy Brooks	29 Sep 1931	8/ 59
Langston, Herbert	Lamar, Justine	2 Dec 1933	8/ 378
Langston, Levy	Barry, Rossie Mae	7 May 1930	7/ 448
Lanier, Aaron	Yowell, Viola Bell	21 Jun 1928	7/ 146
Lanier, Aaron	Davis, Thelma	9 Dec 1929	7/ 382
Lankford, William B.	Eaton, Katherine Elizabeth	4 Nov 1930	7/ 517
Lantz, Garfield James	Willsey, Marie Pauline	23 Jun 1928	7/ 154
Lantz, Robert Leslie [Pinecastle]	Tanner, Bessie Irene [Pinecastle]	22 Jul 1926	6/ 278
Large, Johnnie	Brown, Eva	23 Feb 1929	7/ 253
Larson, Jacob [St. Olif, IA]	Judd, Bertha Althia [Orlando]	7 Aug 1927	6/ 561
LaShance, Hubert Sheldon	Wood, Jocelyn	29 Nov 1928	7/ 212
Last, Augustus	Graham, Essie Mae	6 Jun 1929	7/ 306
Laster, Oliver	Saunders, Fannie	30 Apr 1931	7/ 589
Lastinger, James Nerle	Holtsclaw, Lettie Luella	1 Jan 1930	7/ 394
Latham, James Ryder	McDonald, Bertha	2 Oct 1931	8/ 58
Latour, Louis [Lake Hamilton]	Sandquist, Ellen Marie [Dundee]	9 Sep 1925	6/ 36
Latour, Louis [Lake Hamilton]	Sandquist, Ellen Marie [Dundee]	9 Sep 1925	6/ 42
Latshow, Irwin R. [Ocoee]	Stiles, Sarah [Ocoee]	17 Oct 1925	6/ 65
Lau, Irvin	Ison, Maxie	21 Oct 1931	8/ 66
Laudermilk, Bert Henry [Park Ridge, IL]	Kinzel, Leota I. [Oakland, IL]	21 Mar 1927	6/ 481
Lauster, John Henry [Orlando]	Bower, Sudie Belle [Orlando]	27 Oct 1926	6/ 371
Lavender, Lovick Hollan	Watford, Audry	4 Jul 1928	7/ 156

Lavery, Charles Elmer	Douglass, Nellie Bemrose	4 Nov 1933	8/ 361
Law, Vernie [Orlando]	Bryan, Beatrice [Orlando]	11 Oct 1926	6/ 351
Lawrence, Charles W., Jr [W] [Babson Park]	Grey, Dorothy E. F. [Winter Park]	30 Dec 1925	6/ 124
Lawrence, James William	Williams, Lulu Missouri	15 Nov 1931	8/ 75
Laws, Robert Woolridge	Kalback, Carol Beatrice	2 Nov 1929	7/ 367
Laws, Robert Woolridge [Orlando]	Vigneron, Blanche Yvonne [Orlando]	5 May 1927	6/ 535
Lawson, Cyrus Moseley	McKibben, Sarah Christine	29 May 1928	7/ 123
Lawson, Euarse [Orlando]	Bostic, Susie [Orlando]	16 Oct 1926	6/ 355
Lawton, Oliver	Stroman, Helma	22 Jul 1929	7/ 324
Lea, Louis [Orlando]	Battles, Bessie [Orlando]	8 Aug 1926	6/ 307
Leachardt, B. G. [Titusville]	Baggett, Roberta [Apopka]	18 May 1927	6/ 511
Leary, Fred Lee	James, Rosa Lee	5 Feb 1934	8/ 424
Leavell, Fletcher Corrine	Padgett, Elsie Mae	20 Apr 1929	7/ 291
Lechniak, Walter Edward	Brosche, Frances Elizabeth	17 Jun 1934	8/ 497
Lee, A. W. [Sanford]	Teague, Edith [Sanford]	14 May 1927	6/ 508
Lee, Ben [Orlando]	Wilson, Lucretia [Orlando]	11 Dec 1926	6/ 405
Lee, Charles C. [W] [Center Hill]	Fender, Mary Virginia [Center Hill]	26 May 1925	5/ 580
Lee, Charles Morrison	Chance, Dicie	22 Jan 1934	8/ 415
Lee, Charlie	Blunt, Aldonia	16 Jun 1928	7/ 140
Lee, Clifford Walford	Lively, Lillie Ione	13 Apr 1929	7/ 279
Lee, Empprous	Anderson, Lettie	1 Jun 1930	7/ 462
Lee, Lester [Ocoee]	Howard, Dorothy [Ocoee]	20 May 1927	6/ 514
Lee, Robert E.	Purvis, Ezlee	14 Jun 1934	8/ 496
Lee, Sylvester	English, Louise	5 Sep 1929	7/ 341
Lee, Virgil Eugene	Loper, Sarah Oleana	23 Dec 1933	8/ 389
Lee, Warren C.	Morris, Estelle Daverl	3 Dec 1927	7/ 21
Lee, William Henry [Orlando]	Albert, Anna [Orlando]	30 Jul 1926	6/ 294
Lee, William Sturgis	Kirkland, Thelma Lucile	26 Nov 1929	7/ 378
Lee, Willie	Jackson, Julie	30 Sep 1930	7/ 501
Lee, Willie Horace [B] [Orlando]	Wilson, Irene [Orlando]	19 Dec 1925	6/ 106
Lee, Wm. Giles [Orlando]	Riordan, Mary [Brooklyn, NY]	17 Mar 1926	6/ 188
Leggett, Edwin Ezra	Williams, Dorothy Marie	7 Oct 1930	7/ 506
Lehan, James Joseph	Muiss, Alice M.	14 Feb 1930	7/ 414
Leigh, Elias Clarence [Winter Park]	Boatwright, Virgie [Winter Park]	20 Dec 1926	6/ 412
Leighty, George William [W] [Orlando]	Adams, Christine [Orlando]	8 Jul 1925	6/ 12
Lemon, C. T.	Evans, Susie Mae	17 Oct 1933	8/ 460
Lennartz, Peter Joseph [W] [St Petersburg]	Mossburg, Flora Mae [St Petersburg]	27 Jul 1925	6/ 25
Lenoir, August Francis Xavier [Orlando]	St. John, Ruth Gordon [Eustis]	11 Apr 1926	6/ 217
Lenox, Calvin Wesley	Heaton, Ruth Louise	21 Nov 1932	8/ 219
Lenton, Allen [B] [Winter Park]	Whaley, Annie [Winter Park]	16 Feb 1925	5/ 526
Lentz, John Fred	Haolt, Katherine Marie	29 Dec 1930	7/ 534
Lersch, Donald Ruscher	Rouse, Verna Mae	23 Dec 1931	8/ 92
Leshinsky, Abraham	Rosen, Anna	24 May 1931	8/ 11
Lester, Corrnelius Abner [Winston Salem, NC]	Crout, Lillian Almaree [Pelion, SC]	18 Feb 1926	6/ 162
Lester, James Garland [Pinecastle]	Groh, Esther Elizabeth [Myerstown, PA]	20 Feb 1926	6/ 166
Lester, Ralph	Goodman, Blanche	20 Mar 1928	7/ 83
Letral, Thomas Crimpscheul [Orlando]	Burns, Ida Smith [Orlando]	15 Jul 1926	6/ 299
Lewis, Alvie L. [W] [Zellwood]	Foote, Jennie [Zellwood]	25 Apr 1925	5/ 565
Lewis, Charles Wesley	Peterson, Rosa	8 Jun 1929	7/ 305
Lewis, Curtis Gage	Funnelle, Penelope Earle	2 Nov 1931	8/ 70
Lewis, Edwin C.	Brooks, Nannie Kent	21 Apr 1928	7/ 100
Lewis, Hezekiah	Washington, Vililian	24 Mar 1930	7/ 431

Lewis, Howard	Tollmer, Henritta	26 Jan 1929	7/ 235
Lewis, Jack Clyde	Raiford, Lula Gillon	11 Oct 1930	7/ 505
Lewis, James	Sims, Ruby	19 Oct 1933	8/ 352
Lewis, John Jack	Hammond, Beulah Mae	30 Jan 1933	8/ 251
Lewis, Oscar	Moore, Rosa	26 Nov 1931	8/ 78
Lewis, Walter Henry	Ludlam, Vernon	8 May 1930	7/ 450
Lewis, William	Lanier, Lela	13 Jan 1933	8/ 245
Lewis, Willis Harry	Werner, Ella Ferdinanda	4 Apr 1934	8/ 458
Liby, Alvie Andrew [Daytona]	Hichman, Frieda Laverne	25 Aug 1926	6/ 321
Liddon, W. J.	Cockran, Flora	15 Nov 1928	7/ 204
Lightsey, Purvis	Floyd, Lenora	28 Jun 1933	8/ 317
Ligon, Ellerbee Willie	Pierce, Julia Mae	5 Feb 1934	8/ 425
Ligon, Jean Harry	Davis, Celia Anna	3 Oct 1931	8/ 56
Lillard, Calvin	Dixon, Annie Lee	26 Apr 1932	8/ 148
Lilley, Eulis Melvin	Dunn, Bernice Aline	16 Feb 1929	7/ 252
Lillvik, Andrew Francis	Roberts, Zoe Allegra	26 Mar 1934	8/ 449
Linder, John Robert	Johnston, Sadie Mae	29 Jan 1932	8/ 120
Lindsay, Wayland Archie [W] [Orlando]	Dubberly, Ennie Virginia [Orlando]	7 Feb 1925	5/ 523
Lindsey, Archie Wayland	Bilbray, Annie Mae	1 Jun 1932	8/ 163
Lindsey, William Hays	Carter, Mildred Lewis	20 Apr 1928	7/ 101
Linear, Fred	Edwards, Frankie	3 Jan 1931	7/ 537
Linger, E. Clifford, Jr.	Backster, Adelinda	1 May 1929	7/ 286
Lingo, Robert Lee	Hayes, Emma Frances	13 May 1928	7/ 116
Lipham, Amos Davard [W] [Orlando]	Roeder, Nell Lois [Orlando]	25 Dec 1925	6/ 121
Little, Eldon Hall	Turner, Willie Reedy	24 Sep 1932	8/ 203
Little, Ernest [Ocoee]	Nobles, Sallie Mae [Ocoee]	20 Feb 1926	6/ 160
Little, Robert Gaston [W] [Orlando]	Barr, Betty [Orlando]	2 Jun 1925	5/ 598
Little, Robert Lee [Orlando]	Hume, Margaret Ellene [Orlando]	14 May 1926	6/ 237
Little, St. Elmo	Causey, Iva Belle	16 Apr 1932	8/ 145
Littles, Clifford	Hamilton, Fannie	1 Oct 1929	7/ 352
Littles, Curtis	Graham, Willie Lee	22 Dec 1930	7/ 531
Lively, Hal Wilburn	Parker, Frances Ada	21 May 1932	8/ 159
Livengood, Clifford E. [Charleston, WV]	Harris, Evelyn [Charleston, WV]	19 Dec 1925	6/ 106
Livingston, George A. [Conway]	Barber, Maggie S. [Conway]	21 May 1927	6/ 515
Livingston, George D	Bryant, Julia May	24 Jun 1933	8/ 318
Livingston, Henry Luther [Winter Park]	Johns, Esther Odelle [Orlando]	28 Jul 1927	6/ 556
Livingston, Joe	Merritt, Daisy	3 Jun 1929	7/ 302
Livingston, Joe [Orlando]	Booker, Lizzie [Orlando]	23 Aug 1926	6/ 320
Livingston, Paul	Matson, Elma	14 Feb 1928	7/ 66
Livingston, William Carson [Orlando]	Johnson, Violet Catherine [Orlando]	20 Jun 1927	6/ 547
Lloyd, Hal	Green, Philles	14 May 1928	7/ 113
Lloyd, James	Adams, Viola	14 Jul 1929	7/ 325
Locke, David Clifford	Bekemeyer, Myrtis	4 Mar 1933	8/ 265
Lockhart, Clarence Burgess	Drawdy, Emily Ann	14 Dec 1933	8/ 393
Locklear, Barney Preston	Metcalf, Susan	3 May 1934	8/ 472
Lockwood, Allen Wardlow	Lockwood, Milred F.	26 Jan 1930	7/ 406
Lockwood, Geo. Leslie [Brooklyn, NY]	Coborn, Linda [Washington, DC]	18 Jan 1926	6/ 141
Lofton, Cornelius [B] [Orlando]	Bleckley, Valera [Orlando]	16 Nov 1925	6/ 86
Logan, Augustus [Apopka]	Singleton, Ella [Apopka]	17 Jan 1927	6/ 438
Logan, Henry	Missouri, Robbie Mae	26 Oct 1929	7/ 370

Logan, Jake	Brown, Ida Dora	24 Feb 1930	7/ 421
Logan, Manuel	Harris, Geneva	1 Mar 1930	7/ 421
Logue, George Carlton	Patterson, Bernice Frances	6 Jul 1930	7/ 478
Logue, William Columbus	Elston, Helen Louise	12 Jun 1932	8/ 168
Lohr, Joseph A. [W] [Orlando]	Yerger, Alberta G. [Orlando]	13 Nov 1925	6/ 90
London, Levrett Heber [Tangerine]	Wood, Montine Leona [Eustis]	15 Apr 1926	6/ 210
Lonesome, Wilbur Cornelious	Lighthouse, Effie Mae	7 Sep 1926	6/ 331
Long, James	Ward, Susie Loretta	17 Jan 1934	8/ 417
Long, John Hezzie	Hagen, Dorothy Mae	11 Sep 1929	7/ 344
Long, John Robert [Sanford]	Swanson, Frances Thelma [Sanford]	26 Feb 1927	6/ 465
Longo, Edward Andrew James	Brown, Wava Priscilla	23 Dec 1932	8/ 232
Loper, Norman Clifford	Black, Elsie Catherine	22 Apr 1934	8/ 467
Loper, Roy C.	Carter, Daisy Lee	17 Oct 1928	7/ 195
Lord, Isaac [Orlando]	Williams, Bettie [Orlando]	25 Nov 1925	6/ 89
Lord, Ralph Waldo	Tate, Maree Berenice	17 Oct 1931	8/ 60
Lott, Aaron	Henry, Beulah	29 Jul 1930	7/ 482
Louton, Kenneth	Harden, Mary Jane	2 Mar 1934	8/ 438
Love, Elwood	Ford, Agnes	1 Mar 1934	8/ 438
Love, Leon Haywort	Oakley, Margaret Edna	26 Apr 1928	7/ 106
Lovejoy, John	Gabel, Adriana Francina	12 Apr 1928	7/ 98
Loveless, James Jackson	Bush, Maggie Alive	3 Jun 1928	7/ 129
Lovell, Justin Jacob	Watkins, Virginia Belle	20 Apr 1930	7/ 443
Lovett, Bennie	Collins, Mamie Lue	18 Feb 1934	8/ 434
Low, Emmett Francis	Davis, Nettie Alys	7 Oct 1933	8/ 351
Lower, George Casey [Pinecastle]	Blake, Mildred Bessie [Pinecastle]	1 Jul 1926	6/ 286
Lowry, Robert George [Dawson, GA]	Jenkins, Beauty [Dawson, GA]	16 Aug 1926	6/ 306
Loyd, John [Morristown, TN]	Harris, Cloffie [Orlando]	11 Apr 1927	6/ 491
Lucas, Timothy	Hilton, Leona Bernethel	29 Apr 1931	7/ 588
Lucas, Timothy [Orlando]	Albritton, Lottie [Orlando]	25 Feb 1926	6/ 164
Luce, Frank Almon	Cox, Sarah Jane	11 Apr 1931	7/ 578
Lucius, Earl	Mann, Bernice Juanita	21 Dec 1931	8/ 97
Lucius, Enoch Fred [W] [Orlando]	DeLong, Muriel [Orlando]	12 Jul 1925	6/ 19
Luke, George	Lee, Cathryn	12 Dec 19314	8/ 86
Luke, Love	Roundtree, Willie Mae	9 May 1934	8/ 475
Luke, Love [Orlando]	Gordon, Carrie [Orlando]	3 Aug 1927	6/ 557
Luker, Charles LaFayette	Rehberg, Marie Barco	4 Apr 1933	8/ 285
Lunsford, Aubrey Davis	Richards, Pattimay	26 Jun 1930	7/ 473
Lurie, Cecil [Orlando]	Harrison, Hannah Frances [Youngstown OH]	2 May 1926	6/ 230
Luther, Charles William [Orlando]	Bunch, Roberta [Orlando]	31 Dec 1926	6/ 428
Lutz, Fred [Orlando]	Sherry, Mary [Orlando]	17 Sep 1925	6/ 50
Lynch, Lawrence Sirlee	Thomas, Dorothea	7 Jun 1930	7/ 464
Lynch, Will Jim	McWhorter, Mary Brown	27 Nov 1931	8/ 79
Lyons, Albert S.	Stewart, Jennie	7 Feb 1929	7/ 242
Lyons, Garfield [Orlando]	Cane, Julia [Orlando]	1 Jul 1926	6/ 283
Lytle, Edwin Eugene [Winter Park]	Ahlgrin, Luella Marie [Winter Park]	9 Jun 1926	6/ 262
Lytle, Willian Snyder	Swan, Bettie F.	26 Dec 1928	7/ 222

M

Mack, Bud	Jones, Clyde	10 Oct 1927	6/ 591
Mack, Ervin	Brown, Teresa Mae	17 May 1933	8/ 302
Mack, Louis	Burnett, Ruth	15 Jun 1930	7/ 468
Mack, Robert	Harrison, Sarah	9 Nov 1929	7/ 368
Mack, Rudolph	Harr, Eola	14 Jan 1928	7/ 44
Mack, Ulysses	Thompson, Annie Mae	22 Jan 1934	8/ 423
Mackay, Alexander Thomas	Hurlburt, Helen	25 Dec 1933	8/ 411
MacNeill, Frank Rivers [Sanford]	Lee, Ann [Sanford]	19 Mar 1926	6/ 185
Madden, Sam [Orlando]	Burton, Christine [Orlando]	30 Dec 1926	6/ 423
Madden, William L. [Albany, NY]	Sullivan, Ruth [Omaha, NE]	17 Oct 1925	6/ 67
Maddox, Alexander Bumby	Hays, Alma Agnes	22 Jun 1933	8/ 498
Madison, General	Williams, Ruth	18 Jan 1930	7/ 401
Madison, Jake	Mitchell, Willie Belle	7 May 1929	7/ 292
Madison, James [B] [Orlando]	Massey, Ruth [Orlando]	5 Jan 1926	6/ 128
Madison, Robert	Betsy, Alma	16 Nov 1931	8/ 75
Madison, Thomas	Weston, Olivia	22 Oct 1927	7/ 2
Madrays, Walter	Fossett, Edna	7 Mar 1931	7/ 565
Madrey, Walter [Winter Garden]	Ruffin, Pearl	25 Oct 1926	6/ 363
Magnusson, John James	Stevens, Ruth	28 Nov 1928	7/ 210
Mahler, Frank	Schurz, Grete	12 Apr 1930	7/ 437
Mahli, William	Shaw, Caroline	7 Sep 1931	8/ 48
Mahusen, Abram	Brown, Carrie Lena	14 May 1933	8/ 300
Major, John Henry [Orlando]	Webster, Essie	19 Dec 1926	6/ 418
Malby, Alfred Joseph	Hyfield, Madge Cornelia	16 May 1934	8/ 476
Malcolm, Willie Swep	Isbell, Sara Sue	20 Jul 1928	7/ 165
Mallory, William Fred	Knudson, Agnes Christine	10 Jun 1934	8/ 493
Malloy, Charlie [Ocoee]	Webb, Mary Bell [Ocoee]	20 Jan 1927	6/ 441
Malloy, Himsley Grady	Fender, Doris Juanita	26 Apr 1930	7/ 443
Malone, Lacy	Curtindale, Edith	2 Jun 1928	7/ 125
Maness, Kinney Matherson	Davis, Precious Florence	4 Jun 1931	8/ 15
Manigo, William	Baker, Alice	31 Dec 1930	7/ 537
Maning, Sidney	Gaines, Jessie	17 Aug 1928	7/ 173
Mann, Claude	Wright, Evelyn	25 May 1930	7/ 459
Mann, James Arlin [Winter Garden]	Lord, Merle [Winter Garden]	10 Jul 1926	6/ 301
Mann, Luther Franklin	Parrish, Mary Odessa	10 Mar 1928	7/ 77
Mann, Omer French	Robertson, Jerushia	22 Sep 1929	7/ 349
Mann, Orville Matthews [Orlando]	Kerns, Thelma Bertha	20 Jun 1927	6/ 540
Mann, Raymond DeSota [Ocoee]	Osteen, Laverne Mae	16 Dec 1926	6/ 410
Mann, Roy Francis	Ives, Mary Elizabeth	18 Feb 1932	8/ 119
Manning, Ralph David [Clearwater]	Pansing, Harriet Leola [Orlando]	13 Nov 1926	6/ 387
Manning, Warren [B] [Orlando]	Thomas, Mandy [Orlando]	11 Jul 1925	6/ 14
Manson, Frank George [Orlando]	Haywood, Nellie [Orlando]	30 Apr 1926	6/ 222
Manuel, James	Little, Sarah	12 Oct 1928	7/
Manuel, LeRoy	Jackson, Johnnie Lee	19 Nov 1928	7/ 205
Manuel, Raymond	Williams, Mariah	5 Dec 1932	8/ 225
Manuel, Sam	Tyson, Thelma	6 Jan 1931	7/ 539
Manuel, Walter [Orlando]	Brown, Cora [Orlando]	19 Aug 1927	6/ 567
Marchand, Alton Leonard	Gillespie, Juanita	29 Jul 1933	8/ 329

Marcum, James Washington [Orlando]	Bickerton, Luella [Orlando]	6 Apr 1926	6/ 198
Marden, Ralph Hodges [Orlando]	Griffin, Daisy [Orlando]	20 Jun 1926	6/ 280
Margetts, Claude William [Orlando]	Roberts, Essie Jane [Orlando]	7 Sep 1926	6/ 332
Mark, Mathew [Orlando]	Jones, Lucenia [Orlando]	29 May 1926	6/ 248
Markham, George Emerson [Orlando]	Bailey, Alice Louise [Scheneckday, NY]	25 Nov 1926	6/ 390
Marks, Harris A.	McKinzie, Eulalie	4 Jun 1928	7/ 130
Marks, Louis Talmadge [Orlando]	Morris, Oleita [Orlando]	7 Oct 1925	6/ 58
Marlow, Coleman Mark	Smith, Lillian Roosevelt	21 Jul 1934	8/ 513
Marlow, William Kirby	Clark, Nora Mae	23 Sep 1930	7/ 499
Marmen, Jesse [Pinecastle]	Glaze, Cleaolar [Pinecastle]	14 Mar 1926	6/ 191
Marsh, David S.	Webb, Mamie Clyde	30 Sep 1933	8/ 345
Marshall, Charles	White, Mary	24 Apr 1929	7/ 282
Marshall, Edward	Slayton, Charlie Mae	17 Nov 1930	7/ 522
Marshall, Fred	Spragin, Winona	25 Aug 1928	7/ 175
Marshall, James Eugene	Albertson, Tressie E.	20 Aug 1933	8/ 334
Marshall, L.	Walker, Jimmie	19 Sep 1933	8/ 343
Marshall, Otis	Paul, Ida	6 May 1929	7/ 290
Marshall, Richard [B] [Orlando]	Willis, Hattie [Orlando]	10 Jan 1925	5/ 511
Marten, Clayborne	Wilson, Edna	25 Nov 1931	8/ 78
Martin, David [B] [Orlando]	McPherson, Maggie [Orlando]	29 Jan 1925	5/ 518
Martin, Elmore [B] [Ft Gate]	Gordon, Georgie [Ft Gate]	10 Apr 1925	5/ 557
Martin, Farris Samuel	Smart, Corrie Marie	26 Mar 1933	8/ 277
Martin, Franklin C. Jr [Orlando]	Pickron, Anne Melba [Orlando]	18 Feb 1926	6/ 175
Martin, Ike Junior	Childes, Lucille	2 Apr 1934	8/ 453
Martin, James Calvin	Jackson, Maggie Lee	11 Jan 1934	8/ 409
Martin, Joe	Simmons, Ruby Mae	31 Dec 1927	7/ 36
Martin, John Arthur	Senter, Addie Aurelia	16 Sep 1932	8/ 198
Martin, John H.	King, Mary	24 Dec 1928	7/ 219
Martin, Leo	Gonzalez, Violet	23 Apr 1934	8/ 469
Martin, Robert	Bridges, Nora	11 Jan 1933	8/ 246
Martin, Robert Leon [Orlando]	Farley, Mae [Orlando]	5 Nov 1926	6/ 381
Martin, Roscoe [Morgan crossed out]	Gray, Isadora	16 Jan 1933	8/ 245
Martin, Theodore George	Crosby, Minnie Minerva	21 Dec 1933	8/ 388
Martin, Thomas	Blair, Sophia	17 Feb 1930	7/ 416
Martin, Thomas Wesley	Houston, Mary Irwin	5 Feb 1934	8/ 425
Martin, Willie Edward	Allen, Lillie Mae	11 Jul 1931	8/ 32
Martindale, Clifford Andrew	Grundy, Beatrice May	5 Apr 1929	7/ 275
Mason, Frank	Crosby, Jimmie	5 Sep 1933	8/ 339
Mason, John Robert	Gaskins, Naomi	22 Nov 1929	7/ 375
Mason, Robert Howell	Cowsert, Angie Weaver	26 May 1928	7/ 122
Mathers, Charles	Webb, Virginia	6 Jan 1934	8/ 407
Mathews, Albert [B] [Orlando]	Swift, Annie [Orlando]	23 Jan 1926	6/ 140
Mathews, Gettis	Brown, Lucile	16 Oct 1930	7/ 509
Mathews, Louis	Mack, Cora	12 Sep 1931	8/ 49
Mathews, Rufus G.	Johnson, Phoebe C.	12 Jan 1934	8/ 414
Mathews, Ulysses	McCaskey, Biddie C.	14 Jun 1930	7/ 467
Mathieux, Orie Rawson [Geneva]	Campbell, Kathleen Lord [Oviedo]	27 Dec 1926	6/ 420
Mathis, Andrew Colly [W] [Winter Garden]	Lord, Mattie Mae [Winter Garden]	16 Dec 1925	6/ 102
Mathis, Clarence [W] [Oviedo]	Redditt, Jeanette [Ft Christmas]	10 Jul 1925	6/ 16
Mathis, Ulysee	Williams, Dora	6 Feb 1932	8/ 117
Matthews, Charles Irving [Orlando]	Boland, Kathleen [Orlando]	15 Nov 1926	6/ 384
Matthews, Leslie Lee	Turner, Eva Alma	25 Dec 1930	7/ 550

Mattingley, Thomas Kenneth	Clarke, Constance Mason	8 Jun 1933	8/ 364
Mattox, Ollie	Thorpe, May Willie	5 Nov 1930	7/ 517
Mauldin, Freddie Hastings	Hall, Nettie Evelyn	27 Sep 1931	8/ 54
Maurice, Sturge Charles [Orlando]	Alexander, Nana [Orlando]	14 May 1927	6/ 513
Maus, Burns Rowland	Moore, Mildred Garland	12 Apr 1934	8/ 474
Mawhinney, Donald [Sarasota]	Richmond, Jan Kimball [Fredonia, NY]	12 Feb 1927	6/ 456
Mawson, Raymond William	Boles, Nina Mae	10 Jun 1934	8/ 495
Maxwell, Carl	Sewell, Anida	12 Sep 1927	6/ 581
Maxwell, Francis Marion [W] [Apopka]	Walker, Mary E. [Orlando]	16 Mar 1925	5/ 541
Maxwell, Harold	Cohen, Lula	10 May 1928	7/ 116
Maxwell, Willie	Lewis, Margarette	12 Jan 1931	7/ 543
May, Thomas Grady [Orlando]	Taylor, Thelma [Orlando]	22 Feb 1926	6/ 162
May, William Ramsey [W] [Sanford]	Hand, Doris	1 Feb 1926	6/ 146
Mayer, Gerald Eugene	Mercer, Doris Mildred	27 Dec 1933	8/ 406
Mayer, Herman Oscar	Anderson, Julia Margaret	4 Oct 1928	7/ 193
Mayfield, William Howard	Davis, Mary Thelma	28 Dec 1927	7/ 34
Mays, Charles Berry	Hooten, Juanita	11 Jun 1930	7/ 465
Mazer, Edmund J. [W] [Orlando]	Hall, Rura R. [Orlando]	8 Jun 1925	5/ 595
McAllister, Charles D. [Mt Clements, MI]	Smith, Florence [Winter Garden]	23 Feb 1926	6/ 205
McAllister, Chas. Thomas [Orlando]	Johnston, Sarah Jane [Orlando]	7 Sep 1925	6/ 42
McAllister, Denver Brown	Johnson, Grace Helene	14 Sep 1929	7/ 346
McAllister, John Knox	McDonald, Mabel Emola	2 Jul 1933	8/ 320
McAninch, Harry White	Cartledge, Katie Cordelia	21 May 1932	8/ 160
McAninch, Raymond Sharpe [Orlando]	Mann, Arkatic [Orlando]	5 Feb 1927	6/ 452
McAver, Vance Franklin	Imler, Arvilla	29 Jan 1929	7/ 237
McBride, Anderson Boone	Flanders, Eloise May	22 Mar 1929	7/ 260
McBride, Dallas Milton	Jones, Emily Louise	31 Dec 1927	7/ 40
McBride, Orville Clark	Swallum, Beatrice Elizabeth	25 Jun 1930	7/ 472
McCafferty, Dite	Hall, Mattie Josephine	5 Mar 1931	7/ 564
McCafferty, William Franklin, Jr [Zellwood]	Burnap, Mary [Zellwood]	12 Feb 1927	6/ 459
McCall, Adonijah	Horton, Irene	25 Oct 1930	7/ 513
McCall, Boysie	Sears, Essie	4 Jan 1932	8/ 99
McCall, Kenneteh E. [W] [Maitland]	Webb, Emma Lene [Lane?] [Orlando]	15 Aug 1925	6/ 33
McCalley, Harvey Wallace [Sanford]	Love, Susan Elizabeth [Orlando]	31 May 1927	6/ 518
McCammon, Francis Max	Whitaker, Elma Vivian	15 Jan 1934	8/ 412
McCarthy, Harold Francis	Kirkland, Mary Willis	24 Apr 1934	8/ 467
McCaskill, Boysie	Hilton, Lorenzo Evelyn	12 May 1933	8/ 296
McCaskill, Boysie [W] [Orlando]	Johnson, Annie [Orlando]	21 Jan 1925	5/ 515
McCattry, Alfred [Orlando]	Ford, Mittie [Orlando]	22 Jul 1926	6/ 278
McClain, John [W] [Miami]	Eichstaedt, Amelia Ohelia [Cocoa]	5 May 1925	5/ 568
McClary, Eugene [B] [Oakland]	Butler, Anna Bell [Oakland]	30 May 1925	5/ 583
McClean, Willis Alexander [Winter Park]	Allen, Rose [Sanford]	26 Feb 1927	6/ 466
McClelland, Cecil	McCormick, Edna	8 Feb 1930	7/ 410
McClelland, David [B] [Orlando]	Jayroe, Carrie [Orlando]	20 Jan 1925	5/ 516
McClendon, Joel Thomas	Tompkins, Cleo	19 Jul 1930	7/ 483
McClendon, Torris	Briar, Essie Mae	4 Dec 1927	7/ 21
McCleod, J. B. [Orlando]	Griffin, Mamie [Orlando]	14 Sep 1925	6/ 45
McClure, Fred C. [Orlando]	Laughlin, Mary Gladys [Orlando]	12 Sep 1925	6/ 45
McCollum, Marvin	Echart, Gertrude Ann	15 Aug 1928	7/ 174
McConico, Don Arthur	Lester, Viroah	22 Apr 1932	8/ 146

McConnell, A. Y. [Birmingham, AL]	Smith, Edith [Orlando]	20 Oct 1926	6/ 366
McCord, James Newell	Stansell, Alma	6 Dec 1931	8/ 85
McCormick, Joe	Wilkerson, Jessie	21 Mar 1933	8/ 274
McCormick, Robert Frank, Jr.	Few, Evelyn Sue	10 Oct 1928	7/ 198
McCormick, Theron [Orlando]	Whitehead, Elizabeth [Orlando]	24 Dec 1926	6/ 417
McCoy, Albert Grover	Winfield, Edna	31 Dec 1930	7/ 536
McCoy, Earnest [Winter Park]	Hawkins, Vergie May [Winter Park]	25 Jul 1927	6/ 554
McCoy, William Winslow	Tracy, Doris Margaret	5 Jul 1930	7/ 477
McCrary, Anderson	Williams, Bell Rosalie	23 Jan 1932	8/ 106
McCrary, Jesse	Watkins, Josie Belle	23 Apr 1933	8/ 289
McCray, James	Emzie, Hattie	23 May 1933	8/ 303
McCray, John D. [B] [Orlando]	Wilson, Carrie	7 Mar 1925	5/ 536
McCree, Napoleon	Bowan, Carrie Lu	14 Apr 1928	7/ 98
McCue, D. O.	Rodobaugh, Mary	25 Mar 1931	7/ 571
McCullough, John Tom [W] [Dunedin]	Waller, Norah [Dunedin]	19 May 1925	5/ 575
McCullough, Thomas Lawhorn	Chadwick, Alma Oreta	22 Oct 1932	8/ 207
McCutcheon, Chas. Raymond [Winter Garden]	Oswell, Charlotte [Mt. Lake Park MD]	3 Mar 1926	6/ 175
McDaniel, Henry E. [Orlando]	Pope, Willie [Orlando]	24 Sep 1925	6/ 50
McDaniels, Arthur [Scotlandneck, NC]	Woodley, Laura [Orlando]	27 Apr 1927	6/ 501
McDonald, Mose	Porter, Mattie	5 Oct 1929	7/ 354
McDonald, William [Sanford]	Faye, Ellen [Sanford]	28 Feb 1927	6/ 467
McDowell, James	Smith, Margaret	28 Jan 1931	7/ 548
McDuffie, Leroy	Sanders, Mae Allie	17 Oct 1928	7/ 195
McDuffie, Ozier	Thomas, Aline	27 Nov 1933	8/ 385
McElhaney, Elmer Emerson [W] [Orlando]	Ferguson, Lucy Blanch [Orlando]	17 Nov 1925	6/ 85
McElroy, Sanders	Roundtree, Gertrude	25 Feb 1929	7/ 250
McEwan, William Faris [W] [Daytona]	Puckette, Lutha Annette	23 Jan 1926	6/ 141
McFadden, George	Bryant, Lula	22 Dec 1927	7/ 28
McFadden, Robert [Orlando]	Loza, Susanna [Orlando]	15 Apr 1927	6/ 493
McFall, John	Smith, Elizabeth	10 May 1931	8/ 1
McFarland, Handsome	Siplin, Minnie Lee	25 Jun 1933	8/ 309
McFerrin, Philip Charles	Brewer, Madeline	13 May 1932	8/ 156
McGarity, Victor Hugo	Garrett, Ruby	20 Sep 1929	7/ 348
McGee, John Edward [Orlando]	Tracy, Cathryn [Orlando]	28 Aug 1926	6/ 321
McGee, Mack	Amos, Isabel	10 Aug 1929	7/ 330
McGee, Willie	Hinson, Bessie	21 Jan 1932	8/ 110
McGett, Peter	Johnson, Tessie Mae	19 Jan 1931	7/ 545
McGill, Chester E.	Jones, Mary	14 Feb 1928	7/ 64
McGill, Condley	Sprinks, Emma C.	29 Jan 1929	7/ 237
McGill, George Willie [B] [Sanford]	Miller, Katie [Winter Haven]	17 Aug 1925	6/ 34
McGill, Oscar Forrest [Orlando]	Autrey, Gladys [Orlando]	21 May 1927	6/ 522
McGill, Sidney	Pete, Lucy	10 Mar 1930	7/ 425
McGuire, Orvid Eugene	Risener, Wilma Victoria	29 Mar 1934	8/ 504
McIntosh, James Henry	Massey, Helen Douglass	16 Jul 1929	7/ 323
McIntosh, Luther	Marshall, Willie Mae	30 Mar 1934	8/ 451
McIntosh, Samuel Davis	Minor, Chanie	29 Jan 1932	8/ 110
McIntyre, Henry [Orlando]	Smith, Josie [Orlando]	21 Feb 1927	6/ 462
McIntyre, Robert Eric [Valdosta, GA]	Ralston, Katherine Mae [Omaha, NE]	22 Mar 1926	6/ 187
McKalsen, Charles [Fairville]	Wilson, Margaret Leacy	10 Sep 1926	6/ 335
McKay, Harry Edward	Kimmey, Dorothy Corinne	27 Nov 1932	8/ 221
McKee, Shelly Marvin	Simmons, Anna Belle	20 Jan 1930	7/ 402
McKeever, James Rollins	Alsbrooks, Marian	11 May 1933	8/ 294

McKelvey, Paul Vernon	Dekle, Audrey Edge	17 Sep 1932	8/ 198
McKenzie, James Gotlick [Orlando]	Chaires, Annie Elizabeth	25 Oct 1926	6/ 364
McKenzie, Mack [Taft]	Powers, Ellen [Taft]	28 Jun 1926	6/ 251
McKiernan, John J.	Carpenter, Billie	5 Oct 1929	7/ 356
McKinney, Joseph Andrew	Stine, Bernice Violet	16 Apr 1933	8/ 284
McKinney, Ralph Puckett	Hodson, Francis Myrtle	12 Jun 1929	7/ 308
McKinney, Rufuss Lee [Orlando]	Bailey, Bessie Adell [Orlando]	14 Apr 1926	6/ 209
McKinney, Thomas [W] [Anna Maria]	Sayles, Mary [Indianapolis IN]	6 Apr 1925	5/ 554
McKinnon, Henry	Spicer, Mabel	9 Jun 1928	7/ 134
McKintosh, Kenneth Ross [Bee Ridge]	Hill, Mary Mildred [Orlando]	10 Jun 1926	6/ 264
McKinzie, Jefferson	Lewis, Ethel Mae	28 Apr 1928	7/ 110
McKnie, John	Walden, Alice	17 Sep 1929	7/ 347
McKnight, John Fred	Redding, Doris	17 Mar 1928	7/ 81
McKnight, Louie Frank	Styles, Marie Beatrice	22 May 1934	8/ 481
McKnight, Walter [B] [Orlando]	Gray, Donnie Bell [Orlando]	23 Jul 1925	6/ 22
McLaughlin, Sidney [W] [Kissimmee]	Rolls, Lois [Kissimmee]	17 Jan 1926	6/ 136
McLean, Ewell B.	Meins, Gladys L.	30 Mar 1929	7/ 268
McLean, Howard	Scott, Irene	11 Jun 1929	7/ 307
McLendon, Jesse James	Grayer, Henrietta	11 Nov 1928	7/ 203
McLeod, Clarence Jackson	George, Laura Gertrude	28 Jun 1930	7/ 474
McLeod, Henry Roland [Orlando]	Webster, Martha Alice [Orlando]	18 May 1926	6/ 247
[lic 18 May 1926; recorded 28 May 1926]			
McLeod, Jesse Calvin	Worth, Mabel Louise	2 Apr 1933	8/ 280
McLoud, John Clarence [W] [Sanford]	Bell, Abbie Berry [Orlando]	26 Nov 1925	6/ 94
McLoud, Will	Tucker, Louise May Belle	29 Dec 1930	7/ 534
McMartin, Roland [Orlando]	Chupp, Emily Pauline	4 Oct 1926	6/ 346
McMillen, Delbert	Day, Beulah	20 Apr 1929	7/ 283
McMillen, Hugh [Gastonia NC]	Haile, Jenille [Maitland]	21 Jun 1926	6/ 282
McMiller, Ben	Curry, Marie	4 Jul 1931	8/ 28
McMillian, Ernest Raymond	Tisdale, Leona Anderson	11 Aug 1932	8/ 182
McMillon, James	Rawls, Rosa Lee	31 Oct 1931	8/ 68
McMurray, Robert [Clemont]	Walker, Estelle [Oakland]	13 Jun 1927	6/ 532
McNab, Eddie	Rider, Mary	7 Nov 1932	8/ 214
McNair, James O'Neal	Howard, Mary Elizabeth	14 Feb 1931	7/ 556
McNair, John R. [B] [Orlando]	Lamps, Mamie [Palm Beach]	14 Apr 1925	5/ 561
McNash, Estill [B] [Winter Garden]	Taylor, Almae [Winter Garden]	28 Jul 1925	6/ 28
McNeill, Edw. Alexander [Orlando]	Davis, Willie Mae	8 Sep 1926	6/ 335
McNeill, John Thomas [Orlando]	Young, Florence Adelec [Orlando]	30 Dec 1926	6/ 428
McNish, Albert	Seplin, Rebecca	13 May 1929	7/ 294
McNish, Archer [Orlando]	Jones, Leona [Orlando]	30 Aug 1926	6/ 323
McPherson, Boy	Adams/Odams, Martha	1 Jun 1930	7/ 461
McQueen, Henry [Apopka]	Carmichael, Henrietta [Apopka]	12 Oct 1926	6/ 352
McQueen, Herman	Small, Naomi	19 Nov 1932	8/ 218
McRae, Orman	Wiley, Katie Lee	11 Oct 1928	7/ 192
McRae, Thomas A. [St Petersburg]	Sanders, Jane L. [Atlanta, GA]	18 May 1925	5/ 600
McRainey, George Hampton [Orlando]	Wade, Jerry Blythe [Orlando]	16 Jan 1926	6/ 107
McRee, Richard Walter [Orlando]	Eliz, Margaret [Orlando]	20 Aug 1926	6/ 319
Meadows, Thomas Earl	Jones, Lucille	3 Apr 1931	7/ 581
Meadows, W. T.	Johnson, Lucy	18 Feb 1929	7/ 247
Means, Robert A.	Henderson, Mary	17 Dec 1927	7/ 27

Means, Russell	Wiliams, Thealulu Belle	9 Jan 1934	8/ 408
Medley, Horace [Winter Garden]	Danford, Esther Belle [Winter Garden]	5 Jul 1926	6/ 290
Medlin, Robert Neal	Stanek, Mary Elizabeth	14 Jul 1933	8/ 325
Medlock, John Kenneth, Jr.	Bruce, Pauline Ruby	23 Nov 1933	8/ 374
Meece, Walter [W] [Champaign IL]	Hull, Maggie [Orlando]	30 Mar 1925	5/ 549
Meeks, Floyd William	Skipper, Neva Ruth	19 May 1934	8/ 479
Meiner, Edward	Wagner, Nellie	17 Apr 1929	7/ 280
Melton, Richard Fordyce	Richey, Marion Dolores	8 May 1933	8/ 296
Melton, Robert Frank	Smart, Carrie Marie	2 Jun 1928	7/ 125
Melvin, Dave	Coleman, Anna Lee	3 Jan 1933	8/ 238
Melvin, James [Orlando]	Williams, Fannie Mae [Orlando]	5 Feb 1927	6/ 450
Mendes, Joseph Carricro [Tauton, MA]	Glenn, Margaret [Tauton, MA]	16 Dec 1926	6/ 428
Mendsen, John Cleaveland	Seeds, Thelma Jeanette	8 Aug 1929	7/ 330
Menges, Walter Austin	Williams, Nan Elizabeth	11 May 1932	8/ 154
Mercier, Joseph J. [W] [Orlando]	Deakin, Mary Ellen [Orlando]	24 Apr 1925	5/ 592
Meredith, Otis Byron	Wrye, Margie Geneva	23 Jan 1934	8/ 419
Meredith, William V.	Taylor, Orrie A.	3 Jun 1929	7/ 300
Merier, Henry [W] [Sanford]	Davis, Margie [Sanford]	12 Aug 1925	6/ 33
Meriex, Drew	Kegler, Rubie	12 Jun 1934	8/ 491
Merritt, Clifford S. [Orlando]	Freberg, Esther [Elkland, PA}	28 Oct 1926	6/ 376
Merritt, D. E. [B] [Orlando]	Coleman, Leonora [Orlando]	15 Jul 1925	6/ 22
Merritt, Hassell Brewer [Orlando]	Willy, Mary [Warwick, RI]	20 Oct 1926	6/ 358
Merritt, Ralph	Ashley, Irene	11 May 1931	8/ 2
Merritt, Samuel	Washington, Viola	25 Jul 1934	8/ 514
Merritt, Walter LaFayette	Hudson, Jessie Jewell	1 Feb 1932	8/ 111
Merritt, William Henry	Moore, Ruth	9 Jun 1934	8/ 494
Meschaan, Ralph	Massry, Pauline	1 Jan 1933	8/ 240
Messick, Paul McDonald	Carr, Annie Gertrude	24 Feb 1933	8/ 263
Metcalf, Charles Thomas	Waters, Mary Odell	8 Jan 1933	8/ 246
Metcalf, Harold Franklin [W] [Windermere]	Patterson, Florence Cecelia [Windermere]	22 Dec 1925	6/ 110
Metts, Allen F.	Dull, Carmen	1 Jan 1930	7/ 393
Meurlot, Marvin Ray	Sibthrop, Lillian	12 May 1929	7/ 294
Meuse, Alfonzo	Silas, Elmira Matilda	10 Jan 1934	8/ 408
Meyer, Dorman A. [Apopka]	Lynch, Leota [Apopka]	22 Aug 1925	6/ 39
Mickins, Robert [Oakland]	Henderson, Millie [Winter Garden]	12 Feb 1927	6/ 455
Mickler, Frank Robinson	Cockman, Ella Marie	23 Feb 1933	8/ 261
Mickler, Rolfe	Lanier, Susan Cherry	17 Oct 1931	8/ 62
Middleton, Clyde A. [DeLand]	Buck, Laurie [Orlando]	27 May 1927	6/ 517
Miehls, Alfred J. [W] [Orlando]	Deken, Anna C. [Winter Park]	19 Mar 1925	5/ 544
Mier, John Celia	Mier, Hazel Madeline	17 May 1932	8/ 160
Mignot, Clarence J. [W] [Orlando]	Hatten, Ethel [Orlando]	25 Nov 1925	6/ 87
Mikell, William	Washington, Martha	18 May 1930	7/ 457
Miles, James Lawrence	Haight, Marian Stewart	20 Jan 1934	8/ 413
Miles, John H.	Edwards, Mary	1 Jan 1934	8/ 397
Miles, Vernon Colquitt [Winter Garden]	Boyd, Wilma B. [Winter Garden]	26 May 1927	6/ 516
Miller, Aubrey Hugh	Walker, Helen Florence	2 Dec 1933	8/ 379
Miller, Bert Rule	Barden, Masalea	12 Dec 1930	7/ 529
Miller, Carl Ione	Jerman, Louise Eleanor	18 Nov 1933	8/ 372
Miller, Dayton G.	Whiteman, Nellie	19 Sep 1928	7/ 185
Miller, Elbert Edgar	Brown, Mary Lucile	7 Jan 1933	8/ 240
Miller, Elmer Jennings Bryan [Lockhart]	Prevatt, Annie May [Winter Park]	28 Apr 1926	6/ 221
Miller, F. A. [Orlando]	Taylor, Florence [Orlando]	21 Mar 1926	6/ 182

Miller, Franklyn Wylie	Honour, Mabel Harris	4 Aug 1928	7/ 169
Miller, Gasway	Hill, Mary	30 Nov 1929	7/ 378
Miller, George [Orlando]	Garvin, Rena [Orlando]	16 Oct 1926	6/ 355
Miller, George Whitfield	Hammer, Graace Amanda	17 Oct 1928	7/ 195
Miller, Joe	Comer, Effie Mae	28 Jan 1930	7/ 407
Miller, Judge	Johnson, Corine	24 Dec 1929	7/ 389
Miller, Julius A.	Chesshyre, Ida Mary	3 May 1930	7/ 447
Miller, Otto Conrad	McCain, Charleete	8 Nov 1932	8/ 215
Miller, Raymond Oliver	Persico, Angeline Mary	1 Sep 1932	8/ 191
Miller, Roy Amos	Noyes, Aileen	14 Aug 1932	8/ 184
Miller, Sylvester Tolbert	Pickrell, Beatrice	3 Mar 1928	7/ 77
Miller, Theophile H.	Dobbs, Opal	22 Oct 1927	6/ 598
Miller, Tom	Edwards, Katherine	14 Oct 1930	7/ 506
Miller, Victor M.	Oestreisher, Thelma L.	15 Jan 1929	7/ 232
Miller, Will [B] [Winter Park]	Hutchinson, Ludie [Winter Park]	20 May 1925	5/ 579
Milligan, James Manley	Hauser, Ellawella	21 Apr 1928	7/ 108
Mills, John Barney [Orlando]	Shaffer, Florence Elizabeth [Ocoee]	29 Apr 1926	6/ 227
Mills, John Bunny	Thomas, Gwendolyn	16 Sep 1928	7/ 185
Mills, Oreon Henry	Styles, Helliq	23 Feb 1931	7/ 559
Mills, Phillip Lamar [Maitland]	Benson, Ruth [Orlando]	19 Jun 1926	6/ 279
Mills, Ralph [Winter Park]	Johnson, Cordula [Winter Park]	22 Jan 1927	6/ 446
Mills, Robert Talmadge [Orlando]	Bowden, Virginia [Orlando]	14 Jul 1926	6/ 306
Milton, Carl	Baker, Ella Lou	3 Mar 1930	7/ 422
Milton, James	Gary, Charity	27 Nov 1933	8/ 375
Milton, John	Combs, Nettie	27 Jun 1928	7/ 149
Milton, John	Hall, Sallie	12 Dec 1927	7/ 24
Milton, Joseph Kennedy	Kennedy, Norine Frances	2 Jun 1932	8/ 163
Milton, Mathew	Brown, Helen	12 Feb 1934	8/ 427
Milton, Roy Beatty	Dunn, Gladys Mary	3 Sep 1932	8/ 189
Mims, Fred [Orlando]	Woodard, Emma [Orlando]	19 Dec 1926	6/ 417
Mims, Henry	Smith, Carrie	11 Mar 1929	7/ 259
Minard, Arvin	Outlaw, Burneise	26 Mar 1930	7/ 432
Miner, Joseph Otis [Orlando]	Johnson, Joy Livingston [Morrisburg TN]	27 Mar 1926	6/ 207
Mingo, Louis	Morhead, Adele	11 Nov 1933	8/ 363
Minick, S. H. [Orlando]	Beasley, Nona Alma [Orlando]	30 Jul 1927	6/ 559
Minor, Miles Tell [W] [Crown Point]	McIntyre, Nannie Lou [Ocoee]	19 May 1925	5/ 577
Minx, Freeman	Morris, Ada	2 Feb 1929	7/ 242
Mitchell, Balem	Jones, Lillie Mae	10 Mar 1928	7/ 78
Mitchell, George [Orlando]	Williams, Eva [Orlando]	21 Aug 1926	6/ 317
Mitchell, Herman	Williams, Helen	4 May 1929	7/ 289
Mitchell, James	Spencer, Beatrice	24 Nov 1928	7/ 207
Mitchell, Louis L.	Gallman, Gertrude	9 Jul 1928	7/ 157
Mitchell, Omar Calmese [Altura]	Hannah, Mary Elizabeth	31 Jan 1927	6/ 451
Mitchell, Robert Bagwell	Sigletary, Margaret Mae	5 Jun 1934	8/ 489
Mitchell, Sam	Johnson, Ethel	19 Jan 1929	7/ 233
Mitchell, Samuel	Grizzle, Mary Lizzie	10 Apr 1930	7/ 437
Mitchell, Thomas [Winter Park]	Dixon, Celeste [Winter Park]	17 Apr 1927	6/ 495
Mitchell, Thomas [Sanford]	Blair, Sarah [Sanford]	22 Mar 1926	6/ 185
Mitchell, William [Orlando]	Arnold, Pauline [Orlando]	28 Sep 1926	6/ 344
Mixon, Gilbert	Williams, Abba	26 Dec 1930	7/ 535

Mixon, Harold Gaines	Roberson, Hazel Mai	24 Dec 1930	7/ 538
Mize, Adam Ledford	Bennin, Marie Joanne	21 Dec 1927	7/ 34
Mizelle, Albert Roberson	Caswell, Helen	8 Mar 1932	8/ 124
Mobley, Ben	Davis, Mary Jane	6 May 1929	7/ 291
Mobley, Jerry [B] [Winter Garden]	Jones, Martha [Winter Garden]	5 Feb 1925	5/ 522
Moch, Levy Clinton [Orlando]	Boatwright, Bertha [Winter Park]	9 Jun 1926	6/ 261
Mock, Ernest Bryant	Long, Pearl	14 Sep 1929	7/ 345
Mock, Guyte Roscoe	Fassinger, Martha Florence	15 Mar 1932	8/ 126
Moffett, E. A. [Sanford]	Moffett, Martha [Sanford]	16 Apr 1927	6/ 494
Mole, Wade Law	Brokaw, Martha Geiger	27 Feb 1932	8/ 120
Mollenkapp, John Lewis [Lake Alford]	Law, Carrie [Bessmer, Als.]	16 Feb 1926	6/ 155
Mollinkapp, J. L.	Health, Ora M.	19 Dec 1928	7/ 217
Monforton, Edmour Arthur	Spurling, Florence Birdie	31 Dec 1930	7/ 538
Monroe, Lawrence	Spires, Lavetta Gladys	15 Sep 1931	8/ 50
Monroe, LeRoy	Johnson, Willie Mae	17 Sep 1929	7/ 347
Monroe, William	Lancaster, Margaret	20 Mar 1928	7/ 84
Montana, Henry [B] [Orlando]	Willis, Essie May [Orlando]	12 Nov 1925	6/ 81
Montgomery, Henry	Coney, Martha	23 Sep 1929	7/ 348
Montgomery, Jeff	Mann, Mattie	22 Aug 1931	8/ 43
Montgomery, John William [Mims]	Willman, Bessie [Mims]	1 Jun 1927	6/ 520
Montgomery, Joseph	Thomas, Mamie	2 Mar 1931	7/ 562
Montgomery, William [Eatonville]	Casey, Ella May [Altamonte Springs]	18 Jun 1927	6/ 538
Montreville, Noel Barre	Kinney, Lois Finn	5 May 1929	7/ 291
Moody, Anne [Oviedo]	Grant, Mary [Sanford]	24 Aug 1927	6/ 570
Moody, Milton Paul [Lakeland]	Poole, Margaret Wonson [Orlando]	3 Jul 1927	6/ 546
Moon, Paul Vincent	Beale, Lois Maxciene	17 Mar 1933	8/ 273
Moore, Alvie Alfred	Bells, Jossie	29 Oct 1930	7/ 520
Moore, Benjamin [B] [Orlando]	Robinson, Mattie Lou [Orlando]	25 Jul 1925	6/ 24
Moore, Byron Russel	Sanderson, Pauline	22 Jan 1932	8/ 108
Moore, Clifton	McKinney, Willie May	21 Jan 1928	7/ 52
Moore, Clyde	Batchelor, Neoma Gertrude	4 Nov 1929	7/ 366
Moore, David	Peterson, Amy	1 Jun 1928	7/ 125
Moore, Eddie	Williams, Dora	27 Apr 1931	7/ 586
Moore, Edward [Orlando]	Alexander, Denzae [Orlando]	22 Aug 1927	6/ 569
Moore, Eugene	Doe, Inez	7 Sep 1929	7/ 342
Moore, Eugene A.	Jackson, Kate	30 Aug 1927	6/ 573
Moore, George [Clearwater]	Brown, Hess L. [Daytona Beach]	17 Oct 1925	6/ 65
Moore, Glynn Calvin	Bartlett, Marguerite Mary	1 Aug 1928	7/ 167
Moore, Hosea Curry [Russellville AL]	Butts, Ruth Elaine [Sylagauga AL]	6 Mar 1926	6/ 176
Moore, Jack	Burditt, Hester Charlotte	30 Apr 1929	7/ 268
Moore, James Edward [W] [Orlando]	Godwin, Marie Minerva [Orlando]	2 Apr 1925	5/ 551
Moore, Kingman Colquitt, Jr.	Goodwin, Rose Irene	31 Dec 1933	8/ 398
Moore, Leander	Griggs, Willie Mae	2 Nov 1932	8/ 212
Moore, LeRoy	Wright, Hannah May	26 Sep 1927	6/ 584
Moore, Lynie Roy	Paul, Amelia	17 Jan 1930	7/ 400
Moore, Montgomery [Orlando]	Holmes, Lucy [Orlando]	27 Jun 1927	6/ 528
Moore, Phillip Kiran	Moore, Jennie Lou	8 Mar 1932	8/ 124
Moore, Raymond Lee [Columbus, OH]	Harrington, Eunice [Taft]	11 Jun 1927	6/ 565
Moore, Stanley Albert [Lebanon, IN]	Burdette, Faith Gertrude [Havana, IL]	20 Feb 1926	6/ 159
Moore, William Edward	Castile, Florence Flora	7 May 1932	8/ 151
Moore, William Raymond [Orlando]	Foster, Beatrice [Orlando]	1 Jun 1927	6/ 522
Moore, Willie	Davis, Lucile	20 Jan 1930	7/ 404

Moorer, Curtis	Walker, Luellor	6 Apr 1929	7/ 275
Moorman, Jacob G. [W] [Tampa]	Haselton, Ledona [Orlando]	6 Apr 1925	5/ 556
Moran, Aubrey Evans [Geneva]	LeFila, Lula Frances [Geneva]	5 Jun 1927	6/ 527
More, Len Bridge [B] [Orlando]	Wright, Annie [Orlando]	11 Feb 1926	6/ 153
Morey, Alonzo Albert	Alden, May Frances	2 Jun 1932	8/ 486
Morfatt, Lawrence [W] [Melbourne]	Strader, Dena [Melbourne]	31 Oct 1925	6/ 73
Morgan, Alexander Bradford	Shipp, Kathryn Elizabeth	21 Jun 1932	8/ 174
Morgan, Alvo Holmes	Morgan, Madeleine	16 Feb 1929	7/ 245
Morgan, Benjamin Leonard	Logan, Hortense Ursula	24 Jan 1931	7/ 547
Morgan, Clyde	Bennett, Nora Mae	5 Apr 1931	7/ 576
Morgan, Ed Junior	Williams, Elizabeth	26 Nov 1932	8/ 221
Morgan, Floyd [Cuthbart, GA]	Gilchrist, Minnie [Sanford]	24 Jul 1926	6/ 276
Morgan, Fred Park	Brock, Katherine	5 May 1928	7/ 109
Morgan, Henry	Edge, Remell	18 Apr 1931	7/ 582
Morgan, James	Mitchell, Annie Lou	21 Dec 1928	7/ 218
Morgan, Jesse Vitrue	Bickerton, Thelma Louise	14 Jun 1928	7/ 145
Morgan, Ross James [B] [Winter Park]	Williams, Fannie [Winter Park]	6 Jan 1926	6/ 123
Morgan, William Henry [Sanford]	Ponder, Mae [Maitland]	16 Dec 1926	6/ 409
Morgan, William S.	Barco, Erma	19 Nov 1927	7/ 25
Morman, Henry [Orlando]	O'Neal, Freda [Seville]	16 Dec 1926	6/ 401
Morrell, Horace [Orlando]	Ford, Lilla [Valdosta, FL]	1 Dec 1926	6/ 403
Morris, Albert [B] [Orlando]	Scruggs, Charlotte [Orlando]	7 Nov 1925	6/ 78
Morris, Lloyd [Orlando]	Williams, Katie Belle [Orlando]	27 Dec 1926	6/ 419
Morris, Melvin G.	Sprayberry, Huvian Bridges	24 Jan 1929	7/ 237
Morris, Samuel	Cooper, Anna	29 Sep 1929	7/ 353
Morris, Walter Berry	Brooks, Selena	29 Nov 1930	7/ 524
Morris, William Harley [W] [Orlando]	Rogers, Blanche Catherine [Orlando]	14 Nov 1925	6/ 85
Morris, William Reed	Whitehead, Louise Janet	28 Aug 1928	7/ 181
Morrison, F. J. [Orlando]	Hodges, Inez [Orlando]	26 Feb 1927	6/ 487
Morrison, Fred	Folds, Gladys	29 Dec 1930	7/ 535
Morrison, Robert Henry	Cornelius, Laura Dorothy	2 Mar 1932	8/ 121
Morrison, William Willis	Thomas, Eunice Alberta	30 Apr 1934	8/ 470
Morrow, Archie [Orlando]	Davis, Birt [Orlando]	15 Mar 1927	6/ 474
Morrow, Jonathan Badger [W] [Orlando]	Strouble, Mary King	13 Jun 1925	5/ 587
Morton, Cicero DeForrest	Hargrove, Bessie Mae	10 Jan 1931	7/ 541
Morton, Gustavus Adolphus	Grossenbacher, Fleta	9 Nov 1933	8/ 365
Morton, Phillip Daniel	Seyle, Mary Adele	5 Oct 1932	8/ 205
Mosby, Ira Sylvester [Bunne,ll]	Cowarty, Elsie [Orlando]	5 Feb 1927	6/ 457
Mosby, Richard	Ranger, Mariel Marie	23 May 1932	8/ 159
Mosby, William	Ginlack, Minnie	21 Feb 1934	8/ 438
Moseley, Clayton	Howze, Thelma	22 Dec 1928	7/ 220
Moseley, Ned [Orlando]	Scott, Annie [Orlando]	12 Aug 1926	6/ 316
Moseley, Roy	McClinton, Leslie	17 Jun 1928	7/ 145
Moseley, Thomas Tracy [Orlando]	Shaw, Irene [Orlando]	7 Jul 1927	6/ 547
Moseley, Tom [Fairvilla]	Roy, Lillie [Fairvilla]	19 Jun 1927	6/ 539
Moseley, Warren	Lee, Mary Erma	19 May 1932	8/ 160
Moses, Claude Swanson	Ramsey, Rose Little	25 Jun 1933	8/ 317
Moses, Edmond Boxley	Rowe, Ruth McCall	5 Jun 1928	7/ 135
Moses, Joe	Stinson, Annie	16 Jun 1931	8/ 19
Moses, Willie	Mitchell, Nettie Belle	2 Jul 1932	8/ 175

Mosley, Elmer [Wrightsville, GA]	Hughes, May [Orlando]	25 Dec 1926	6/ 427
Mosley, Joe	Hill, Isabelle	25 Feb 1933	8/ 275
Mosley, John Henry	Meadows, Marie	26 Feb 1930	7/ 420
Moss, Christopher Thomas	Motgomery, Dorothy Corinne	12 Dec 1933	8/ 383
Mote, James Rochester	Llod, Sallie Mae	22 Apr 1932	8/ 146
Mote, L. O. [W] [Orlando]	Keel, Ida [Orlando]	15 Nov 1925	6/ 84
Motl, Charles Rudolph	Mosley, Emma Adeline	29 Jul 1933	8/ 330
Mott, Clifton Bryant	Roberts, Ruby Burns	24 Dec 1933	8/ 404
Mott, James	Mitchell, Jennie	10 Feb 1934	8/ 426
Mower, Edward Sylvester [Orlando]	Reinsch, Anna	31 Dec 1926	6/ 424
Mowery, William A. [Winter Park]	Ginn, Robbie Viola [Winter Park]	17 Apr 1926	6/ 212
Moye, John	Ward, Rosetta	14 Nov 1933	8/ 366
Moye, Virgil Scott	Patterson, Lela Adrian	28 Jul 1933	8/ 329
Moze, William Belmont [Sanford]	Joyner, Kathryn Agnes [Orlando]	14 May 1927	6/ 508
Mueller, Harold Carl	Patrick, Claire Elizabeth	1 Jan 1930	7/ 408
Muldow, John	Williams, Ella	11 May 1933	8/ 306
Mullon, Harry Burrows [Winter Park]	Crosgrove, Dorothy [Winter Park]	24 Feb 1926	6/ 166
Mumford, Donald Lewis	Laroque, Mary Florence Olivia	31 Aug 1931	8/ 46
Mumford, Elmo [Orlando]	Kenney, Agnes [Orlando]	18 Mar 1926	6/ 183
Mumford, Samuel [B] [Conway]	Milton, L. T. [Orlando]	10 Apr 1925	5/ 557
Munnell, Dan M.	Thompson, Elizabeth Ellen	16 Jul 1932	8/ 181
Munnerlyn, Herbert Lee	Prentice, Helen Marie	9 Aug 1933	8/ 333
Munroe, James	Green, Viola	8 Jan 1934	8/ 404
Murnan, Hubert Fred	Sullivan, Blanche	16 May 1928	7/ 114
Murphy, James F. [Orlando]	Davis, Gladys [Orlando]	5 Dec 1926	6/ 405
Murphy, LeRoy	Ford, Willie Esther	12 Nov 1927	7/ 12
Murphy, Ralph	Frazier, Melissa	1 Nov 1930	7/ 516
Murphy, Robert Raymond	Moran, Pauline Amelia	12 Jun 1934	8/ 493
Murphy, Samuel	Sheffield, Amy	30 May 1931	8/ 7
Murray, James [Orlando]	Strong, Minnie Mae [New York, NY]	4 Oct 1926	6/ 348
Murray, Jimmie A. [Orlando]	Hartman, Lillian Belle [Orlando]	17 Jun 1926	6/ 280
Murray, John	Coar, Ruby	7 Jul 1928	7/ 156
Murray, Joseph Durham	Saylors, Willie Lorine	21 Oct 1928	7/ 198
Murray, Onez	Phillips, Trulie	11 Mar 1933	8/ 269
Murray, Thomas	Pollard, Cleo	4 Aug 1931	8/ 40
Murrell, Robert Lee [Cocoa]	Helms, Aldia Antoinette	14 Jul 1926	6/ 295
Muse, George	Williams, Bernice	15 Jul 1932	8/ 178
Musselwhite, Troy Cornelius	MacGilvery, Gladys Zilla	9 Sep 1933	8/ 340
Myers, Elvyn LeRoy	Wade, Mary Jane	2 Feb 1929	7/ 238
Myers, George Bowman [Titusville]	Parrotte, Della [Titusville]	16 Aug 1926	6/ 306
Myers, George Leon	Emerson, Alma Ruth	6 Apr 1929	7/ 278
Myers, Harold W.	Emery, Helen E.	10 May 1930	7/ 450
Myers, Horace Rowland	Hurley, Harriette Etheleon	19 Mar 1932	8/ 128
Myers, Lewis Albright [W] [Orlando]	Coalman, Helen Charline [Orlando]	4 Dec 1925	6/ 102
Myers, Mils Murden	Von Oehlhoff, Jane Tudor	30 Mar 1929	7/ 267
Myers, Sam	Boone, Eva	17 Jun 1933	8/ 314
Myers, Willie	Smith, Sarah	27 Apr 1931	7/ 586

N

Nable, Gustavus Raymond	Raybon, Oradell Matilda	30 Aug 1931	8/ 45
Nall, Stephen Frank	Cribbs, Vallie Pearl	3 Dec 1928	7/ 210
Nance, Johnie [Orlando]	Claypool, Edna [Orlando]	28 Mar 1927	6/ 482
Nardone, John [W] [Mt Dora]	Chaney, Nina Marylin [Orlando]	5 Feb 1926	6/ 149
Nash, Ralph Elester	Drawdy, Eva	10 Jul 1931	8/ 30
Nason, Roger Slater	Clover, Margaret Elizabeth	15 Mar 1930	7/ 432
Nauman, Edward Hamilton	Carpenter, Leila M.	6 Jan 1933	8/ 239
Naumann, William August [Orlando]	Royal, Esta Fidela [Orlando]	3 Dec 1926	6/ 397
Nealley, James Howard, Capt.	Newman, Jean Tupper	18 May 1929	7/ 295
Neel, Whidby Connard	Locklear, Verdia Isabelle	19 Dec 1931	8/ 90
Neely, George Barnes	Folger, Euladie	14 Feb 1928	7/ 67
Neff, Floyd Eugene [Loma Linda, CA]	Yeargin, Edith Ilene [Orlando]	9 Jun 1926	6/ 265
Neiding, Lester	Dyke, Grace	19 Feb 1929	7/ 249
Neil, Lee	Jones, Bessie	12 Jan 1929	7/ 229
Nelson, Amos Waldemar [W]	Case, Maybelle [Orlando] [Higganum CT]	11 May 1925	5/ 573
Nelson, Arthur Regnald [W] [Orlando]	Engebretson, Pearl Alice [Sioux City, IA]	10 Jun 1925	6/ 3
Nelson, Brent G. [Orlando]	Hudson, Christine [Orlando]	24 Jan 1927	6/ 443
Nelson, Charles Marvin	Walker, Mildred Molina	17 Aug 1932	8/ 184
Nelson, Edgar Cecil [W] [Orlando]	Johnson, Dorothy Strong	24 Jan 1925	5/ 519
Nelson, Eugene Delworth	Motlow, Etta Irene	28 Nov 1931	8/ 80
Nelson, George [Orlando]	Alford, Ida [Orlando]	17 Apr 1926	6/ 212
Nelson, Kenneth Franklin [W] [Tampa]	Chambers, Gwendolyn [Orlando]	5 Apr 1925	5/ 555
Nelson, Lawrence	Byrd, Nettie	15 Mar 1928	7/ 80
Nelson, Lee Napoleon Bonaparte [Orlando]	Mileham, Inez Harriet	14 Aug 1926	6/ 304
Nelson, Leon	Green, Oziedell	27 Nov 1930	7/ 525
Nelson, Leroy	Williams, Martha Pauline	7 Mar 1932	8/ 124
Nelson, Lonnie [B] [Orlando]	Ginlack, Erma Mae [Orlando]	22 Dec 1925	6/ 110
Nelson, Oscar Lee	Redfern, Marion	12 Mar 1930	7/ 429
Nelson, Samuel [B] [Orlando]	Love, Elise [Orlando]	9 Nov 1925	6/ 80
Nelson, Will [Winter Park]	Allen, Hattie Mae [Winter Park]	26 Apr 1926	6/ 220
Nelson, Wilmot Oren	Bass, Madge	3 Sep 1927	6/ 575
Nesbitt, Major Braxton [W] [Cocoa]	Caselman, Minnie [Cocoa]	24 Apr 1925	5/ 563
Nettles, John Bryant	Hickson, Maggie Lavonda	9 May 1933	8/ 291
Nettles, William [Orlando]	Kirby, Effie Rexine	23 Dec 1926	6/ 419
Nettleton, Harry Willard [Orlando]	Washington, Montez [Orlando]	8 Apr 1926	6/ 201
Newberg, Elof Albin	Slone, Evelyn Amanda	17 Dec 1931	8/ 89
Newbold, Harold Wilber	Pollock, Inez Vivian	12 Mar 1932	8/ 129
Newby, LeRoy Winfred [Orlando]	Morris, Augusta Clark [Orlando]	30 Jan 1926	6/ 158
Newcomb, Gilbert Sheldon	Moye, Emma Elizabeth	2 Sep 1932	8/ 200
Newcomer, Don Richard	Smith, Helen Frances	2 Dec 1929	7/ 379
Newell, Arthur W. [W] [Orlando]	Morgan, Agnes [Orlando]	3 May 1925	5/ 570
Newell, Edward S. [W] [Orlando]	Curry, Okle V. [Orlando]	21 Jan 1925	5/ 521
Newell, Harold Francis [Orlando]	Morgan, Lola Virginia [Orlando]	3 Sep 1926	6/ 350
Newell, James	Porch, Agile	19 Jan 1929	7/ 234
Newell, Sidney Phillip [Orlando]	Cobb, Eleanor Hope [Orlando]	16 Jun 1926	6/ 272
Newham, Lorin Ben	McManus, Myrtle Jessie	26 Jun 1934	8/ 500
Newham, Ralph E.	McLeod, Lucile	19 Nov 1932	8/ 219

Newhaus, Carl C.	Odem, Mertice	21 Jul 1928	7/ 163
Newman, Cleaveland [Orlando]	Lee, Lillian Sulather [Orlando]	2 Jul 1927	6/ 543
Newman, Marion David	Gilbreath, Ora Belle	5 Jul 1933	8/ 325
Newman, Wilber Clyde [Orlando]	Lafler, Mildred May [Orlando]	22 Dec 1926	6/ 432
Newsom. Charley	Jones, Jossie May	2 May 1929	7/ 287
Newton, Chap C.	Warren, Gertrude	7 Feb 1928	7/ 59
Newton, Henry [Orlando]	Tanner, Myrtle [Orlando]	26 Jul 1927	6/ 555
Newton, John [B] [Orlando]	Culverson, Sallie [Orlando]	30 Nov 1925	6/ 94
Newton, John Thomas [W] [Ocoee]	McDaniel, Mary Helena [Ocoee]	5 Feb 1925	5/ 522
Nicholas, Ray F.	Hedrick, Margaret Ostola	3 Sep 1929	7/ 344
Nichols, Ernest [Winter Garden]	Beaufort, Ossie [Winter Garden]	7 Jun 1926	6/ 259
Nichols, Forrest R. [W] [Winter Haven]	Dubois, Lillie Mae [Lake Hamilton]	16 Jun 1925	5/ 587
Nichols, Frank	Paulk, Mary	13 Jan 1934	8/ 410
Nichols, Robert Dicke	Munnerlyn, Florence	18 Feb 1928	7/ 67
Nicholsen, Cecil Wallace	Nicholson, Sadie Kzyer	19 May 1930	7/ 456
Nicholsen, Robert G.	Brewer, Lucy	28 Dec 1928	7/ 224
Nicholson, Albert [Orlando]	Dixon, Annie [Orlando]	23 Dec 1926	6/ 415
Nicholson, Jack [B] [Orlando]	Byrd, Minnie C. [Orlando]	26 Jun 1925	6/ 4
Nicholson, William James	King, Mary Louise	14 May 1931	8/ 3
Nickels, Paul	Ludke, Alma	23 Feb 1929	7/ 253
Nickels, Thomas White	Richards, Mary Alice	1 Jun 1934	8/ 487
Nickles, Benjamin Jordan [W] [Orlando]	Hayden, Anna Leonole [Orlando]	27 Dec 1925	6/ 119
Nickles, Willie	Young, Alberta	31 Oct 1932	8/ 212
Niles, Willard [Orlando]	Anderson, Mary [Orlando]	31 Dec 1926	6/ 424
Nipper, George Alex	Thomas, Alma	4 Mar 1932	8/ 122
Nipper, Orin Larkin Cloy	Nipper, Myrtis Alma	14 Mar 1932	8/ 125
Nisbet, David S.	Williams, Sarah Curtis	16 Aug 1934	8/ 523
Niven, Paul Harrison	Fussell, Myrtle Edith	22 Dec 1932	8/ 230
Nix, Ralph	Bryant, Sammie	10 Jul 1929	7/ 321
Nix, Ralph Kenny [Orlando]	Long, Louise [Orlando]	22 Sep 1926	6/ 342
Noack, Charles Frederick	Hinson, Amelia	20 Sep 1927	6/ 589
Noble, John	Cheatam, Anna	19 May 1931	8/ 4
Noble, Paul	Foster, Yules	18 Oct 1930	7/ 511
Nobles, Charlie	Hughes, Flossie	13 Jan 1928	7/ 43
Nobles, James Edward Jr.	Martin, Edna Willella	3 Feb 1933	8/ 275
Nolle, Alton Jefferson	Witherby, Helen Ida	2 Jun 1929	7/ 304
Nordgren, Eric Bertil	Gustafson, Harriet	28 Jun 1932	8/ 175
Norfleet, Clarence [B] [Orlando]	Brown, Mamie Virginia [Orlando]	15 Nov 1925	6/ 111
Norman, Jack Homer	Farmer, Julia May	7 Sep 1932	8/ 192
Norman, Newton Jones, Jr. [Orlando]	Austin, Julia Katherine [Orlando]	17 Jul 1926	6/ 296
Norman, Rolley [Winter Park]	Morrison, Willie May [Winter Park]	11 Sep 1926	6/ 336
Normandeau, Robert Nathan	Jordan, Algatha	9 Aug 1934	8/ 522
Norris, Louis Bartow [Winter Park]	Coffee, Jennie Lee [Orlando]	27 Nov 1926	6/ 395
Norsman, Edgar	Murray, Harriet Elizabeth	19 Mar 1932	8/ 130
Norsworthy, Jared Esselman	Karnes, Helen Maxine	12 Mar 1934	8/ 444
Norton, Edward Fiske	Fuller, Emma Lucretia	19 Dec 1931	8/ 91
Norton, John C. [Clermont]	Stanfield, Ethel Hattie [Orlando]	17 Apr 1926	6/ 214
Norton, Marion [Clarcona]	Johnson, Earline [Clarcona]	22 Nov 1926	6/ 388
Nowell, Luther Theodus	Bean, Annie Lou	27 May 1933	8/ 305

O

O'Berry, Albert Lewis	Reaves, Mary Donie	23 Dec 1932	8/ 231
O'Brien, Daniel Joseph [Orlando]	Doering, Marie [Hialeah]	18 Mar 1926	6/ 181
O'Connor, Thomas Luke	Peter, Alice May	4 Feb 1928	7/ 57
O'Hara, Leon	Tucker, Lillian	26 Sep 1931	8/ 53
O'Neill, Joseph Anthony [Orlando]	Giroux, Leah Marie [Orlando]	8 Feb 1927	6/ 451
O'Steen, Frank Herring	Branch, Roberta	29 Sep 1931	8/ 55
O'Steen, Jennings Cone	Burns, Grace	26 Mar 1932	8/ 133
Oakley, James Horne [W] [Indianapolis, IN]	Thompson, Katherine [Indianapolis, IN]	19 Dec 1925	6/ 121
Oamun. Richard Halley	Bossie, Elma Rose	1 Feb 1930	7/ 408
Odell, Benjamin Bradford	McIntire, Louise Elizabeth	5 Jan 1933	8/ 238
Odem, William Clyde	Weiden, Gertrude Mary Kathryn	24 Dec 1931	8/ 96
Odom, Paul John [Orlando]	Partin, Mildred Marie [Orlando]	l Jun 1926	6/ 254
Odum, John Diffin	Davenport, Mary Alice	30 Dec 1933	8/ 398
Odum, Oscar	Williams, Mamie	19 Jan 1933	8/ 247
Oestricher, Albert Raymond	Dodane, Henriette Hyacinthe	25 Jul 1929	7/ 325
Ogden, George Hewitt	Robbins, Alice L.	5 Sep 1927	6/ 574
Ogden, Roscoe [Clarksburg, WV]	Allen, Willie May [Winter Park]	27 Nov 1926	6/ 393
Ogletree, James Taft	Clark, Lura Mae	12 Mar 1934	8/ 444
Oliphant, James	Hilton, Alene	29 Apr 1929	7/ 288
Oliver, David	Brawdy, Martha	16 Oct 1927	6/ 594
Oliver, Floyd [Winter Park]	William, Princella [Winter Park]	30 Aug 1926	6/ 324
Oliver, Joseph	Braswell, Luelle	2 Mar 1930	7/ 440
Oliver, Nelson [B] [Laughman]	Taolever, Dequlia [Ocala]	27 Nov 1925	6/ 92
Oliver, Perry	Butler, Leila A.	2 Mar 1933	8/ 265
Oliver, Peter Samuel	Bechtol, Mary Petersohn	16 Nov 1933	8/ 367
Olson, Carl Walder [Oakland]	Adson, Lonie [Oakland]	17 Nov 1926	6/ 385
Olson, Oscar Albert [Orlando]	Wood, Eleanor Adelaide [Orlando]	11 Mar 1926	6/ 176
Orr, Clifton Wise [orlando]	Yowell, Lydia Gertrude [Orlando]	2 Nov 1926	6/ 380
Osborn, Kendred L.	Clark, Dorothy Uphans	11 Feb 1928	7/ 64
Osborn, Ralph Caleb	Abbott, Rebecca Morea	20 Aug 1929	7/ 334
Osteen, Derrik [Maitland]	Woodard, Bertie [Maitland]	21 Feb 1926	6/ 168
Osteen, Enoch	Tootle, Demanrice	14 Dec 1929	7/ 384
Osteen, James A. [Winter Park]	Hobby, Ione [Winter Park]	6 Aug 1927	6/ 561
Osteen, William	Wainer, Inez	19 May 1928	7/ 123
Osteen, William D. [W] [Ocoee]	Holland, Hathel [Ocoee]	19 Nov 1925	6/ 88
Oswalt, Aubrey	Brasefield, Elizabeth Ruth	27 Mar 1928	7/ 89
Outlaw, Bud	Davis, Creola	21 Dec 1928	7/ 218
Outlaw, John Tomas	Clark, Kathleen	27 Aug 1932	8/ 188
Outler, Tom	Smith, Kizzie	10 Jan 1932	8/ 105
Overby, Fred Patterson	Crane, Corinne Betty	1 Jan 1933	8/ 236
Overholt, Ray	Lovely, Louise	12 Apr 1928	7/ 101
Overstreet, Joe	Trawick, Trixie	8 May 1929	7/ 287
Owen, James Caney	Booker, Turner Mae	25 Aug 1928	7/ 176
Owen, Martin Boyd	Smith, Olive Jeannette	l Mar 1928	7/ 72
Owens, Emannuel [Orlando]	Tinsley, Pearl [Orlando]	6 Mar 1926	6/ 170
Owens, Henry	Jones, Janie	24 Aug 1932	8/ 187
Owens, Richard	Hestor, Mary	3 Dec 1927	7/ 19
Owens, Trueman	Goodwyne, Doris Louise	11 Feb 1933	8/ 257

Owens, Walter Lee	Giddians, Nannie Elizabeth	2 Jul 1931	8/ 27
Oxindine, Edward Allison [Orlando]	Stuckey, Mildred [Orlando]	16 Sep 1926	6/ 338

P

Paddock, Earl Lewis [Orlando]	Paul, Edna Helena [Burlington, MI]	17 Jan 1926	6/ 107
Padgett, Arthur [W] [Ocoee]	Elledge, Inez [Ocoee]	9 Dec 1925	6/ 99
Padgett, Fred Lee [Orlando]	Filipek, Betty [Orlando]	25 Dec 1926	6/ 423
Padgett, John P.	Stiles, Mildred Elizabeth	9 Mar 1933	8/ 268
Padgett, Luther	Johnston, Jessie Pearl	27 Apr 1934	8/ 469
Padgett, Richard [Winter Garden]	Malloy, Annie [Winter Garden]	20 Apr 1926	6/ 214
Page, Archie Thomas	Howard, Mary Lillian	29 Nov 1933	8/ 378
Page, Byron Jerome [Dover, NH]	Fernald, Leona May [Rochester, NH]	19 Apr 1927	6/ 497
Page, Jessie [Winter Garden]	Kelly, Idean [Winter Garden]	10 Oct 1925	6/ 59
Page, Julius Wilford	Hoffman, Theresa Sophia	14 Jul 1934	8/ 511
Palmer, Callie Albertus	Corliss, Arie Lee	30 Nov 1932	8/ 223
Palmer, Charles E.	Burlingame, Martha L.	24 Mar 1928	7/ 87
Palmer, John Eugene	Jones, Lola Irene	16 Feb 1928	7/ 65
Pappas, John [W] [Orlando]	Pack, Velma [Orlando]	6 Aug 1925	6/ 29
Paramore, Eugie Alexander [W] [Ocoee]	Pierce, Lily Mae [Ocoee]	14 Dec 1984	6/ 100
Parham, Albert Harrison [also at 8/335 with date: 15 Aug 1933]	Rhodes, Opal	10 Jun 1933	8/ 314
Parish, A. C. [Orlando]	Parish, Bonnie [Blountstown]	28 Aug 1927	6/ 571
Park, Holly [W] [Elizabeth, WV]	Carney, Bessie [Parkersburg, WV]	15 Dec 1925	6/ 101
Parker, Donald Delos	Rhyne, Augusta	9 May 1928	7/ 112
Parker, Donald Henry	Steinbach, Anita Louise	4 Nov 1933	8/ 361
Parker, Earl	Wilson, Ida Lee	12 Mar 1932	8/ 125
Parker, Fisher Lee	Holimon, Altamese	2 Apr 1933	8/ 283
Parker, Harvey Clyde [Winter Garden]	Thompson, Lillie Belle [Winter Garden]	23 Apr 1926	6/ 216
Parker, James [B] [Bainbridge GA]	Hall, Annie Bell [Bainbridge, GA]	21 Dec 1925	6/ 109
Parker, John Robert	Rowland, Lilly	27 May 1930	7/ 460
Parker, Lawrence	Roberson, Essie Mae	12 Feb 1934	8/ 428
Parker, Luther	Hagins, Dorothy Lee	21 Jun 1929	7/ 312
Parker, William Clayton [W] [Ft Meyers]	Kelly, Anna Marbury [New York, NY]	22 Dec 1925	6/ 112
Parker, William Laurence [Maitland]	Bennett, Rita Mae [Maitland]	16 Jun 1926	6/ 271
Parkham, Leonidas Norris [Windermere]	Lawrence, Virginia Margaret [Windermere]	30 Dec 1926	6/ 443
Parkinson, William Henry	Lerach, Ellen Marguerite	15 May 1931	7/ 592
Parks, William	Pope, Curnealia	28 Nov 1927	7/ 17
Parmer, Henry	Williams, Mamie Lee	22 Oct 1927	6/ 596
Parnell, Leo	Paulk, Lizzie	24 Jan 1928	7/ 51
Parramore, Manuel G.	Armstrong, Eunice Lucretia	25 Sep 1933	8/ 345
Parrish, Dewey	Weeks, Mauddie Lee	12 Dec 1931	8/ 85
Parrish, Earl William	Crittenden, Alice	21 Feb 1931	7/ 559
Parrish, James Willis [W] [Taft]	Keith, Lucy [Taft]	4 Jul 1925	6/ 15
Parrish, Raymond Curtis [Winter Garden]	Brockman, Mary Lee [Winter Garden]	10 Jun 1926	6/ 263
Parrish, William	Rollins, Elizabeth	14 Apr 1933	8/ 284
Parrott, George Edw. [Apopka]	Conway, Lucille [Apopka]	7 Jun 1927	6/ 530
Partin, Elbert [Orlando]	Cruttenden, Beulah [Pinecastle]	1 May 1927	6/ 510
Partin, Emil Ellis [Orlando]	Corley, Annie Laurie	27 Dec 1926	6/ 420
Partin, Guy [Orlando]	Malloy, Pearl [Ocoee]	19 Jan 1927	6/ 440
Partin, James Hiram [Orlando]	Malloy, Carrie Anne [Ocoee]	9 Jul 1927	6/ 548
Partin, Lawrence [W] [Orlando]	Tyson, Kate	9 Jan 1926	6/ 130

Partin, Theodore	Burlingame, Evelyn E.	16 Jul 1934	8/ 510
Pascoe, Joe [Orlando]	Love, Eva [Orlando]	29 Nov 1926	6/ 395
Pass, Claude Wills [Winter Garden]	White, Leslie Lee [Winter Garden]	1 Jun 1927	6/ 520
Patman, Lee Floyd [Orlando]	Powell, Belle [Taft]	14 Sep 1925	6/ 45
Patrick, John Henry [Orlando]	Felton, Pearlie [Orlando]	27 May 1927	6/ 517
Patrick, Milton Shelton	Williams, Eva	10 May 1930	7/ 452
Patrick, Noah DeLisle [Orlando]	Johnson, Vivian Ina [Orlando]	27 Jun 1927	6/ 543
Patrick, Ollie	Clark, Sallie	4 Sep 1931	8/ 45
Patrick, Rentz Gerald	Hall, Kittie Ellen	13 Mar 1933	8/ 273
Patrick, William Allison [Orlando]	Harton, Clarice Belle [Orlando]	22 Jun 1926	6/ 282
Patterson, Bennie	Stringfield, Rosa Mae	28 Oct 1933	8/ 359
Patterson, Earl	Holmes, Zadie	11 May 1932	8/ 153
Patterson, Ernest Willie	Lewis, Ella	13 Jan 1934	8/ 409
Patterson, Felix Leslie	Welch, Ruth	2 Feb 1929	7/ 240
Patterson, Frank Reyser	Lyles, Mabel Lee	20 Jul 1931	8/ 34
Patterson, Harris [B] [Kissimmee]	Smith, Julia [Kissimmee]	27 Jun 1925	6/ 10
Patterson, Joseph [Orlando]	Tucker, Callie [Orlando]	26 Jul 1926	6/ 296
Patterson, Leonard	Fulford, Lula	21 Feb 1929	7/ 249
Patterson, Lloyd	Richardson, Ophelia	7 Jul 1930	7/ 476
Patterson, Mack [Killarney]	Hampton, Clara [Killarney]	10 Jan 1927	6/ 435
Patterson, Willie [B] [Orlando]	Williams, Mamie [Orlando]	24 Dec 1925	6/ 114
Pattison, Earl S. [W] [Jacksonville]	Weed, Louise [Orlando]	13 Dec 1925	6/ 119
Pattison, John H.	Burnett, Lucille Belle	3 Dec 1927	7/ 20
Patton, Benjamin Frank	Wettstein, Charlotte	8 Jun 1929	7/ 307
Patton, Edward T. [W] [Orlando]	Miller, Mabel A. [Orlando]	6 May 1925	5/ 570
Patton, Robert A. [Daytona]	Hutchinson, Irene [Daytona]	27 May 1926	6/ 246
Paul, Allen	Kinsey, Agnes	19 Nov 1928	7/ 205
Paul, Emery	Morgan, Sarah	14 Oct 1930	7/ 506
Paul, George [Winter Park]	Bryant, Elsie [Winter Park]	5 Apr 1926	6/ 197
Paul, Lewis	Harts, Bernice May	26 Dec 1933	8/ 394
Paul, Moses	Bradley, Effie Mae	13 Nov 1933	8/ 365
Paul, Shedrick	Sullivan, Georgie	1 Apr 1931	7/ 573
Paul, Stephen Chas. [Orlando]	Delsman, Kathryn Estelle [Orlando]	26 Apr 1926	6/ 220
Paul, William Perry [Orlando]	Crawford, Sallie [Orlando]	12 Mar 1927	6/ 472
Paulk, William Thomas	Shaw, Eston	3 Jan 1928	7/ 39
Payment, Albert Rudolph	Butler, Orvina	3 Apr 1934	8/ 457
Payne, Albert [Orlando]	Dixon, Frances [Madison]	8 Dec 1926	6/ 404
Payne, Carroll Morey	Kelsey, Mary Evelyn	12 Oct 1930	7/ 507
Payne, Ellis Raymond	Burnsed, Lillie Blanche	8 May 1931	7/ 596
Payne, Lucius L.	Smith, Mary Lucy	21 Nov 1927	7/ 13
Peach, Joseph George [Orlando]	White, Juanita [Orlando]	25 Oct 1925	6/ 71
Peach, Sidney	Loache, Flora D.	10 Sep 1928	7/ 183
Peacock, William Ira	Sligh, Ethel Adeline	7 Aug 1931	8/ 88
Peaden, Porter Lee [Orlando]	Barker, Corinne May	25 Aug 1927	6/ 577
Peadon, Robert Randolph	Cox, Doris Aleane	31 Dec 1933	8/ 398
Peaks, Donald Eustis	Penny, Lucy Annelle	26 Mar 1932	8/ 139
Pearce, Edward Foster	Bowen, Mattie	8 Jun 1932	8/ 167
Pearcy, Frank [Orlando]	Wright, Hattie May [Orlando]	20 Feb 1926	6/ 161
Pearl, Elvin Bachelder	Price, Bessie Watson	10 Jun 1929	7/ 308
Peavey, Andrew Lewis	Robinson, Mary May	10 Aug 1929	7/ 331

Peek, John Clinton	Gates, Mary Joyce Scott	28 Oct 1933	8/ 356
Peel, Walter Ernest [Orlando]	Ainsworth, Elizabeth Ethel [Orlando]	15 Oct 1925	6/ 64
Peeler, Joseph [W] [Athens, GA]	Kelly, Lillian [Big Stone Gap, VA]	25 Nov 1925	6/ 92
Peeples, Charles Beny	Godwin, Addie	15 Jan 1928	7/ 47
Peery, George Atwood	McCready, Rachel Narcissa	14 Sep 1932	8/ 197
Peffer, Thomas Oscar [Orlando]	Murray, Laura Jean [Orlando]	13 Mar 1926	6/ 179
Penberthy, Pierce Edward	Sisney, Eloise Lucile	26 Nov 1931	8/ 78
Penn, George F. [W] [Orlando]	Thompson, Sallie [Orlando]	1 Apr 1925	5/ 553
Penney, Chester Ulyses	Knight, Adelle	15 Dec 1927	7/ 25
Pennington, Paul	Baggett, Selma	31 Aug 1930	7/ 493
Penny, Charles Holmes [W] [W. Palm Beach]	Deuch, Rosa [Orlando]	21 Mar 1925	5/ 548
Peoples, Willie [Orlando]	Hicks, Albert [Orlando]	18 Feb 1926	6/ 156
Pepper, James	Conner, Maggie Mae	13 Apr 1932	8/ 142
Pepper, Leslie Carroll [Phoenix, AZ]	Williford, Akel [Orlando]	6 Feb 1927	6/ 453
Percival, Harry Elwood [Orlando]	Richards, Dorothy May [Orlando]	27 Mar 1927	6/ 484
Perdue, Robert Gordon, Jr.	Dunaway, Edith	6 Jul 1932	8/ 176
Perkins, David Roscoe	Davis, Lillian Labon	28 Jan 1934	8/ 420
Perkins, Walter	Meriweather, Willie Bell	2 Jan 1929	7/ 227
Perlots, Hillie	Dinkins, Abbie	7 Jul 1930	7/ 480
Pernell, Fred	Robinson, Sarah	11 Feb 1929	7/ 249
Perrin, James [Orlando]	Ware, Rosalee [Orlando]	29 Aug 1926	6/ 334
Perrott, Henry Vernon [Pinecastle]	Ray, Ida [Orlando]	5 Oct 1926	6/ 349
Perry, Alfonso	Harrell, Mozelle	22 Sep 1930	7/ 498
Perry, Clyde [Winter Garden]	Williams, Bessie [Winter Garden]	2 Apr 1927	6/ 488
Perry, Jim [B] [Orlando]	Wall, Annie [Orlando]	7 Nov 1925	6/ 77
Perry, Oliver	Synhoff, Claire	11 Jan 1928	7/ 43
Persons, George Mack	Mizelle, Ethel Maxine	19 Mar 1933	8/ 273
Peschall, E. Ray	Taylor, Ava	5 May 1928	7/ 111
Pete, Lonnie [Orlando]	Thomas, Callie [Orlando]	1 Feb 1927	6/ 448
Peterkin, Walter	Gruver, Mildred	4 Jan 1932	8/ 100
Peters, Edward Wells	Baurette, Lydia	17 Mar 1928	7/ 82
Peters, Samuel Arthur	Clark, Joan Carey	27 Dec 1927	7/ 33
Peterson, Andrew J.	Deason, Loree	26 May 1929	7/ 299
Peterson, George	Herring, Bessie	25 Feb 1928	7/ 69
Peterson, John Louis	Moore, Marian Lorna	16 Apr 1929	7/ 280
Peterson, Matthew [W] [Orlando]	Hilliard, Margaret [Orlando]	11 Apr 1925	5/ 558
Petris, Willis Edward	Wright, Kathryn Jane	24 Jun 1931	8/ 39
Petry, Luke Duncan	Queen, Bessie	25 May 1933	8/ 304
Pettit, Clark R. [Cocoa]	Hickox, Mirtie [Cocoa]	17 Aug 1927	6/ 569
Petty, Raiman [River Head, NY]	Benjamin, Jennie [River Head, NY]	13 Feb 1926	6/ 158
Petty, Tom	Moody, Eliza	5 Jan 1932	8/ 100
Pfeifer, Joseph Felix [Orlando]	Winn, Maudie Mae [Orlando]	2 Jun 1926	6/ 255
Pfister, Edwyn Eugene [Orlando]	Worrell, Katherine A. [Orlando]	3 Apr 1926	6/ 200
Pflough, Floyd F. [Orlando]	Johns, Blanche Marie [Orlando]	30 Jun 1926	6/ 300
Pharr,.Wendell W	Spurgeon, Lillian Louise	11 Aug 1929	7/ 333
Phiffer, Lonnie	Nimmons, Rosener	20 Jan 1934	8/ 414
Phillips, A. J.	Johnson, Emma	19 Dec 1931	8/ 89
Phillips, Euston Chancy	Martin, Elma Aleene	30 Apr 1933	8/ 293
Phillips, Frank Thomas [Tampa]	Sherer, Neomi Catherine [Tampa]	16 Mar 1926	6/ 180
Phillips, Homer	Hilliard, Lizzie Mae	25 Mar 1933	8/ 276
Phillips, James	Cody, Birtha	29 Apr 1929	7/ 284
Phillips, Preston	Walls, Mary Emma	11 Nov 1933	8/ 363

Phillips, William Taylor	Williams, Mamie Ruth	12 Aug 1931	8/ 41
Philo, Charles [Tampa]	Broxie, Julie [Tampa]	23 Nov 1926	6/ 389
Piatt, Charles Edward	Sculley, Bessie	25 Jan 1930	7/ 405
Pichard, Clarence Alfred	Brewer, Vera Catherine	22 Mar 1934	8/ 484
Pickens, Chappie Willard [W] [Orlando]	Humphries, Flossie [Orlando]	14 Dec 1925	6/ 99
Pickerell, Henry Edwin	Harrod, Ida Evans	18 Feb 1929	7/ 248
Pickerell, Paul Thaddeus [W] [Orlando]	Wernert, Mildred Francis [Orlando]	1 Jan 1926	6/ 134
Pickett, Fred	Francis, Anna	1 May 1929	7/ 285
Pickett, William Marvin [St. Petersburg]	Williams, Susie Mae [Richmond, VA]	20 Oct 1926	6/ 359
Pickrell, David R.	Holt, Patsie Ruth	25 Feb 1928	7/ 74
Pierce, Harry Raymond	Poetzinger, Marguerite	17 Mar 1934	8/ 447
Pierce, Kenneth	Watson, Alice	14 Mar 1929	7/ 263
Pierce, Ray Lucius [Orlando]	Tucker, Mary Francis [Orlando]	15 Feb 1927	6/ 460
Pierce, Richard	Ratliff, Ellen	25 Feb 1931	7/ 560
Pierce, Rudolph	Batchelor, Netamae	28 Nov 1932	8/ 226
Pierson, Jay Lord	Decker, Pearl Anne	1 Mar 1934	8/ 442
Pike, J. C.	Yarbrough, Eunice	28 Nov 1928	7/ 207
Pilat, Hugo	Brown, Aubrey Mae	5 Jun 1931	8/ 13
Pinar, Arthur	Ishmael, Dora	9 Apr 1931	7/ 581
Piner, Nellie [Orlando]	Lyson, Lottie [Orlando]	19 Jun 1926	6/ 275
Pinkney, Henry [B] [Orlando] [gives address]	Wilson, Lillie [Orlando] [gives address]	26 Dec 1925	6/ 118
Pinkney/Pickney, Ephriam [Orlando]	Singleton, Jennie [Orlando]	2 Jul 1926	6/ 285
Pinkston, Jeff [Orlando]	Heath, Dorothy	14 Dec 1926	6/ 407
Pipkin, Hughie	Jones, Annie	4 Feb 1928	7/ 57
Pistole, William Melvin [W] [Mobile, AL]	Hilton, Marjory/Marjorie [Haines City]	16 Dec 1925	6/ 103
Pitman, Arthur Earl	Rockett, Thyra Anis	17 Sep 1932	8/ 198
Pitman, Henry [B] [Orlando]	Ingram, Sophie	24 Dec 1925	6/ 113
Pitt, Cratus Hall	Sullivan, Viola	29 Jul 1931	8/ 37
Pittman, James Andrew [Orlando]	Stone, Martha Innes [Orlando]	17 Apr 1926	6/ 213
Pittman, William F. [W] [Orlando]	Gaston, Lena [Orlando]	30 Dec 1925	6/ 123
Pitts, Frank [B] [Sanford]	Hall, Mattie [Sanford]	20 Jan 1925	5/ 530
Pitts, Herman	Prigden, Adlena	6 May 1933	8/ 292
Pitts, Paul Payton	Thomason, Vera Mae	17 Dec 1933	8/ 386
Pleus, Robert James	Sleeper, Virginia Tallman	22 Nov 1927	7/ 18
Plowden, Charlie [B] [Apopka]	Roberts, Lola [Apopka]	21 Dec 1925	6/ 109
Plumb, Hugh Jr. [Augusta, GA]	Dabney, Mary [Atlanta, GA]	3 Mar 1926	6/ 173
Plummer, Bernard	Brooks, Lida Yancey	7 Mar 1932	8/ 123
Plummer, Messiah	Wycke, Jeanie Mae	9 Sep 1929	7/ 342
Plummer, Raymond Bryan	Browns, Sue Rives	29 Jun 1929	7/ 317
Plunk, Arthur	Alderman, Nona Mae	19 Jun 1934	8/ 515
Podmore, John Arthur	Bethea, Mary Eugenia	5 Nov 1927	7/ 9
Pogue, Henley W.	Dean, Gladys Virginia	4 Sep 1930	7/ 497
Polds, Eldridge	Byrd, Ruby Lee	28 Jun 1930	7/ 477
Polhill, R. L.	Willis, Ophelia	20 Mar 1928	7/ 83
Pollard, Elijah [Oakland]	Phillips, Lucy [Winter Garden]	1 Nov 1926	6/ 371
Pollard, Elishia	Manns, Viola	12 Sep 1932	8/ 195
Ponder, Loring Clinton, Jr.	Waters, Naomi	1 Jan 1934	8/ 397
Pone, Willie	Wesley, Elberta	12 Mar 1928	7/ 79
Pontius, Freda O.	Kahlenback, Dorothy H.	6 Apr 1930	7/ 436
Pool, Julius	Pierce, Celesta	27 May 1930	7/ 460

Poole, Fort Henry	Green, Alvaro Elizabeth	14 May 1932	8/ 155
Poole, Willard Cleveland	Rochow, Norma	6 May 1933	8/ 292
Poor, William Washington	Nale, Hannah Marie	18 Mar 1931	7/ 568
Pope, Clifford	Bass, Assie Belle	20 Oct 1927	6/ 595
Pope, Dallas	McNish, Beaulah	1 Apr 1929	7/ 269
Pope, Fred Wallace	Beeman, Dorothy Alynda	2 Jun 1932	8/ 164
Pope, Leon	Belton, Laurie	25 Dec 1933	8/ 391
Pope, Thomas D.	Bland, Nellie	1 Sep 1928	7/ 180
Poppel, John Alexander	Matthews, Nellie	8 Sep 1927	6/ 575
Porter, David	Martin, Ella Louise	16 Dec 1927	7/ 28
Porter, David Roscoe [S. Jacksonville]	Kelley, Elizabeth [Philadelphia, PA]	16 Mar 1926	6/ 180
Porter, Jas. Hardy	Atwood, Nora Lee	27 Oct 1927	7/ 3
Porter, Lauris F. [W] [Orlando]	Heller, Katherine Margaret	30 Mar 1925	5/ 550
Porter, Robert [Orlando]	Donnell, Dorothy [Orlando]	22 Oct 1925	6/ 70
Porter, William [Orlando]	Francis, Anna [Orlando]	10 May 1926	6/ 241
Portlock, Armand	Belle, Emma	8 Mar 1930	7/ 424
Posada, Eddie	Strickland, Vera	22 Mar 1932	8/ 130
Postell, Alfonso [Oakland]	Myers, Louise [Oakland]	5 Nov 1926	6/ 378
Posten, Willie	Revels, Myrtle	30 Dec 1929	7/ 393
Potter, Paul W. [W] [W. Palm Beach]	Hall, Fay Alethea [Anderson, SC]	9 Jun 1925	5/ 589
Potter, Philip Richardson [Orlando]	Wood, Marguerite [Farmington, MI]	17 Feb 1926	6/ 172
Potter, William Redding [Orlando]	Rutherford, Janice Dorothy [Orlando]	2 Jul 1927	6/ 564
Potter, Wister James	Styles, Chrizzelle Evelyn	31 Dec 1928	7/ 225
Potts, Charles Arlington [Tampa]	Bernard, Ethel Morton [Island, KY]	10 Apr 1926	6/ 204
Pouder, Walter	Parnell, May	4 Feb 1928	7/ 56
Poulton, Ernest Russell	Williams, Verna	14 Jul 1928	7/ 161
Pouncy, John [Winter Garden]	Nells, Effie [Winter Garden]	16 Jan 1926	6/ 135
Pounds, Lemeul	Blackall, Gertrude E.	11 Jan 1928	7/ 42
Pounds, Wm. Bennin [Ocoee]	West, Mable Rooker [Ocoee]	6 Oct 1925	6/ 58
Powell, Albert [Winter Garden]	Willis, Mary Elizabeth [Winter Garden]	11 Sep 1926	6/ 335
Powell, Albert Foy	Lavender, Carolyn Dylla	9 May 1932	8/ 153
Powell, Benjamin Ira	Price, Lona Belle	25 Nov 1933	8/ 377
Powell, James	Williams, Rena	21 Dec 1929	7/ 387
Powell, Tee	Manley, Rena	29 Apr 1931	7/ 591
Powell, Tommie Lee	Morall, Annie Mae	30 Jan 1933	8/ 251
Powell, Walter [B] [Winter Garden]	Jacobs, Susie [Winter Garden]	24 Dec 1925	6/ 113
Powell, William Jack	Warren, Elizabeth Lola	2 Apr 1934	8/ 453
Powell, Willie [Orlando]	Davis, Lola [Orlando]	21 Mar 1927	6/ 479
Powers, Robert	Green, Edna O.	25 Mar 1929	7/ 267
Pratt, Robert Alva [New Haven CT]	Anmann, Edith Louise [Orlando]	18 May 1926	6/ 242
Prensky, Adolph Roth	Berman, Sylvia Regina	25 Mar 1934	8/ 450
Presley, William H. [Orlando]	Moseley, Missouri [Orlando]	7 Aug 1926	6/ 313
Pressley, John Henry [Orlando]	Ham, Martha Elizabeth [Orlando]	25 Dec 1926	6/ 434
Preston, Andrew C.	Courath, Mary Catherine	6 Jun 1933	8/ 315
Preston, Cleveland	Harvin, Mamie	10 Dec 1928	7/ 214
Price, Enoch	Cole, Anna	23 Oct 1929	7/ 360
Price, Franklin Lee [B] [Orlando]	Evans, Charicy Lee [Orlando]	24 Dec 1925	6/ 114
Price, John Thomas	Moore, Myrtle	16 Jan 1929	7/ 231
Prichard, Joe Wynne	Edwards, Posey	7 Oct 1933	8/ 350
Pritchard, Marcus Warren	Richardson, Faye Elizabeth	13 Apr 1934	8/ 461
Proxton, John	Ball, Enola	28 Apr 1928	7/ 108
Proyer, Robert [Orlando]	Nelson, Ida Mae [Orlando]	26 Apr 1927	6/ 497

Pruet, Cyril Hugo	Hurley, Mildred	6 Jun 1928	7/ 134
Pruett, Amos Randall [Orlando]	Jansen, Hilda [Orlando]	22 Aug 1926	6/ 318
Pruett, John Dalton, Jr.	Tyson, Ada Lucile	2 Oct 1933	8/ 350
Pryer, A. B. [B] [Orlando]	Davis, Pinkie [E. Orlando]	27 Apr 1925	5/ 565
Pullens, Willie Lee	Whitaker, Frances Rebecca	28 Oct 1933	8/ 358
Pulliam, Horace	Branson, Evelyn Dorothy	7 Apr 1934	8/ 459
Pullins, James Ralph	Brickley, Ester Pearl	4 May 1933	8/ 289
Purcell, Charles Sage	Chapman, Ferol Stewart	4 Sep 1932	8/ 192
Purcell, Floyd Buffin	Chamberlain, Helen Elizabeth	10 Jul 1932	8/ 177
Purcell, Lloyd Bain	Theobold, Virginia Frances	19 Jun 1931	8/ 38
Purcell, Tilifred Flemmon	Arnold, Janet Margaret	2 May 1931	7/ 594
Purvis, Charles Henry [W] [Tampa]	Whittington, Dollie [Tampa]	3 Jun 1925	5/ 599
Putman, Leon	Drawdy, Bertha	11 Sep 1932	8/ 195
Putney, Austin Talbot [W] [Jacksonville]	Monnett, Lida G. [Orlando]	7 Jun 1925	5/ 596

Q

Qualls, Joe F.	Johnson, Sallie	17 Nov 1928	7/ 206
Quellette, Robert Henry	Hayner, Mae	23 Apr 1928	7/ 105
Quigley, Edward J. [Orlando]	Merle, Freda Marie [Endicott, NY]	12 Sep 1925	6/ 44
Quina, John Joseph	Stiles, Helen Carolyn	20 Jun 1931	8/ 22
Quinn, Edwin Yates [W] [Orlando]	Quinn, Catherine Wilkinson [Orlando]	2 May 1925	5/ 566

R

Raab, Samuel	Hatyria, Barbara	13 Mar 1928	7/ 80
Raab, Theodore	Stockman, Caroline	16 Oct 1927	6/ 595
Rachelle, Littleton [Orlando]	Welch, Lucretia [Orlando]	1 Jun 1927	6/ 520
Rackley, Charlie J.	Johnson, Lillie Mae	23 Jan 1928	7/ 50
Rackley, Isaac [Winter Garden]	Whitlock, Rosa Lee [Winter Garden]	15 Nov 1926	6/ 383
Rackley, Wm L. D. [W] [Mt Vernon GA]	Rackley, Mary Jane [Orlando]	3 Feb 1925	5/ 527
Radditt, John	Cox, Bertie	11 Oct 1930	7/ 504
Radebaugh, Cushman Shelton [Orlando]	Giles, Edna Adelina [Orlando]	7 Jun 1927	6/ 526
Radebaugh, Otis Barclay, Jr.	Gaskin, Ethel Spencer	12 Jun 1934	8/ 492
Rains, George Washington	McCarthy, Sarah	6 Jun 1928	7/ 130
Rains, Joe [Winter Park]	Hayes, Lula [Winter Park]	11 Aug 1926	6/ 310
Rajcany, Frank Carl [W] [Orlando]	Keeler, Dorothy Florence [Orlando]	17 May 1925	5/ 575
Raleigh, James Morris [W] [Orlando]	Kaiser, Anna [Orlando]	14 Jan 1925	5/ 513
Ramsay, Henry Clyde	Roberts, Lucille Mline	11 Mar 1928	7/ 80
Rand, Albert	Harris, Mamie	15 Nov 1932	8/ 217
Rand, LeRoy	Kingsley, Ethel Mae	30 May 1932	8/ 162
Randall, Elijah	Martin, Rosa	17 Mar 1934	8/ 445
Randall, Lee Deforest [Orlando]	Pickett, Katherine Gertrude	7 Feb 1927	6/ 451
Randall, Walter Doane	Brown, Ruth Mary	25 Feb 1931	7/ 563
Randles, John Wallace	Wells, Olin	1 Feb 1932	8/ 112
Randley, David [B] [Thomasville, GA]	Sherman, Louise [Orlando]	19 May 1925	5/ 576
Ranier, Tony Romeo [Orlando]	Echols, Regeina [Kissimmee]	18 Jun 1926	6/ 273
Rankin, Twain Galyon	Kelley, Juanita Louise	17 Aug 1929	7/ 334
Rankin, Walter A. [W] [Orlando]	Wehr, Mamie L. [Orlando]	13 Nov 1925	6/ 82
Ranous, William James	Fyffe, Martha	23 Apr 1934	8/ 466

Raspberry, John	Henderson, Nannie	3 Oct 1933	8/ 348
Rast, Claude Lonsdale [W] [Taft]	Batten, Nettie Lucile [Orlando]	11 Jan 1926	6/ 135
Rauch, Harvey Jacob	Fetters, Gertrude Vertal	29 Mar 1934	8/ 451
Raulerson, Joseph Gordon	Lent, Olive Josephine	20 Dec 1931	8/ 91
Rausch, Francis E.	Giroux, Delima A.	12 Oct 1927	6/ 591
Rawson, Bernard Anderson	Johnson, Louise Ella	11 Jan 1933	8/ 243
Rawson, Ray Glenn [Apopka]	Hayes, Cora [Apopka]	18 Dec 1926	6/ 410
Ray, George Troy [W] [Winter Garden]	Miller, Margaret Elizabeth [Winter Garden]	27 Jul 1925	6/ 26
Ray, Herman	Wever, Margaret	19 Mar 1930	7/ 430
Ray, Moses West	Vinning, Daisy	7 Jun 1928	7/ 131
Ray, Roy	Sanders, Tabitha	14 Nov 1929	7/ 376
Ray, Willie	Spriggens, Irella	15 Jun 1933	8/ 313
Rayborn, Marion Lamar [Delray]	Holman, Martha [Orlando]	26 Dec 1926	6/ 432
Rayburn, Aubrey Arthur	Glover, Orlean	6 Dec 1930	7/ 528
Raymond, Harold Lewis	Carter, Annette Mary	30 Jun 1930	7/ 475
Rayston, Reginald	Shaw, Ruth A.	1 Sep 1928	7/ 179
Read, Robert Lewis [Orlando]	Harper, Marie Louise [Orlando]	18 Feb 1926	6/ 157
Reams, Charley Fletcher	Saylors, Mamie Grace	17 Jan 1933	8/ 248
Reaves, Adell [Orlando]	Keeley, Mattie [Orlando]	6 Nov 1926	6/ 375
Redd, Edwin Hall	McCarthy, Mittie	29 Aug 1931	8/ 44
Redden, Willie [Sanford]	Wilson, Leah [Cordele, GA]	14 Oct 1925	6/ 63
Redding, Louie Oscar [B] [Orlando]	Moorhead, Effie [Orlando]	13 Jun 1925	5/ 591
Redditt, Charles Marvin	Keeping, Florence Mable	10 Apr 1932	8/ 141
Redditt, Eddie Middleton	Green, May Slomia	27 Mar 1932	8/ 134
Redmond, Cleo [B] [Winter Garden]	Davis, Alberta [Winter Garden]	6 Aug 1925	6/ 30
Reed, Cecil William	Cumbie, Mildred Reid	29 Sep 1927	7/ 58
Reed, Charles Stewart [Orlando]	Annis, Eva Violet	10 Jan 1927	6/ 440
Reed, James	Ambrose, Lillian	28 Sep 1928	7/ 188
Reed, Jim [Orlando]	Williams, Henrietta [Sanford]	26 Jun 1926	6/ 250
Reed, Jimmie	Willies, Ardella	7 Oct 1932	8/ 204
Reed, Omer Lee	Roebuck, Eugenia Edna	31 May 1934	8/ 484
Reed, Robert LeRoy	Jarrell, Mildred Bernice	29 Dec 1933	8/ 395
Reese, Henry Lee [Orlando]	Stokes, Margureite [Orlando]	15 Jun 1926	6/ 267
Reese, Ran [Orlando]	Jackson, Mattie [Orlando]	30 Oct 1926	6/ 369
Reeves, Mertin Whinery [Orlando]	Smith, Elsie Blanche [Orlando]	10 Feb 1926	6/ 157
Regan, Edward Arthur	Helms, Corinne Florence	4 Mar 1933	8/ 266
Rehberg, Antoine Eddie	Champion, Josephine Lucile	20 Jan 1934	8/ 416
Reid, Charles Estes	Osborne, Alice Lillian	21 Mar 1932	8/ 131
Reihl, Berhard A.	Angle, Martha	23 Sep 1928	7/ 186
Renfro, Williams	Childs, Marie	31 Mar 1934	8/ 452
Renneberg, Harold [Cocoa]	Penfield, Jennie Maud [Cocoa]	28 Aug 1926	6/ 322
Revels, Harry	Robinson, Nattie Belle	15 Aug 1932	8/ 183
Revert, Harry [Orlando]	Anderson, Ruby [Orlando]	11 Mar 1926	6/ 192
Rex, Charles Walter	Autrey, Lottie Mae	15 Sep 1927	6/ 583
Rex, Reuben H.	Cannon, Jane	1 Apr 1933	8/ 280
Reynish, William Jenkins [W] [Liberty, NE]	Perry, Rachel Brooks [Chillicothe, OH]	24 Jan 1925	5/ 518
Reynolds, Andrew [Orlando]	Keaton, Charlie May [Orlando]	19 Feb 1927	6/ 461
Reynolds, Howard	Hull, Laura Jane	8 Dec 1928	7/ 214
Reynolds, Raymond Augustus	Tireman, Marion Pierson	11 Apr 1931	7/ 579
Reynolds, Robert William [Orlando]	Richards, Edna Eula [Orlando]	29 Jun 1926	6/ 292
Ribsam, Nicholas John	Houghton, Edith Irene	29 Jan 1931	7/ 549
Rice, James Junior	Ramsey, Minerva	2 Oct 1932	8/ 201

Rich, Jim [Tildenville]	King, Lucy [Winter Garden]	24 Aug 1925	6/ 38
Rich, Thomas L.	Hartnett, Alma Smith	2 May 1931	7/ 593
Rich, Willie [Winter Garden]	Wilson, Malonia [Winter Garden]	7 Jun 1926	6/ 260
Richards, Max Theodore	Moflar, Frances Mary	1 May 1931	7/ 592
Richardson, Aninias	Cooper, Georgia	29 Jun 1932	8/ 26
Richardson, Charles Pierce [W][Miami Beach]	Stevens, Bertha [Jacksonville]	27 Jun 1925	6/ 9
Richardson, Cleveland [B] [Orlando]	Vaughns, Willie [Orlando]	6 Jul 1925	6/ 10
Richardson, David	Cornett, Nina Elwyn	10 Nov 1933	8/ 364
Richardson, Herman [B] [Orlando]	Rutherford, Marie [Orlando]	3 Jan 1925	5/ 506
Richardson, James	Young, Nora L.	7 May 1932	8/ 152
Richardson, Leroy	Laidler, Rosa Lee	11 Mar 1929	7/ 260
Richardson, Leslie Earl	Medlock, Jamie Griffin	16 Feb 1933	8/ 258
Richardson, Luther Lionel	Jones, Ila Louise	18 Jun 1932	8/ 172
Richardson, Maribo Binion	Noah, Ruby Irene	7 May 1932	8/ 155
Richardson, Robert [B] [Plymouth]	Miller, Piney [Lockhart]	13 Jan 1926	6/ 133
Richardson, Rufus F.	Moseley, Lucile Harriet	1 Dec 1927	7/ 18
Richardson, Theodore [B] [Orlando]	Anderson, Bertha [Orlando]	27 Jul 1925	6/ 25
Richl, Clifford	Partin, Emma	24 Apr 1928	7/ 102
Ricketson, Clem	Simmons, Ola Lillian	25 Apr 1931	7/ 585
Rickey, Edward H. [W] [Orlando]	Johnson, Margaret Ann [Orlando]	2 May 1925	5/ 567
Rickman, Perry Richard	Martin, Lois Vera	27 Dec 1927	7/ 36
Riecken, Charles George	Ramsdell, Josephine Elizabeth	15 Feb 1930	7/ 417
Riew, August Christ	Heine, Josephine	12 Mar 1929	7/ 265
Rigdon, Robert Holland	Garwood, Ethel Marie	6 Apr 1929	7/ 273
Rigdon, Willis Joseph	Mathews, Hazel Pauline	11 Aug 1934	8/ 521
Riggs, Frank W. [St. Petersburg]	Murch, Florence Alvina [Philadelphia PA]	9 May 1927	6/ 505
Riggs, Harold Coleman	Macklin, Ella Taylor	29 Nov 1928	7/ 210
Riley, Benie [Winter Garden]	Medley, Modena [Winter Garden]	12 Jul 1926	6/ 303
Riley, Ernest Alfred [W] [Orlando]	Hooker, Dorothy [Orlando]	20 Dec 1925	6/ 111
Riley, Will [B] [Ocala]	Isham, Joemimia [Orlando]	25 Apr 1925	5/ 564
Rippey, Frederick Vance	Orr, Elsa Irene	5 Dec 1930	7/ 526
Risener, Frederic L. [W] [Apopka]	Harbind, Mildred M. [Apopka]	8 Nov 1925	6/ 80
Ristig, James Paul	Nye, Marion Alice	2 Jul 1929	7/ 317
Ritchey, Roy Sherman [Quitman, GA]	Childers, Mary Gladys [Orlando]	14 Jun 1926	6/ 268
Ritherford, Charlie	Bryant, Louise	26 Dec 1933	8/ 393
Ritter, Henry Edwin [W] [Orlando]	Warner, Gertrude [Orlando]	7 Mar 1925	5/ 535
Ritzi, Paul Andrew	Whitecombe, Frances	4 Jun 1928	7/ 130
Rivers, LeRoy [B] [Kissimmee]	Grant, Rubelle [Kissimmee]	31 Jan 1925	5/ 521
Roach, Thomas Leo	Meadows, Mickey	17 Mar 1929	7/ 265
Robbins, George, Jr. [Winter Garden]	McDaniels, Zula [Winter Garden]	13 Dec 1926	6/ 406
Robbins, Howard Horace [Winter Park]	Padoline, Nora [Winter Park]	19 Apr 1926	6/ 206
Robbins, John Oswald	Cornelison, Pauline Marie	23 Aug 1926	6/ 319
Robbins, Joseph [B] [Orlando]	Barber, Ada [Orlando]	23 Jan 1926	6/ 139
Robbins, William S. [W] [Sanford]	Haugabook, Harriet J. [Sanford]	21 May 1925	5/ 578
Roberson, Joe	Genrewt, Estelle	31 Mar 1930	7/ 433
Roberson, Julius Lanzo [Orlando]	Wheeler, Minna [Orlando]	20 Nov 1926	6/ 387
Roberson, Lewis	Merritt, Willie Maude	2 Feb 1934	8/ 421
Roberson, Louis	Wiley, Mary Alice	18 Mar 1933	8/ 270
Roberson, Percy Eugene	Scott, Lessie Lee	7 Jul 1931	8/ 29
Roberson, Raymond Clifton	Holliday, Maycelle Grace	8 May 1933	8/ 293

Roberson, William	Hull, Rose	16 Feb 1932	8/ 117
Roberts, Charles Herbert	Walker, Margaret Alice	8 Jul 1934	8/ 508
Roberts, Donald Pryor	Fuller, Lelia	15 Jan 1930	7/ 410
Roberts, Fanciel Lavier [Orlando] [Lavier, Fanciel on lic.]	Jackson, Bernice [Orlando]	8 Feb 1926	6/ 158
Roberts, Jessie [Winter Park]	Adams, Leola [Winter Park]	11 Apr 1927	6/ 490
Roberts, Joe	Wright, Georgia Elizabeth	6 Apr 1929	7/ 273
Roberts, John [Orlando]	Williams, Julia [Orlando]	14 Aug 1926	6/ 305
Roberts, Joseph Frank	Flynn, Thelma Alice	19 Jan 1930	7/ 402
Roberts, Relford [Orlando]	Sherman, Bertha May [Orlando]	2 May 1927	6/ 500
Roberts, Richard	Buford, Georgia Ann	18 Nov 1933	8/ 369
Roberts, Richard [B] [Winter Garden]	Jackson, Jennie [Winter Garden]	3 Feb 1925	5/ 521
Roberts, Scott	Ray, Patand	16 Jan 1932	8/ 104
Roberts, William Manning [Orlando]	Ellman, Mary Matilda [Orlando]	16 Aug 1925	6/ 38
Robertson, Guy F.	Chandler, Elizabeth	7 Jun 1928	7/ 132
Robertson, Ross Edward	Kluckhohn, Florence Ruth	24 Jun 1932	8/ 174
Robertson, Wayne	Moody, Gladys	22 Jun 1928	7/ 150
Robinson, Alexander Mitchell [W] [Orlando]	Nordheim, Edna Fredericka [Lake Worth]	16 Jan 1926	6/ 139
Robinson, Artis Lee	Frazier, Alice	3 Feb 1934	8/ 423
Robinson, Asa [Orlando]	Montgomery, Anna [Orlando]	22 Jun 1926	6/ 250
Robinson, Charlie [Orlando]	Betsey, Birdie [Orlando]	13 Apr 1927	6/ 491
Robinson, Daniel Webster [Orlando]	Nelson, Margaret [Orlando]	23 Nov 1926	6/ 389
Robinson, Dave	Tollver, Mollie Rose	19 Apr 1930	7/ 454
Robinson, Eston Earl	Heck, Mary Viola	12 May 1934	8/ 475
Robinson, Eugene [Orlando]	Wallace, Ethel Mae [Orlando]	18 Oct 1926	6/ 367
Robinson, Frederick [Orlando]	Hogans, Odessa [Orlando]	6 Jul 1926	6/ 288
Robinson, Frederick Moody	Fields, Rose Catherine	14 Oct 1933	8/ 351
Robinson, J. M.	Williams, Minnie	29 Jul 1934	8/ 515
Robinson, Jack [Tampa]	Foster, Mead [Orlando]	29 Mar 1926	6/ 193
Robinson, Jake	Anderson, Henrietta	6 Sep 1927	6/ 574
Robinson, James [Orlando]	Pitts, Irvilla	20 Sep 1926	6/ 342
Robinson, John [B] [Orlando]	Ballard, Lena [Orlando]	14 Nov 1925	6/ 83
Robinson, Joseph Lunion [W] [Orlando]	Dietrich, Grace Permilia [Orlando]	No Date	6/ 128
Robinson, Matthew/ Mattew [Maitland]	Curry, Ione [Maitland]	10 Oct 1925	6/ 60
Robinson, Prezy	Davis, Virdee Mae	23 Sep 1929	7/ 349
Robinson, Samuel Alonzo [W] [Thomasville, AL]	Beverly, Eulene Exa [Thomasville, AL]	15 Jul 1925	6/ 20
Robinson, Sol	Riley, Clementine	8 May 1933	8/ 290
Robinson, Stuart	Allen, Betty J.	27 Jul 1928	7/ 166
Robinson, Timothy	Warren, Lillian	30 Nov 1931	8/ 82
Robinson, Tom	Patterson, Elzadie	9 Sep 1929	7/ 342
Robinson, Wiley [Titusville]	Randolph, Maggie [Titusville]	17 Oct 1925	6/ 67
Robinson, William T. [W] [Seffner]	Williams, Dorothy E. [Seffner]	23 Apr 1925	5/ 565
Robinson, Willie	Irving, Daisy	19 Jan 1927	6/ 440
Robinson, Willie	Williams, Idella	26 Aug 1931	8/ 44
Roche, Richard Kerwin [W] [New Orleans, LA]	Turnboro/Turnbow, Lucile [Brookhaven, ME]	16 Mar 1925	5/ 543
Roche, William Lawrence [Sanford]	Purvis, Virginia [Sanford]	15 Feb 1926	6/ 162
Rodenbaugh, Cecil Harris [Winter Park]	Denniman, Genevieve Grace	7 Feb 1927	6/ 453
Rodgers, James Joseph	Vogel, Loretta Emma	24 Nov 1932	8/ 220
Roebuck, John	Yates, Eunice	4 Nov 1927	7/ 6
Rogers, Cecil [Orlando]	Burfield, Mae [Orlando]	22 Mar 1926	6/ 188

Rogers, Charlie Griffin	Saunders, Margaret	22 Dec 1932	8/ 236
Rogers, Charlie Jack	Beier, Charlotte Ann	2 Jun 1932	8/ 164
Rogers, F. F. [Holopaw]	Wilson, Nell P. [Orlando]	30 Oct 1926	6/ 370
Rogers, Floyd	Ihrig, Vera	10 Feb 1929	7/ 250
Rogers, Fred	Henry, Johnnie Mae	2 Feb 1928	7/ 91
Rogers, Fred Dowell	Pennington, Inez Louise	1 Oct 1932	8/ 202
Rogers, James	Pickett, Daisy	16 Mar 1931	7/ 568
Rogers, James Raffen	Smith, Flossie Mae	31 Jan 1931	7/ 550
Rogers, James Ruffen	Lazers, Flonnie Lee	6 May 1933	8/ 297
Rogers, John William	Mathews, Nellie	25 May 1931	8/ 10
Rogers, Robert E. Lee	Schmitt, Lillie J.	27 Nov 1931	8/ 83
Rogers, Robert Preston [Water Valley, MS]	Cherry, Florence Edmonson [Orlando]	9 Jan 1927	6/ 436
Rogers, Walter Brevard	Koon, Juanita Elizabeth	1 Jul 1929	7/ 318
Rogers, William King	Cuthbertson, Dorothy Belle	8 Sep 1933	8/ 356
Roland, Roy Luther	Whitten, Florence Lorne	21 Dec 1928	7/ 217
Role, John	Burns, Sarah	8 May 1930	7/ 450
Roller, L. E. [W] [Orlando]	Thompson, Florence G. [Orlando]	13 Dec 1925	6/ 103
Rollerson, Frank	McPherson, Edna	6 Feb 1930	7/ 409
Rollin, Earl James	Smith, Janie Blanche	26 May 1934	8/ 482
Rollins, Charlie [Apopka]	Willis, Naomi [Apopka]	27 Nov 1926	6/ 391
Rollins, Connelious S.	Reed, Razzie Belle	5 Jan 1929	7/ 228
Rollins, Eulea [Plymouth]	Richards, Edna May [Plymouth]	9 Aug 1926	6/ 314
Rollins, Fred	Bland, Agnes	30 May 1928	7/ 122
Rollins, Louis Cannon	Thompson, Mary Pauline	30 Jan 1928	7/ 54
Rollins, Taft [B] [Orlando]	Williams, Josie [Orlando]	28 Dec 1925	6/ 127
Rollins, Taft Earl	Lumpkin, Elizabeth	12 Mar 1933	8/ 269
Rollins, Will [B] [Plymouth]	Pollard, Mabel [Plymouth]	7 Mar 1925	5/ 535
Rollins, William Lee [Winter Garden]	Thornton, Lois Estelle [Winter Garden]	18 May 1927	6/ 511
Rom, Carl William	Pinder, Mary Louise	5 Aug 1928	7/ 169
Romfh, John Randolph [W] [Orlando]	Trantham, Flossie [Orlando]	22 Apr 1925	5/ 563
Rone, Linden Jasper	Merchant, Gladys Richardson	10 Jun 1934	8/ 492
Rood, Francis Gleason	Eldridge, Bernice Winifred	29 Jan 1933	8/ 252
Roof, Henry Charles Knisler [Orlando]	Smith, Ellen Susan [Cheboybon, MI]	27 May 1927	6/ 519
Roof, Horace E.	Darling, Iona	24 Mar 1928	7/ 89
Roper, Ezra Roosevelt	Williams, Cora Louise	14 May 1933	8/ 299
Roper, Joseph Thomas	Bumby, Pauline	9 Mar 1930	7/ 425
Rorabach, Frank Wesley [W] [West Palm]	Davenport, Helen Montgomery [West Palm]	11 Nov 1925	6/ 82
Rose, Loise D.	Atkins, Marian Roberta	4 Jul 1934	8/ 506
Rose, Mike [Orlando]	Bryant, Anne [Orlando]	28 Aug 1926	6/ 322
Rose, Ralph [Orlando]	Christensen, Johanna [Orlando]	7 Oct 1925	6/ 74
Rosen, Al [Orlando]	Taffet, Minnie [Orlando]	9 Jun 1926	6/ 265
Rosenfelt, William Raymond [Winter Park]	Hertz, Pauline Margaret [Winter Park]	7 Apr 1926	6/ 201
Rosew, Oscar	Bauer, Margarte	15 Feb 1928	7/ 65
Ross, Andrew Brantley [Orlando]	Ross, Leila Edwards [Orlando]	24 Apr 1926	6/ 218
Ross, Donald Alonzo [Orlando]	Kimes, Mary Geneva [Orlando]	4 Apr 1926	6/ 205
Ross, Frank William	Luke, Lillie Jane	5 Jul 1934	8/ 506
Ross, James	Gillis, Mattie	21 Nov 1931	8/ 76
Roth, Irwin Kennedy	Bailey, Margaret	5 Jul 1934	8/ 507
Roton, Harris William	Harrison, Donnie Dell	1 Feb 1930	7/ 408
Roumillat, William H.	Whidden, Dillon	10 Aug 1929	7/ 331

Rouse, Leon Jesse	Bethis, Jewel	27 Mar 1929	7/ 266
Rouse, Sampson	Casseman, Mary	28 Nov 1928	7/ 208
Roussian, Marshall	Minor, Mary Edna	9 Apr 1928	7/ 96
Routh, Paul Kenneth	Carroll, Marie Lillian	15 Feb 1930	7/ 415
Routzahn, Gideon	Chancellor, Sara	18 Nov 1931	8/ 75
Row, Jacob Howard Sr.	Colley, Nettie	19 Aug 1934	8/ 523
Rowe, Abner Peter	Davis, Irene	2 Aug 1934	8/ 518
Rowe, Jimmie Theodore	Butler, Levada	12 May 1931	7/ 591
Rowe, Thomas H. [Orlando]	McCormack, Virginia [Orlando]	6 Sep 1925	6/ 46
Rowland, William Marshall	Ressor, Myrtle Virginia	9 Jun 1928	7/ 137
Rowley, Coit [Ravenwood, WV]	King, Margaret Louisa [Orlando]	29 Jul 1926	6/ 295
Royal, Edward	Hill, Nellie Mae	11 Feb 1930	7/ 412
Rozier, Albert	Chisolm, Lillie Mae	3 Nov 1930	7/ 516
Rubin, Albert	Cohen, Ruby	20 Apr 1931	7/ 583
Rucker, Charles Thomas	Baker, Martha	28 Sep 1927	6/ 587
Rucker, Henry Vincent	Wallett, Bessie LeDerle	20 Dec 1930	7/ 533
Ruff, Wayne Randall	Moflar, Katrina Anna	24 Dec 1933	8/ 391
Ruhl, Walter Houser	Crawford, Bettis Elizabeth	28 Feb 1931	7/ 560
Ruland, Frederick James [W] [Bridgeport CT]	Scott, Thelma H. [Bridgeport, CT}	2 Apr 1925	5/ 550
Runertson/Robertson, Joseph Lewis [Orlando]	Goyette, Doris Gertrude	7 Jan 1927	6/ 433
Rupp, James	Williams, Margaret	2 Nov 1927	7/ 5
Russell, Ardie Bloxham [Orlando]	Russell, Edith Jane	26 Aug 1927	6/ 570
Russell, Cloyde Harlan	Cole, Ruth Hazelton	13 Jan 1934	8/ 410
Russell, Leo Joe	Summer, Maggie Lean	8 Feb 1931	7/ 553
Russell, LeRoy Rogers	Johnson, Ellen	3 Jun 1928	7/ 139
Rutherford, Clarence [Orlando]	Jenkins, Luella [Orlando]	7 Sep 1925	6/ 41
Rutherford, Eugene Curtis	Mitchell, Avey Aline	14 Nov 1932	8/ 216
Rutledge, James [Orlando]	Washington, Dorothy [Orlando]	7 Sep 1925	6/ 41
Rutledge, Jessie	Seelars, Maud	6 Sep 1930	7/ 494
Rutledge, Walton [Apopka]	Craig, Virgie [Apopka]	28 Mar 1927	6/ 483
Rutledge, Zollie Jackson	Bledsoe, Ora Dell	15 Jul 1929	7/ 322
Ruzenstein, Joseph [Sanford]	Rettenmar, Minnie Talbert [Sanford]	28 Jan 1927	6/ 445
Ryals, Oscar Guston	Cash, Francis Gertrude	8 Mar 1934	8/ 443
Ryan, Mark Vernon [Apopka]	Blalock, Annie Morgan [Tallahassee]	26 Jun 1926	6/ 252
Ryans, Matthew [Orlando]	Young, Annie [Orlando]	13 Aug 1927	6/ 566

S

Saba, John Maure	Smart, Amelia	22 Dec 1930	7/ 524
Sackett, Charles Edwin	Kirkland, Mattie	20 May 1933	8/ 301
Sackett, Charles Edwin [Orlando]	Middlekauf, Mary Ella [Orlando]	3 Jun 1927	6/ 531
Sadler, Thomas	Williams, Sallie Mae	29 Jan 1934	8/ 419
Sael, William York	Anderson, Edna	3 Jun 1930	7/ 463
Saffer, Rex Eugene [W] [Tavares]	Downey, Helen Orpha [Orlando]	9 May 1925	5/ 582
Safford, Oscar [Winter Park]	Rollerson, Readus [Winter Park]	10 Oct 1925	6/ 59
Salmon, Henry [Clarcona]	Kimbrell, Marie [Clarcona]	25 Jan 1927	6/ 445
Salter, Adam [Orlando]	Telliver, Pearlie [Orlando]	19 Oct 1925	6/ 65
Salter, Dan [Orlando]	Allen, Essie May [Orlando]	7 Oct 1925	5/ 58
Salter, Lemar	Ivory, Osceola	30 Sep 1928	7/ 189
Samakis, James [Boston, MA]	Cornish, Marjorie [Rumford, ME]	24 Mar 1927	6/ 481
Sammons, Ervin [Hartford, AL]	Hammack, Annie Laurie [Daleville, AL]	1 Mar 1927	6/ 469

Samples, Freddie Lee	Mobley, Ada Lee	25 Mar 1934	8/ 448
Samples, Robert	Wright, Hattie Lee	5 Sep 1932	8/ 191
Sampson, Frank [Orlando]	Brown, Lillie [Orlando]	13 Mar 1927	6/ 473
Sampson, John Ben	Wilson, Julia Will	15 Jan 1934	8/ 411
Sampson, Victor [Orlando]	Solomon, Maggie E. [Orlando]	28 Jun 1927	6/ 542
Samuel, Joseph [Winter Park]	Morris, Essie Lee [Winter Park]	10 Apr 1926	6/ 203
Samuel, Otis	McDuffie, Elizabeth	20 Oct 1931	8/ 62
Samuels, Allison	Gary, Hattie	28 Sep 1930	7/ 514
Samuels, Eddie [B] [Orlando] [gives address]	Brown, Carrie [Orlando] [gives address]	26 Dec 1925	6/ 117
Sandage, Elmer	Meadows, Elizabeth	25 May 1929	7/ 305
Sandage, Walter Franklin	Morrison, Susie Lee	26 Jun 1929	7/ 315
Sanders, Albert Joseph	Gelm, Mary Agnes	1 Jan 1933	8/ 237
Sanders, Douglas	Turner, Hester	1 Dec 1930	7/ 525
Sanders, John Fletcher	Cooke, Viola	5 Jul 1931	8/ 31
Sanders, Oscar James	Russ, Helen May Arnis	18 Jun 1932	8/ 171
Sanders, William Henry [Orlando]	Dugan, Murreitta Ann [Orlando]	22 May 1926	6/ 245
Sanderson, Charles William [DeLand]	Nott, Margaret Cowles [DeLand]	17 Jun 1926	6/ 269
Sandfort, Fred H., Jr.	Stansell, Viola	7 Nov 1928	7/ 202
Sandifer, William Roper	Smith, Hazel Augusta	5 Sep 1929	7/ 340
Sandrock, Henry	Walsh, Emma Lucy	10 Jun 1931	8/ 16
Sands, Orilas Leslie	Henderson, Leona Estelle	15 May 1932	8/ 163
Sanford, Milo D.	Anderson, Mabel Louise	8 Dec 1927	7/ 25
Sanford, Rase	Carr, Lois Maye	10 Jan 1928	7/ 42
Sansbury, John Herman	Cowart, Bessie Eula	7 Dec 1930	7/ 530
Santo, Frank [Daytona]	Cassidy, Myrtle Hazel [Tampa]	15 Apr 1926	6/ 211
Sapp, Charlie [Orlando]	Masongale, Ella Mae [Orlando]	23 Dec 1926	6/ 415
Sapp, Forrest Dean	Newton, Myrtle Virginia	22 May 1933	8/ 303
Sappington, John Peurifoy [Orlando]	Ford, Clifford Louise [Orlando]	1 Jul 1926	6/ 290
Sargeant, Melvin Bliss	Hisle, Neva Campbell	7 Apr 1928	7/ 97
Sargent, John [W] [Titusville]	Palmer, Marie [Titusville]	7 Mar 1925	5/ 539
Satterwhite, Franklin Pierce	Weitman, Beulah	19 Dec 1932	8/ 229
Saucer, Joseph Moses	Phillips, Loze Marie	13 Jun 1929	7/ 308
Sauls, Rolfe A. [W] [Orlando]	Owen, Anita [Orlando]	8 Mar 1925	5/ 539
Saunders, William Everett	Kembro, Ruthie Mae	9 Jun 1930	7/ 471
Savage, Henry	Sampson, Florence	27 Oct 1927	7/ 2
Savage, Rex Linbaugh	Webb, Juli-Su	5 Jul 1930	7/ 479
Sawyer, Jessie William	Hawkins, Carrie	3 Nov 1927	7/ 6
Sawyer, Treadwell	Stephens, Ruby	28 Nov 1933	8/ 376
Sayer, Joseph Claude	Harnage, Mildred Elto	25 Jun 1930	7/ 472
Sayers, Dan John	Daley, Lillie Margaret	3 Nov 1932	8/ 213
Scarboro, Russell A. [Orlando]	Lowrey, Christine Fitts [Orlando]	16 Aug 1927	6/ 573
Scarbrough, John E. [W] [Ocoee]	King, Evie Z. [Ocoee]	2 Jan 1926	6/ 125
Scarbrough, Lee [Orlando]	William, Ruby [Orlando]	18 Feb 1927	6/ 461
Scarbrough, Vilie [Winter Garden]	Carlton, Lessie [Winter Garden]	24 Jun 1926	6/ 283
Schack, Mayland Alfred	Heil, Ellen Cecilia	17 Jan 1931	7/ 545
Schak, William (W) [Orlando]	Smith, Emma Maxey [Asheville, NC]	5 Dec 1925	6/ 104
Schawber, Albert	Engram, Julia A.	31 May 1934	8/ 485
Schenerlein, Roy Wilbur [W] [Winter Garden]	Martin, Mary Elizabeth [Winter Garden]	9 Nov 1925	6/ 83
Schoettzer, Herman Deidrich [Fontanelle, NE]	Franke, Emma Anna [Fontanelle, NE]	3 May 1927	6/ 502
Schofield, Ben	Jones, Gertrude Belle	23 Nov 1931	8/ 77

Schomberg, William Worth	Godfrey, Kittie Newton	1 May 1930	7/ 447
School, Carl George [Sanford]	Long, Lena Gretchen [Sanford]	15 Feb 1926	6/ 156
Schoolfield, James Collins	Hook, Gladys Viola	23 Jan 1928	7/ 53
Schoonover, R. A. [W] [Orlando]	Peterson, Mabel Annie [Orlando]	19 Jul 1925	6/ 24
Schrader, Arthur Louis [Winter Park]	Harris, Margurite [Winter Park]	16 Jun 1926	6/ 271
Schuirmann, Fred James	Schuirmann, Carol Pauline	5 Nov 1932	8/ 213
Schuler, Harold Arnold [Miami]	Ballard, Marion [Miami]	9 Aug 1926	6/ 312
Schultz, Fred Robert [W] [Orlando]	Wells, Ruth Evangeline [Orlando]	11 Jul 1925	6/ 15
Schunck, Joseph John	Hopkins, Anna Agnes	1 Apr 1929	7/ 268
Schwenn, Ernest	Hawley, Wesley Coke	29 Oct 1929	7/ 362
Scobie, George Reed	Boye, Marie	1 Aug 1931	8/ 39
Scoggins, Oscar [Orlando]	Bass, Gwendolyn [Orlando]	14 Mar 1927	6/ 477
Scott, Benjamin Turner	Jones, Henrietta Rock	10 May 1934	8/ 476
Scott, David Everett [Orlando]	Norris, Bessie [Orlando]	15 Mar 1927	6/ 473
Scott, Douglas Ward	Scott, Aletha	24 May 1932	8/ 159
Scott, Frederic Sterling [Clearwater]	McKenny, Annette [Orlando]	30 Apr 1926	6/ 230
Scott, Gordon Winfield	Tew, Sarah Margaret	29 Oct 1932	8/ 211
Scott, Harold Austin	Miller, Sue	17 May 1934	8/ 479
Scott, James [Hamilton, Ont, CND]	Bray, Annie Harriett [Hamilton, Ont, CND]	6 Feb 1926	6/ 152
Scott, John	Martin, Georgia	23 Jan 1928	7/ 50
Scott, John Maxwell [Orlando]	Ewing, Mildred [Erington, OH]	15 Feb 1927	6/ 463
Scott, John William [Orlando]	Parkerson, Birdy Estelle [Orlando]	9 Dec 1925	6/ 98
Scott, Napoleon	Hascock, Lula	9 Jul 1932	8/ 177
Scott, Thomas Everett	Haven, Norberta	3 Oct 1929	7/ 354
Scott, William	Morton, Flora McKinnon	16 Feb 1931	7/ 556
Scott, Willie, Jr. [Orlando]	Barrington, Ella Mae	2 Feb 1927	6/ 448
Scovill, Edwin P. [W] [Orlando]	Curts, Saphrona Mary [Griffin, GA]	1 Jun 1925	5/ 585
Scraggs, Finch Thomas, Jr. [Orlando]	Brown, Elizabeth Hammond [Orlando]	6 Jul 1926	6/ 290
Scribner, Clyde Herman	Avent, Calista Catherine	7 May 1933	8/ 295
Scrivens, Joe	Worthy, Daisy	5 Jul 1932	8/ 176
Scruse, Prince Albert [Orlando]	Williams, Annie Bell [Orlando]	21 Feb 1927	6/ 462
Scruton, Joseph Lorenzo [W] [Orlando]	Callahan, Ruth Virginia [Rochester, NY]	6 Feb 1926	6/ 151
Seaborn, Nathaniel	Dukes, Mattie Lee	17 Jun 1929	7/ 310
Sealover, Charles Scott	Eickmeyer, Mildred Ann	4 Jun 1934	8/ 488
Searcy, Clifford Franklin [W] [Arcadia]	Tichenor, Eloise [Orlando]	22 Oct 1925	6/ 73
Seaver, Boyd James [Orlando]	Chamberline, Helen Lucile [Orlando]	19 May 1927	6/ 512
Seeds, George [Winter Park]	Theobald, Dorothy [Winter Park]	30 Apr 1926	6/ 239
Seegar, Solomon John Thomas	Sims, Lillie	3 Mar 1932	8/ 121
Segers, Joe Laing [Plymouth]	Allin, Lizzie [Plymouth]	29 Jun 1926	6/ 253
Segraves, John Edmund	Sheppard, Dallas	22 Oct 1927	6/ 596
Segraves, Marvin	Wheddon, Lillie Mae	28 Dec 1929	7/ 390
Segrest, Erastur Franklin	Stephens, Annie	21 May 1928	7/ 115
Seidel, Gustave Adolph [Gotha]	Wood, Anna Fredonia [Orlando]	14 Jul 1927	6/ 551
Sellers, David Durwood	Jewell, Mary Selina	9 Mar 1930	7/ 426
Sellers, Harvey Leon	Morgan, Ruby Estelle	28 Nov 1929	7/ 377
Sermons, Bassie [B] [Orlando]	Hawkins, Bettie [Orlando]	25 Apr 1925	5/ 569
Servetas, Evangelos V.	Hoffman, Doris	28 Feb 1928	7/ 72
Seth, John R.	Hill, Evelyn C.	4 Sep 1928	7/ 181
Seven, Robert Ray	Bavar, Vania Margaret	30 Aug 1930	7/ 492
Sewell, Aubrey James	Johns, Birdie	18 Aug 1933	8/ 335
Sewell, Auby Ray	Condrey, Roxane Rosalind	5 Mar 1933	8/ 274
Sewell, Charles William	Story, Marjorie	24 Mar 1934	8/ 448

Sewell, Frank [W] [Leesburg]	Morgan, Mary [Bushnell]	22 Nov 1925	6/ 89
Sewell, John Ray [Winter Garden]	Thigpen, Etta [Ocoee]	3 Jan 1927	6/ 434
Sewell, Willie Herbert	Golden, Sarah Marie	21 Apr 1931	7/ 589
Sewell, Willie [Eatonville]	Davis, Arngetta [Eatonville]	17 May 1926	6/ 236
Sexton, James David	Boyd, Elsie Atkinson	13 May 1932	8/ 155
Seyle, Gustave Lee, Jr.	Morton, Ethellee Louise	8 Aug 1933	8/ 332
Seymour, King Frank	McFarlane, Elvira Maude	15 Oct 1927	6/ 598
Shadle, Thos. I.	Shaw, Evelyn V.	12 Nov 1927	7/ 10
Shaffer, Eugene [Apopka]	Greer, Annie E. B. [Leesburg]	4 Apr 1927	6/ 486
Shaffer, Joseph Ward [W] [Orlando]	Allen, Lillian Elizabeth	8 Jan 1926	6/ 143
Shaffer, Walter Warren	Marble, Doris Roberts	2 Apr 1934	8/ 454
Shambow, George H.	Storer, Bertha	6 Nov 1930	7/ 518
Shammy, Abdo	Jeandiville, Clara	7 Oct 1928	7/ 192
Shannon, Chester [Orlando]	Thomas, Clima Mae [Orlando]	4 Dec 1926	6/ 399
Shannon, Earl Hurden [Winter Park]	Wagner, Jean Wallace [Winter Park]	25 Nov 1926	6/ 394
Shannon, Richard Cutts	Jennings, Bertha Marguerite	3 Jun 1933	8/ 312
Shannon, Samuel	Genrett, Amelia	30 Nov 1933	8/ 376
Sharp, Cyrus Henry	Cadman, Janet Margery Radclyffe	10 Jun 1931	8/ 17
Sharp, Frank [Orlando]	Brower, Josephine [Orlando]	16 Mar 1926	6/ 179
Sharp, John Henry	Swanson, Enid L.	16 Jan 1932	8/ 108
Sharpe, Clyde Samuel	Johnson, Lucile Elizabeth	21 Aug 1926	6/ 333
Sharpe, Varney Melvin	Colson, Ruby Beryl	16 Dec 1932	8/ 229
Sharpe, William Raymond	Edmonson, Berta Mae	2 Nov 1927	7/ 7
Sharrill, William Edwin	Harvis, Ollie Mae	4 Feb 1930	7/ 409
Shaw, Bradford	Brown, Doretha	27 Apr 1929	7/ 283
Shaw, Byron A.	O'Hara, Lillian V.	8 Oct 1927	6/ 590
Shaw, Harry E. [W] [Philadelphia, PA]	Smith, M. Marguerite [Atlantic City]	5 Dec 1925	6/ 76
Shaw, John	Jones, Lillie Mae	24 Dec 1927	7/ 30
Shaw, Louis Talton [Orlando]	Anderson, Vera [Orlando]	20 Mar 1927	6/ 480
Shaw, Sam	Stamper, Minnie Lee	15 Oct 1920	7/ 194
Shealey, Jesse	Turner, Florence L.	14 Jan 1928	7/ 44
Shealy, John Andrew [W] [Dade City]	Carmack, Ida [Winter Garden]	24 Jun 1925	6/ 2
Shearer, Dewey Henry	Smith, Beatrice	8 Jul 1933	8/ 324
Shearon, Marion Eugene	Smith, Lula	21 Dec 1929	7/ 387
Shears, Richard Leon [Orlando]	Harrison, Dorothy Elberta [Orlando]	6 Jul 1926	6/ 288
Sheffield, Colquitt	White, Minnie Lee	15 Oct 1928	7/ 194
Shelley, Walter	Davis, Pearl	13 Aug 1929	7/ 335
Shelman, Charles F. [Cartersville, GA]	Leyonmarck, Georgiana H. [Chicago, IL]	1 May 1927	6/ 503
Shepard, Herschel Elwood	Fletcher, Martha Catherine	11 Jan 1929	7/ 229
Shepherd, Vernon [Orlando]	Kent, Emma B. [Lake City]	7 Dec 1926	6/ 402
Shepherd, W. B. K. [Ashtatula]	Carter, Effie [Ashtatula]	5 Oct 1925	6/ 57
Shepler, Martin Luther [Orlando]	Bauer, Jessie Marie [Orlando]	9 Jun 1926	6/ 265
Sheppard, Cecil Samuel	Morton, Annie Mae	14 Mar 1930	7/ 427
Sheppard, James Leonard [Lockhart]	Carter, Jeanette [Lockhart]	10 Nov 1926	6/ 379
Sherman, Hinre	Mathis, Corinna	14 Nov 1927	7/ 11
Sherman, Willie	McQueen, Rose	15 Feb 1932	8/ 117
Shipp, Ewen Cameron	Koenig, Caroline Harriet	3 Apr 1933	8/ 281
Shiver, Foy/Roy Lee [Orlando]	McAfee, Juanita Allene [Orlando]	15 Jan 1927	6/ 438
Shiver, J. H.	Shafter, Pearl	27 Jun 1934	8/ 500
Shores, Daniel N. [W] [Lakeland]	Lamb, Sidna Leola [Gotha]	31 May 1925	5/ 585

Short, Orvil John	Fink, Mary Louise	28 Jun 1930	7/ 474
Short, Raymond Charles [Orlando]	Baker, Belle [Winter Park]	1 Jul 1926	6/ 285
Shorter, Willie [B] [Orlando]	Ginyard, Geneva [Orlando]	3 May 1925	5/ 569
Shoup, Jacob H	Burgos, Adela Fales	17 Dec 1931	8/ 87
Shrewsbury, Robert Sidney	Dickinson, Nancy Victoria	25 Dec 1929	7/ 396
Shrigley, James William Jr.	Towns, Mary	16 Nov 1932	8/ 361
Shuler, Lincoln	Barnes, Martha	3 May 1931	7/ 593
Shumate, Charles Hugh	Upton, Dorothea Alice	27 Jun 1931	8/ 25
Shumater, Savage	Johnson, Lessie Mae	20 Dec 1930	7/ 531
Shunck, Ray Marshall [Toledo, OH]	Crabill, Phyllis [Toledo, OH]	23 Apr 1926	6/ 218
Sigal, Frank Henry	Safer, Ethel Mollie	12 Aug 1934	8/ 522
Silsby, Oliver Perry [W] [New Smyrna]	Woodward, Pearl Idella [New Smyrna]	23 Feb 1925	5/ 529
Silverstein, George Wallace	Lieberoff, Ida	14 Aug 1932	8/ 187
Simerly, Charles Thomas [W] [Orlando]	Doyen, Faye [Orlando]	20 Dec 1925	6/ 112
Simes, Hubert Eugene	Watson, Mildred Carol	17 Aug 1932	8/ 185
Simkees, Clyde	Treat, Anna	26 Aug 1930	7/ 491
Simmons, Alvin James	Howard, Naomi M.	7 Mar 1931	7/ 565
Simmons, Chris [Orlando]	Gardner, Mary [Winter Park]	22 Jul 1927	6/ 554
Simmons, E. H. [W] [Orlando]	Cooper, Gertrude [Orlando]	30 Jan 1926	6/ 146
Simmons, Elzo	Mike, Ros	4 Aug 1930	7/ 484
Simmons, Gennie	Hampton, Eloise	7 Apr 1931	7/ 576
Simmons, George Ralph	Prine, Lilah Thomas	2 Apr 1929	7/ 270
Simmons, Guy Frank	Tucker, Flossie Mae	10 Jun 1934	8/ 491
Simmons, Henry	Dodds, Edna Elizabeth	11 Jul 1931	8/ 32
Simmons, Jessie [Winter Park]	Washington, Ada [Winter Park]	28 Aug 1926	6/ 323
Simmons, Jewell Jackson	Hawks, Geneva L.	23 Dec 1932	8/ 231
Simmons, John [B] [Auburndale]	James, Hattie [Auburndale]	22 Apr 1925	5/ 562
Simmons, John Lacey	Daniel, Eddie Sue	11 Aug 1928	7/ 171
Simmons, Johnny	Jones, Lura Byrd	13 Aug 1928	7/ 171
Simmons, Pleasant Henry Askew	Green, Minnie	2 Dec 1933	8/ 377
Simmons, Robert	Thomas, Retha Mae	12 Sep 1932	8/ 197
Simmons, Sherman	Hamilton, Rosa Alice	4 Oct 1928	7/ 190
Simmons, Thomas Davis [Winter Park]	Ross, Lillie Rebecca [Orlando]	3 Feb 1927	6/ 452
Simonet, Floyd B.	Jacobsen, Katherine Anna	30 Aug 1929	7/ 338
Simonton, Amos Davidson	Goesswin, Sadie Emma	4 Jul 1928	7/ 160
Simpson, Dan Arthur	Sanders, Lelia Essie	15 Feb 1930	7/ 415
Simpson, David	Griffin, Altamese	4 Jun 1928	7/ 131
Simpson, Leslie	Written, Bernice	14 Apr 1932	8/ 142
Sims, Charles Oscar [Orlando]	Booth, Averil Kathaleen [Orlando]	14 Jun 1926	6/ 267
Sims, David [Orlando]	Miller, Assie/Ossie	22 Dec 1926	6/ 417
Sims, Frank Hall	Price, Rena Estelle	12 Sep 1932	8/ 195
Sims, George [Orlando]	Hinson, Bertha [Orlando]	1 May 1926	6/ 223
Sims, Harry	Baxter, Bessie G.	16 Mar 1930	7/ 459
Sims, James Henry	Jackson, Gracie Jane	18 May 1933	8/ 300
Sims, Lawrence	Hawks, Annie Sue	25 Mar 1928	7/ 87
Sims, Willie [Orlando]	Norman, Lucy [Orlando]	23 Oct 1926	6/ 361
Sims, Willoughby Bankston	Killen, Dimple	26 Mar 1932	8/ 135
Singer, Stanley Meyer [Orlando]	Fischer, Esther Helen [Orlando]	23 May 1926	6/ 245
Singleton, Abraham [Winter Park]	Grimes, Nadine [Winter Park]	22 Apr 1927	6/ 496
Singleton, Charlie	Jones, Melissa	13 Sep 1927	6/ 579
Singleton, Jessie [Winter Garden]	Johnson, Lucille [Winter Garden]	26 Apr 1926	6/ 219
Singleton, John R. [W] [Miami]	Peschman, Susanna Elizabeth [Winter Park]	10 May 1925	5/ 571

Siplin, Cornelius	Pool, Alice	30 May 1931	8/ 8
Siplin, Isrieal	Lee, Pauline	20 Feb 1932	8/ 118
Siplin, Issac	Richardson, Annie	4 Jan 1932	8/ 99
Siplin, William	Bennett, Susie Anna	6 Nov 1932	8/ 214
Sircy, Rosavelt [Orlando]	Butler, Hannah [Orlando]	16 May 1927	6/ 507
Sirlin, Simon Aloysius	Becker, Elsie Helen	7 Apr 1929	7/ 276
Sirmons, Theodora [Orlando]	Blue, Emma Jane [Orlando]	12 Jul 1926	6/ 303
Sissions, Arthur Lucas [Lockhart]	Outlaw, Mae [Lockhart]	1 Mar 1927	6/ 467
Sistrunk, Alvin Amos	Wade, Lillie Mae	27 Nov 1932	8/ 222
Sistrunk, Roy Edgar	Hart, Dorothy Emily May	27 Aug 1930	7/ 491
Siwerson, Sever Hanson [W] [DeLand]	Ross, Charlotte M. [DeLand]	18 Apr 1925	5/ 562
Skates, Leonard Guy	Gentry, Gladys Margaret	2 Dec 1933	8/ 383
Skellenger, Charles Leonard	Gould, Lillian	28 Jan 1930	7/ 407
Skelton, Kenneth William	Holloway, Clarise Beryl	6 Dec 1929	7/ 382
Skidmore, Hugh Puples	Fuller, Mary Ellen	16 Jun 1928	7/ 151
Skillman, Joseph Hagerman	Bridges, Lucy Mae	20 May 1932	8/ 161
Skipworth, Robert G.	Smith, Florence Irene	7 Jul 1928	7/ 157
Slade, Cab	Holloway, Estelle	15 Jun 1931	8/ 19
Slade, Joseph Madison	Browne, Kathleen Ruth	4 Jun 1934	8/ 488
Slager, Herman Emil [Orlando]	Cleary, Margaret Magdalen [Orlando]	20 May 1926	6/ 242
Slaughter, Harold Sylvanus	Roach, Sadie Harwell	6 Sep 1927	6/ 576
Slavik, Robert Latsy [Oviedo]	Brown, Kress [Goldenrod]	23 Sep 1925	6/ 51
Slayden, Travis LeGrande	Reppard, Alice Reville	28 Nov 1933	8/ 378
Slayton, Polk Decator	Dodd, Stella Mary	12 Jun 1933	8/ 312
Slemons, James Barco	Yon, Beatrice Octavia	2 Feb 1934	8/ 424
Sligh, Clarence Melvin	Tyndale, Alma Jewell	26 Mar 1932	8/ 133
Sloan, Anderson [Orlando]	Grant, Maggie [Orlando]	13 Oct 1925	6/ 61
Sloan, George Dexter	Weller, Maude	1 Oct 1929	7/ 355
Sloan, William Edward [B] [Orlando]	Simmons, Anna [Orlando]	7 Jan 1926	6/ 132
Slone, Odie Putnam	Poole, Verennia Willie	7 Sep 1929	7/ 341
Small, Benjamin C. [Miami]	Herndon, Eva A. [Miami]	12 Sep 1925	6/ 47
Small, Rosevelt	Branch, Mary	8 Jan 1934	8/ 405
Small, Walker [W] [Maitland]	Anderson, Ida [Maitland]	25 Mar 1925	5/ 547
Smalls, Hermona	Strafford, Willie Mae	16 Dec 1927	7/ 26
Smart, Arthur Francis	Ragland, Nellie Thomas	25 Jan 1932	8/ 111
Smart, Henry [B] [Orlando]	Lawhorn, Jessie Mae [Orlando]	5 Jan 1925	5/ 507
Smedley, William George	Humphries, Alberta June	30 Jun 1931	8/ 28
Smiley, Walter Wallace	Patey, Sophie Ann	15 Feb 1929	7/ 245
Smith, A. Grady [Orlando]	Slaughter, Minnie Gertrude [Orlando]	25 Oct 1925	6/ 69
Smith, Allen	Douglass, Katie	9 Dec 1926	6/ 404
Smith, Arthur DeForrest	Cadenhead, Nettie Mae	13 Feb 1932	8/ 116
Smith, Arthur William	Carter, Tempy Amanda	17 May 1934	8/ 477
Smith, Byron Jack	Schumaker, Gertrude Clarkin	15 Jul 1931	8/ 33
Smith, Cecil Kendrick	Buechnew, Clara Smith	21 Feb 1934	8/ 437
Smith, Charles Redding	Lee, Jessie Violette	5 May 1929	7/ 411
Smith, Charley Roger	Adkins, May Belle	12 Mar 1932	8/ 125
Smith, Clarence [B] [Orlando]	Hunter, Willie Mae [Orlando]	30 Mar 1925	5/ 549
Smith, Cord	Brown, Emma Lou	6 Apr 1929	7/ 274
Smith, Cordie B. [Winter Park]	Berry, Mattie Belle [Winter Park]	22 Mar 1926	6/ 185
Smith, Dorland O. [W] [Orange City]	McCarroll, Eleanor Leonora [Eustis]	30 Jul 1925	6/ 27

Smith, Edward Ellerbe [Orlando]	Walker, Carolyn [Kissimmee]	8 Feb 1926	6/ 152
Smith, Edward Owen	McFadden, Marie	22 Aug 1929	7/ 335
Smith, Frank Aloysius	Sager, Vera Marjorie	8 Apr 1929	7/ 277
Smith, Fred H. M. [Winter Garden]	Dodson, Loulie [Winter Garden]	9 May 1926	6/ 231
Smith, Frederick Burton [Winter Park]	Allemon, Anna Hinkle [Orlando]	26 Jun 1926	6/ 300
Smith, Frederick J., Jr.	Peterson, Nancy	3 Apr 1929	7/ 272
Smith, George [Orlando]	Bryant, Anna [Orlando]	4 Oct 1926	6/ 346
Smith, George [Orlando]	Daniels, Lillian [Orlando]	3 May 1926	6/ 226
Smith, George Eugene	Davenport, Elizabeth	18 Jul 1934	8/ 516
Smith, George M.	Keens, Johnnie Lee	26 Feb 1928	7/ 76
Smith, George W.	Sanders, Florence	28 Nov 1928	7/ 208
Smith, Glenn F.	Mahoffey, Lorena	8 Oct 1929	7/ 357
Smith, Handy	Mays, Georgia	9 Apr 1929	7/ 276
Smith, Harold Francis	Godbee, Anna Lou	19 Nov 1933	8/ 370
Smith, Harry Marion	Rogers, Kathryn Wyrelle	7 Jan 1929	7/ 231
Smith, Hector [Orlando]	Grizzle, Allie Mae [Orlando]	28 Mar 1927	6/ 483
Smith, Henry	Hill, Doris	14 Mar 1934	8/ 445
Smith, Herbert Joseph	Davis, Avie	14 Jul 1934	8/ 508
Smith, Horace Lord	McCardle, Eula Lee	27 Jan 1931	7/ 549
Smith, Horace Young	Row, Vivinne Leora	3 Mar 1929	7/ 261
Smith, Howard	Nix, Edith	29 Dec 1927	7/ 35
Smith, Howard Shirley	Grainge, Dorothy Emerick	20 May 1929	7/ 297
Smith, Ira [Plymouth]	Wilkeson, Willie Mae [Plymouth]	21 Sep 1926	6/ 348
Smith, James [Winter Garden]	Philips, Lula Lee [Winter Garden]	4 Apr 1927	7/ 127
Smith, James Daniel	Singleton, Ethel Irene	23 Oct 1933	8/ 354
Smith, James Willard [W] [Pinecastle]	Macey, Mildred [Pinecastle]	4 Jan 1925	5/ 509
Smith, James William	Smock, Dorothy Bernice	26 Nov 1931	8/ 81
Smith, John [Maitland]	Smith, Irene [Maitland]	10 Nov 1926	6/ 407
Smith, John Clay	Dunmire, Ida Mae	2 May 1928	7/ 108
Smith, John Edward	Grant, Elsie Rose	16 Nov 1927	7/ 13
Smith, John Henry	Rawls, Marguerite	20 Mar 1928	7/ 84
Smith, John Henry	Toy, Maggie	20 Jan 1929	7/ 234
Smith, John William	Champneys, Willie Mae	24 May 1928	7/ 120
Smith, Joseph Briggs [W] [Orlando]	Burns, Dora Lillian [Orlando]	23 Nov 1925	6/ 90
Smith, Joseph Frederick	Hayes, Delsa	17 May 1932	8/ 157
Smith, Junius [B] [Orlando]	Lester, Viola [Orlando]	5 Jan 1926	6/ 129
Smith, Leroy	Lewis, Annie Mae	4 Feb 1933	8/ 255
Smith, LeRoy [Orlando]	Thomas, Jennie [Orlando]	18 Oct 1925	6/ 68
Smith, Lloyd	Reid, Minnie	10 Nov 1927	7/ 11
Smith, Major Colra	McClyde, Samantha	5 Apr 1928	7/ 92
Smith, Manuel	Smith, Doretha	6 Jan 1934	8/ 403
Smith, McKinley	Patterson, Johnnie May	10 Oct 1927	6/ 591
Smith, Michael McKenzie, Jr.	Richardson, Virginia Lee	27 Dec 1930	7/ 534
Smith, Mike [Orlando]	Price, Olive Ethel [Kokomo, IN]	14 May 1926	6/ 235
Smith, Nelson	Dickson, Dorothy	4 Aug 1930	7/ 483
Smith, Oscar	Pickett, Willie Eugenia	18 Jul 1931	8/ 33
Smith, Otis Julian [Plymouth]	Stroup, Anna Belle [Plymouth]	11 Aug 1926	6/ 309
Smith, Paul LaVern	McReynolds, Leah Jane	10 Dec 1933	8/ 383
Smith, Paul [Winter Park]	Watson, Alberta [Winter Park]	3 May 1926	6/ 226
Smith, Ray Wilson [W] [Orlando]	Nichols, Esther Marie [Wichita, KS]	25 Nov 1925	5/ 97
Smith, Raymond	Winner, Birdie	29 Dec 1927	7/ 39
Smith, Rhea Marsh	Lockhart, Dorothy	5 Jun 1932	8/ 166

Smith, Robert Hampeliton	Williams, Ruth Winnie	13 Aug 1934	8/ 521
Smith, Robert [Orlando]	James, Easter [Orlando]	27 Mar 1926	6/ 191
Smith, Ruby Elmer	Boatwrigtht, Virgie	23 Jun 1929	7/ 314
Smith, Russell Taylor	Phillips, Ruth	3 Jun 1928	7/ 124
Smith, Sandy [B] [Birmingham, AL]	Jenkins, Lillie [Chatanooga TN]	14 Mar 1925	5/ 539
Smith, Talmadge G. [W] [Orlando]	Touchberry, Mattie [Orlando]	18 Nov 1925	6/ 84
Smith, Theodore William Henry [St. Cloud]	Entrican, Charlotte Garfield [Orlando]	14 Nov 1926	6/ 383
Smith, Thomas Ira	Rowell, Lillie	10 Feb 1932	8/ 115
Smith, Walter [Orlando]	Anderson, Geneva [Orlando]	26 Oct 1925	6/ 71
Smith, Wilis A.	Sigler, Virginia M.	30 Dec 1927	7/ 40
Smith, Will Foster [W] [Holopaw]	Regan, Ruby D. [Groveland]	30 Nov 1925	6/ 94
Smith, William Daniels	Bruner, Rose Corrine	22 Aug 1931	8/ 43
Smith, William Elliott	Brown, Mary Frances	3 Jun 1933	8/ 309
Smith, Williams	Bingham, Alberta	5 Jul 1929	7/ 329
Smith, Willie	McNair, Alice	13 Mar 1929	7/ 262
Smith, Ysadore [Orlando]	Smith, Hattie [Orlando]	8 Jul 1926	6/ 302
Smock, F. Monroe	MacDonald, Lena May	27 Feb 1930	7/ 421
Smothers, Frances Willard	Williams, Wynelle Gwendolyn	11 Jun 1930	7/ 466
Sneed, Ivroy	Ward, Lula	4 Apr 1929	7/ 272
Snider, Earl Baillie [Lake Worth]	Loidley, Janet Seales [Charleston, WV]	16 Nov 1926	6/ 386
Snodgrass, Albert Irvin	Rouse, Irma Valerie	21 Dec 1833	8/ 390
Snook, Jacob Levi	Burkheiser, Lydia	1 Apr 1929	7/ 272
Snow, Peter [Umatilla]	Casey, Lillian [Orlando]	7 Mar 1926	6/ 174
Snowden, Samuel Deward	Wilson, Willie Mae	14 Mar 1934	8/ 445
Snyder, George Thomas	Tanner, Pauline	28 Aug 1929	7/ 337
Snyder, Guy Marvin [Orlando]	Beach, Addie Lee [Orlando]	9 Apr 1926	6/ 202
Snyder, Houston Edward [Barberton, OH]	Bisnette, Lyda Critchfield [Miami]	8 Mar 1927	6/ 471
Sobliski, Ben [Petosky, MI]	Lucas, Niada [Petosky , MI]	10 Mar 1926	6/ 173
Soloman, Gordon [B] [Orlando]	Owens, Janie [Orlando]	18 Jul 1925	6/ 19
Solomon, Frank [Winter Park]	Williams, Carrie [Orlando]	8 Aug 1926	6/ 307
Solomon, George	Wesley, Mauziebelle	29 Sep 1932	8/ 201
Somers, Charles W.	Gilbert, May Alice	6 Jan 1930	7/ 396
Sommerville, James	Wallace, Jeanie Dorothy	30 Apr 1928	7/ 107
Sommons, Mosby	Anderson, Mabel	3 Oct 1929	7/ 357
Sooper, Australia	Davis, Sarah	14 Apr 1933	8/ 282
Sparkman, Guy Raymond	Easterly, Helen Erline	13 Jan 1934	8/ 413
Sparks, Q. P. [Winter Garden]	Prince, Ruth [Winter Garden]	27 Nov 1926	6/ 391
Sparling, Frank	Roberts, Marie	6 May 1929	7/ 290
Spear, Earl Wilford [Lakeland]	Childs, Nannie Christine [Pinecastle]	31 Jan 1926	6/ 172
Spear, Erle Williford	Ritzmann, Grace Louise	19 Feb 1933	8/ 260
Spease, Hanie Nathaniel [Winston Salem, NC]	Segler, Neurel [Ariton, AL]	25 Nov 1926	6/ 393
Speer, Samuel William	McGuire, Susie Carmaleta	21 Nov 1933	8/ 371
Speight, Robert	Irving, Dolly	25 Oct 1931	8/ 67
Speights, Abraham	Tanner, Beulah	3 Feb 1934	8/ 429
Spencer, William Brooks	Grissom, Dorothy E.	23 Feb 1928	7/ 72
Sphaler, Hollis [Orlando]	Hall, Zella [Orlando]	17 Oct 1925	6/ 66
Sphaler, Oscar	Futch, Ethridge	10 Apr 1929	7/ 277
Spinks, Jack A.	Graham, Gladys Fielde	28 Jun 1934	8/ 505
Spinks, Roy A.	Saunders, Helen A.	27 Mar 1928	7/ 89
Spires, Abraham	Stokes, Josephine	12 Mar 1930	7/ 425

Spivey, Amos Daniel	Hogan, Fauniece	7 May 1933	8/ 296
Spivey, Cornelius R.	Grantham, Ruby	30 Mar 1929	7/ 270
Spivey, Edward L. [Orlando]	Tomlinson, Lorna [Orlando]	24 Oct 1925	6/ 72
Spivey, John Morgan	Johnson, Carrie	25 Sep 1933	8/ 344
Spivey, John Wallace	Brown, Evelyn	22 Nov 1933	8/ 372
Springs, Eddie	Allen, Alma	1 Dec 1927	7/ 17
Sprolden, Glennie Anderson	Clemons, Mabel	13 Jul 1931	8/ 32
Stacey, Ralph Anderson [Orlando]	Reynolds, Dorothy Agnes [Orlando]	25 Apr 1927	6/ 501
Stacy, Adrain L. [W] [Orlando]	Dye, Clyde E. [Orlando]	16 Dec 1925	6/ 121
Stadlinger, Peter Alfred	Hoefler, Minnie A.	3 Apr 1934	8/ 457
Stafford, Donald [B] [Lake City]	Mitchell, Helen Veroy [Orlando]	25 Oct 1925	6/ 80
Stair, Ollie [Sanford]	Garmon, Jeppie [Lake Monroe]	4 Jun 1927	6/ 524
Staley, Edmund M.	Harris, Sarah	22 Nov 1927	7/ 15
Stallings, Everett Elic [W] [Orlando]	Betts, Eunice Davis [Winter Park]	23 Dec 1925	6/ 116
Stalnaker, C. G. [Orlando]	Hubbard, Marie [Orlando]	9 Jul 1926	6/ 315
Stalnaker, Corliss Gray	Hancock, Vivian Belle	4 Jan 1932	8/ 99
Staluacker, Sam [Pinecastle]	Davie, Rachel [Pinecastle]	21 Aug 1926	6/ 320
Stanaland, Eart	Henderson, Jewell	10 Nov 1928	7/ 202
Stanfield, Lawrence Monroe	Wilder, Edith Merritt	7 Mar 1932	8/ 123
Stanford, Clarence Leslie [Oakland]	Sadler, Clara Edith [Oakland]	29 Oct 1926	6/ 384
Stanley, Guy Mitchell	Davis, Pansy Belle	27 Jan 1934	8/ 418
Stanley, Henry [Orlando]	Smith, Jessie [Orlando]	18 Jun 1927	6/ 538
Stanley, Ira [W] [Winter Park]	Woodard, May Baird [Winter Park]	8 Jun 1925	5/ 596
Stanley, James Savage Jr.	Lucius, Thelma Oleeta	28 Jul 1934	8/ 517
Stansell, Herbert	Cadwell, Bertha	5 Feb 1929	7/ 241
Stansill, Ethridge [Winter Garden]	Thornton, Hilda [Winter Garden]	12 Feb 1926	6/ 157
Staples, Clarence Eugene [Orlando]	Goodman, Ruby Lee [Orlando]	20 Sep 1926	6/ 340
Stapleton, George Edward	Griffin, Janice	16 Mar 1930	7/ 428
Stark, Ervin A.	Mathews, Helen	3 Oct 1929	7/ 353
Stark, Kenneth Espy	Steele, Grace Elizabeth	31 Oct 1931	8/ 71
Starkweather, Clarence Hugh	Johnson, Virginia	5 May 1932	8/ 153
Starling, Alvin A.	Robbins, Ada Mae	2 Jun 1928	7/ 128
Starling, Carson Gary	Thompson, Dorothy Carlyn	30 Jun 1928	7/ 153
Starling, Elijah	Phillips, Annie	28 Jul 1928	7/ 166
Starling, William Thomas	Elliott, Anna Caroline	9 Aug 1930	7/ 503
Starr, Frank M. [W] [Kissimmee]	Breed, Rae Elizabeth [Kissimmee]	30 Dec 1925	6/ 122
Starr, Heth Caufield	Price, Bessie Frances	11 Jun 1928	7/ 137
Statt, Francis	Barn, Catherine	16 Jun 1928	7/ 141
Stebbins, Charlie Clayton	Koonce, Celeste Susie	18 Oct 1933	8/ 353
Stebbins, Frank Whitfield	Daniels, Eleanor Josephine	29 Dec 1928	7/ 226
Steck, Richard Carroll	McKenney, Helen	2 Dec 1927	7/ 26
Steed, Walter [B] [Orlando]	Gelison, Carrie W. [Orlando]	29 Jun 1925	6/ 6
Steele, Richard Floyd	Hickman, Elsie Elizabeth	3 Apr 1933	8/ 279
Steele, Sam	Blount, Mary	10 Sep 1927	6/ 580
Steely, Ezek [Carbondale, IL]	Phifer, Bonnie [Carbondale, IL]	17 Feb 1927	6/ 460
Stein, Louis Templeman [Tampa]	Baldwin, Lillian Taylor [Tampa]	10 Jun 1926	6/ 266
Stephens, George Edward	Davis, Marian	2 Feb 1928	7/ 152
Stephens, Joseph Benjamin	Douberly, Mary B.	12 Apr 1930	7/ 438
Stephens, Proctor Cullen	Smith, Emily Beatrice	17 Jun 1933	8/ 317
Stephens, William Arthur	Jordan, Thelma Rutledge	11 Oct 1932	8/ 209
Stephenson, Howard Edmondson	Austin, Elsie Christine	14 Dec 1929	7/ 385
Steplight, Andrew [B] [Oakland]	Jefferson, Gertrude [Oakland]	19 Jul 1925	6/ 23

Steplight, Augusta [B] [Oakland]	Hampton, Ella [Oakland]	15 Nov 1925	6/ 88
Stevens, Albert [Orlando]	Reed, Daisy [Orlando]	15 Mar 1927	6/ 476
Stevens, Felton Stanley	Hamilton, Edna	18 Jul 1932	8/ 179
Stevens, Jesse James	Marlor, Lois Geneva	18 Nov 1929	7/ 372
Stevens, Joe	Mason, Nell	3 Feb 1933	8/ 266
Stevens, Joe	Hinson, Mamie	1 Jan 1930	7/ 393
Stevens, Joe [Orlando]	Hamilton, Mary [Orlando]	6 Mar 1926	6/ 170
Stevens, Mallachi [Orlando]	Carter, Vera [Orlando]	16 Jul 1927	6/ 552
Stevens, Reuben	Lee, Doris	24 Dec 1931	8/ 95
Stevens, Thomas Jefferson	Odom, Eleanor	2 Dec 1933	8/ 381
Stevenson, Wheeler [Orlando]	Wells, Leona [Orlando]	8 Sep 1926	6/ 334
Steverson, Ed [B] [Orlando]	Johnson, Leola Gertrude [Orlando]	5 Jan 1925	5/ 507
Steverson, Mallie C.	Freeman, Ida Mae	17 Dec 1930	7/ 530
Steward, Charles James	Sirmons, Lillie	15 Oct 1928	7/ 193
Steward, James Henry [Orlando]	Code, Hattie [Orlando]	20 Feb 1926	6/ 161
Stewart, Bishop [B] [Orlando]	Simmons, Elizabeth [Orlando]	7 Jun 1925	5/ 592
Stewart, Jimmie Walker	Swope, Mary Orton	7 Apr 1934	8/ 456
Stewart, Junious	Spaulding, Gertrude	23 May 1933	8/ 303
Stewart, Nathaniel Lewis	Sams, Jane Sheldon	20 Sep 1931	8/ 51
Stewart, Samuel David	Alford, Norma Catherine	1 Feb 1934	8/ 421
Stewart, Samuel David	Knight, Margaret Beatrice	25 Feb 1928	7/ 70
Stewart, Troy [Orlando]	Wallace, Jimmie Lee [Orlando]	24 Mar 1926	6/ 188
Stewart, Walter Hillbold [Jacksonville]	Watterson, Marguretta [Kalida, OH]	15 Oct 1926	6/ 376
Stewart, William	Windsor, Eunice Lee	23 Jun 1933	8/ 315
Stickland, John Amos	Ellis, Irma Dean June	15 Feb 1930	7/ 420
Stimpson, David Harold	Calhoun, Hettie Irene	28 Apr 1928	7/ 106
Stimpson, Kenneth Luther	Robinson, Ardath Gregg	1 Jun 1934	8/ 484
Stingel, John M. [W] [Orlando]	Millington, Amanda [Orlando]	1 Aug 1925	6/ 27
Stinson, James Arthur	Eaton, Fannie Louise	20 Jun 1931	8/ 38
Stockton, Elza Pizoria	Brooks, Annie Lee	27 Aug 1928	7/ 177
Stockton, Rex Dewey	Dean, Sarah Lee	13 Sep 1930	7/ 496
Stockton, Robert Franklin	Miller, Mary Elizabeth	16 Feb 1934	8/ 434
Stoecker, Ernest Gottlieb	Griffin, Willie Mae	27 Sep 1932	8/ 200
Stokes, Joe	Jackson, Roberter	18 Dec 1930	7/ 532
Stokes, Oliver Obed [W] [Apopka]	Newmans, Senia [Apopka]	6 Feb 1925	5/ 522
Stokes, Thomas Mathew	Sightler, Blanche	1 Oct 1932	8/ 202
Stokes, William German	Thompson, Lela Mai	18 Jan 1930	7/ 403
Stolze, Otto Frederick [St.Louis, MO]	Thatcher, Viola Ruth	4 Sep 1926	6/ 339
Stone, Guy Christian	Humphries, Sallie Mae	14 Jan 1930	7/ 401
Stone, Hector Ambrose [W] [Orlando]	Ammons, Leola [Sumerton, NC]	7 Apr 1925	5/ 555
Stone, Hubert	Roundtree, Patsy	10 Apr 1933	8/ 282
Stone, Jerome [W] [St Cloud]	Parkinson, Catherine Porter [St Cloud]	4 Mar 1925	5/ 534
Stone, Roy B.	Bullard, Eunice	13 Jun 1929	7/ 316
Stoneburn, William	Froelich, Minnie	27 Sep 1927	6/ 587
Stontamire, Paschal Wesley [Salem, VA]	Petrie, Jessie Margaret [Mitchell, SD]	24 Feb 1926	6/ 168
Story, Collie	Thompson, Mary Pauline	25 Jun 1934	8/ 501
Story, Warren L. [W] [Lake Gem]	Redditt, Sophia Margaret [Orlando]	29 Jun 1925	6/ 8
Stoudenmire, John Lee	Bridzman, Sarah Margaret	18 Dec 1929	7/ 385
Stout, Wm. Alfred [Huntington, WV]	Stout, Lena V. [Huntington, WV]	11 Mar 1926	6/ 176
Stover, John Truesdale [W] [Maitland]	Gatlin, Annie [Maitland]	11 Jun 1925	5/ 594

Stover, Leonard Amos [Orlando]	Cruze, Elsie Bonita	22 Jun 1927	6/ 540
Stover, Marion Rogers	Clark, Ruby Neel	25 Dec 1927	7/ 31
Stowe, Elmer Harvey	Jones, Ruth Hazel	1 Jan 1932	8/ 98
Stowe, Robert Eugene	Brabant, Meyon Marie	28 May 1931	8/ 7
Strain, Samuel [Formosa]	Jones, Bertha Inez [Red Springs, NC]	6 Dec 1926	6/ 403
Stranahan, Elmer Wiley [W] [Apopka]	Kirkland, Myrtle [Apopka]	28 Nov 1925	6/ 93
Streetman, L .M.	Hancock, Clara Emerson	14 Oct 1933	8/ 351
Stribling, William Levi	Howard, Mertie Lee	29 May 1929	7/ 299
Strickland, Quitman A.	Sweat, Edna Louise	16 Jan 1930	7/ 405
Strickland, Samuel Gaulden	Paul, Frances Rita	8 Sep 1929	7/ 343
Strickland, William Goss	Weinberg, Elinor Wesley	26 Jun 1933	8/ 24
Strickle, Roy Samuel	Roberts, Helen Frances	8 Jul 1933	8/ 323
Stricklen, Grady [Winter Garden]	Danford, Lulu May [Winter Garden]	3 Oct 1925	6/ 56
Strickler, Bowman Herbert [Vero Beach]	Colburtson, Bess May [Vero Beach]	2 Mar 1926	6/ 192
Stringer, O. Krehl	Hinkley, Margaret Jennie	9 Aug 1932	8/ 182
Strobert, Abraham [Orlando]	Favors, Dauk [Orlando]	12 Mar 1927	6/ 472
Stroud, James Adele	Selleck, Hazel Frances	21 May 1932	8/ 158
Strozier, Fred Lewis [Tarpon Springs]	Clickley, Annie Lee [Tarpon Springs]	20 Aug 1927	6/ 570
Stryker, Frank Richard	Titus, Bertha Rose	15 Apr 1928	7/ 99
Stubb, Robert [B] [Orlando]	Lawrence, Bessie [Orlando]	7 Jan 1925	5/ 510
Stucker, Cliff	Rivers, May	22 Aug 1930	7/ 489
Stuckey, Lem	Lewis, Rebecca	26 Mar 1931	7/ 571
Stuckey, Linzus [Orlando]	Turner, Juanita [Orlando]	30 Aug 1926	6/ 324
Stukes, Jarot	Arnold, Rosa	21 May 1930	7/ 458
Sturdivant, Robert	Chapman, May	5 Sep 1931	8/ 48
Sturges, Charles Herbert	Bush, Lizzie Louise	11 Oct 1930	7/ 508
Sturges, George Stilson	Cain, Mable June	19 Mar 1932	8/ 128
Suggs, Jno. Henry [W] [Orlando]	Stiles, Mabel [Ocoee]	30 May 1925	5/ 583
Sullivan, Egel L.	Jackson, Annie Lizzie	13 Oct 1928	7/ 190
Sullivan, Marcus Mattison	Stanton, Emma Harvie	28 May 1932	8/ 171
Sullivan, Prater [Winter Park]	Young, Lola [Winter Park]	27 Dec 1926	6/ 420
Summers, George Cameron [Gotha]	Lamb, Maggie Lean [Gotha]	24 Jun 1927	6/ 529
Summers, Robert Gray [W] [Orlando]	Moore, Frances Katherine [Orlando]	17 Jun 1925	5/ 587
Summers, William Cornelius	Dungan, Elizabeth	24 Dec 1927	7/ 60
Sumner, David Franklin [Orlando]	Jones, Pearl [Orlando]	24 Jan 1927	6/ 447
Sungster, Dewey	Farmer, Liona	18 Jan 1929	7/ 233
Surrency, Millard Houston	Spriggs, Janie	26 Apr 1931	7/ 592
Sutch, John Albert, Jr. [Winter Park]	Enlow, Beatrice [Winter Park]	1 Jun 1927	6/ 523
Sutherland, Oscar [New Smyrna]	Hetrick, Helen [Mt Gilead, OH]	16 Mar 1926	6/ 179
Sutherland, Paul Alexander	Cunningham, Edythe Lucille	16 Apr 1934	8/ 462
Sutliff, Orja Leslie [W] [Winter Park]	Beall, Catherine Elizabeth [Winter Park]	9 Jun 1925	5/ 590
Sutton, Alexander	Day, Essie May	17 Sep 1929	7/ 351
Sutton, Shedrick	Winters, Rosetta	24 Jun 1929	7/ 314
Sutton, William Leonard [Orlando]	Harrison, Thelma Phyllis [Orlando]	29 Jul 1926	6/ 294
Swain, Roosevelt [Orlando]	Williams, Ethel Lee	20 Feb 1926	6/ 161
Swain, William Bryan	Pease, Bernice	3 Apr 1931	7/ 574
Swann, Ben	Hill, Mattie	3 Sep 1932	8/ 189
Sweet, Lloyd Milford	O'Connor, Mary Virginia	2 Apr 1932	8/ 137
Swilley, James Thompson	Berry, Hazel May	10 Apr 1933	8/ 281
Swindel, Dewey	Drysdale, Evelyn Moore	30 Sep 1929	7/ 354
Swope, Sidney Macum	Deale, Jean	24 Mar 1932	8/ 134
Swope, Templeton Wilson [Orlando]	Masteller, Sarah Elizabeth [Orlando]	1 Jun 1926	6/ 257

Sylvester, LeRoy	Sloane, Rosa	7 Dec 1929	7/ 381
Symonds, Charles Alfred	Johanne, Emily	20 Apr 1930	7/ 442
Symonds, Kenneth Rowland	Connell, Wilma	26 Nov 1932	8/ 224
Szugs, Stephen H. [Miami]	Swink, Lillian Keren [Titusville]	7 Aug 1927	6/ 572

T

Tabor, Carl Ed [W] [Clermont]	Bekemeyer, Margaret Ernestine [Winter Garden]	11 May 1925	5/ 571
Talbott, Donald Owen	Anders, Cora Belle	9 May 1933	8/ 298
Talbott, Thomas Metcalfe [W] [Orlando]	Vaughn, Thelma C. [Orlando]	5 Dec 1925	6/ 120
Talmage, Robert W. [Orlando]	Bethes, Elizabeth Stewart [Orlando]	11 Oct 1926	6/ 352
Talman, Howard Parker [San Francisco, CA]	Patronella, Claire [Winter Park]	31 Jul 1926	6/ 293
Talton, Delmos Jackson	Cayll, Juliet Thelma	4 Oct 1931	8/ 55
Tamney, Maurice [Orlando]	Selemann, Marie [Orlando]	20 Jul 1926	6/ 278
Tandy, William H.	Whitfield, Ruth	18 Aug 1928	7/ 177
Tankersley, Willie [Orlando]	Lewis, Tressie [Orlando]	13 Mar 1926	6/ 178
Tanner, Asa Monroe	Mack, Sara Lee	30 Mar 1929	7/ 270
Tanner, Cleveland [Orlando]	Davis, Clara Mae [Orlando]	18 Mar 1927	6/ 479
Tanner, Elwood Mitchell [W] [Winter Garden]	Phillips, Mary Vea [Winter Garden]	2 Jun 1925	5/ 598
Tannery, Kletner Carleton [W] [Orlando]	Hudson, Kate Pauline [Orlando]	26 Dec 1925	6/ 122
Tarker, Lorenzo	Tyler, Hazel	16 Apr 1928	7/ 103
Tate, Harrison	Wheeler, Ethel Madeline	17 Feb 1929	7/ 246
Tate, Haywood	Keagler, Marie Lou	11 Feb 1929	7/ 244
Tate, Iven	Scott, Senetta	22 Jul 1931	8/ 35
Tatlow, Job Malcolm [Plymouth]	Yeatman, Clara Arlene [Cairo, GA]	30 Jun 1926	6/ 284
Tatum, Robert Reid [W] [Winter Park]	Deane, Ruth Ernestine [Winter Park]	23 Dec 1925	6/ 116
Taylor, Adolph Julius [Orlando]	Cody, Geneva [Orlando]	4 Nov 1926	6/ 374
Taylor, Alvah Milton	Solomon, Annie Julia	29 Jan 1928	7/ 54
Taylor, Charlie [B] [Orlando]	Dubose, Ida [Orlando]	7 Jun 1925	5/ 592
Taylor, Clyde	Schnur, Mary Ann	3 Sep 1932	8/ 193
Taylor, Dan	Roan, Joseph Catherine	21 Apr 1934	8/ 464
Taylor, Earl	Hudson, Emma	16 Oct 1930	7/ 508
Taylor, Eddie	Johnson, Daisy	4 Apr 1931	7/ 574
Taylor, Frank Albert	Ivey, Anna Della	19 Nov 1933	8/ 373
Taylor, Frank Shannon	Russell, Edith Jane	24 Sep 1931	8/ 53
Taylor, Frederick Leslie	Fresh, Lillie Alliene	21 Apr 1934	8/ 466
Taylor, Hamp [B] [Orlando]	Baker, Ada [Orlando]	7 Nov 1925	6/ 78
Taylor, Henry	Davis, Estelle Brooks	21 Mar 1932	8/ 128
Taylor, James Baker	Harris, Verona Lillian	2 Dec 1931	8/ 83
Taylor, Joe [Orlando]	Harris, Hester [Orlando]	11 Jun 1927	6/ 537
Taylor, John Henry	Wilson, Robella Sallie	21 Dec 1930	7/ 532
Taylor, L. D.	Brown, Novella	16 Jan 1932	8/ 106
Taylor, L. T.	Collins, Ruby Lee	13 Jan 1929	7/ 230
Taylor, Lewis Lynch [Orlando]	Coleman, Essie Leigh [Orlando]	22 Apr 1926	6/ 223
Taylor, Maxie	Walter, Sadie	21 Jan 1933	8/ 248
Taylor, Merno	Brown, Thelma Lee	17 Oct 1931	8/ 60
Taylor, Oliver	Rand, Essie Mae	26 Oct 1927	7/ 1
Taylor, Willie [Orlando]	Turner, Maggie [Orlando]	26 May 1926	6/ 249
Taylor, Wm. [Orlando]	Burr, Helen [Orlando]	10 Apr 1926	6/ 202

Teague, Francis Andrew	Hammond, Margaret Louise	23 Aug 1928	7/ 182
Teal, William Paul [Winter Garden]	Fulmer, Robbye [Winter Garden]	3 Oct 1926	6/ 346
Teate, Austin	Jackson, Lela Mae	31 Oct 1929	7/ 363
Teate, Jeffrey	Williams, Gladys	19 Oct 1932	8/ 205
Tedder, Charlie Wyatt [Orlando]	Varner, Vera [Orlando]	25 Mar 1926	6/ 189
Telden, Robert Willis	Bryant, Eveley	10 Feb 1930	7/ 414
Tell, Harvey Frederick	Baker, Frances Virginia	5 Jul 1928	7/ 157
Ten Brink, Arthur Albert [Orlando]	Mathis, Viola [Orlando]	10 Apr 1926	6/ 203
Ternest, Albert Lee	Smith, Jennieve	28 Jun 1934	8/ 503
Terrel, Sylvester	Warren, Beulah	27 Oct 1933	8/ 355
Terry, Lawrence [Orlando]	Patrick, Gertrude [Orlando]	23 Dec 1926	6/ 414
Teston, Ollie Lee	Faulkner, Helen	28 Apr 1928	7/ 105
Testsment, Will	Weaver, Millan	12 Nov 1930	7/ 520
Thames, Otha Terrill	Scarborough, Georgia Anna	26 May 1934	8/ 486
Thayer, Lawrence Lyle [Bunnell]	McFarland, Margaret Elizabeth [Ocoee]	27 Apr 1927	6/ 502
Therry, Gerald Edward	Edwards, May Rogers	21 Jul 1932	8/ 179
Thieme, Martin Nathaniel	Fischer, Sophia Anna	3 Nov 1933	8/ 363
Thigpen, A. M.	Crawford, Margaret Evelyn	18 Aug 1934	8/ 524
Thigpen, George Homer	Soles, Lula Inez	25 Jan 1934	8/ 417
Thigpen, John L.	Barks, Lois	12 Jan 1929	7/ 230
Thollander, Egon Maron	Sulstycki, Ruth Romone	22 Jul 1930	7/ 481
Thomas, Allen [Orlando]	Neblack, Hattie [Orlando]	11 Jun 1927	6/ 533
Thomas, Asbey [Orlando]	Carelock, Ina [Orlando]	31 Aug 1926	6/ 325
Thomas, Chester Emmett [B] [Orlando]	Potts, Hattie [Orlando]	8 Jan 1925	5/ 509
Thomas, Earnest [B] [Orlando]	Quarterman, Juanita [Orlando]	14 Mar 1925	5/ 540
Thomas, Emory Curtis	Wright, Velma Gladys	16 Nov 1927	7/ 15
Thomas, Essie	Roberson, Louise	17 Mar 1930	7/ 427
Thomas, Eugene	Bowen, Agnes Ethel	8 Jun 1931	8/ 13
Thomas, Fred [Orlando]	Ween, Alvesta [Orlando]	19 Jun 1926	6/ 274
Thomas, Fred James	Harvey, Lucy	15 Sep 1931	8/ 50
Thomas, George Allen	Goodwyn, Sarah Ruth	29 Apr 1932	8/ 150
Thomas, Gus [Orlando]	Simmons, Victoria [Orlando]	21 Aug 1926	6/ 317
Thomas, Henry	Leonard, Annie Lizzie	11 Jan 1932	8/ 102
Thomas, Henry	Townsend, Laura	14 Mar 1932	8/ 126
Thomas, Herman J.	Wilson, Alma	24 Dec 1927	7/ 37
Thomas, Howard Lewis	Strickland, Lorie	16 May 1932	8/ 157
Thomas, Joe [Orlando]	Horn, Ida [Orlando]	9 Jul 1927	6/ 548
Thomas, John	Keaton, Eugene	26 Nov 1933	8/ 375
Thomas, John	Tiner, Nancy	18 Aug 1928	7/ 173
Thomas, John [B] [Apopka]	Mitchell, Emma [Apopka]	30 Apr 1925	5/ 566
Thomas, John Willie	Price, Willie Ett	23 May 1928	7/ 118
Thomas, Joseph Morrison	Deloach, Zona	12 May 1931	8/ 2
Thomas, Laurie Jean [W] [Orlando]	Butler, Ruby Earl [Orlando]	2 May 1925	5/ 567
Thomas, Manzie	Culver, Minnie Belle	26 May 1928	7/ 119
Thomas, Offa [Orlando]	Ray, Joette [Orlando]	27 Sep 1925	6/ 54
Thomas, Owen W. [Orlando]	Smith, Kathryn [Orlando]	8 Dec 1926	6/ 406
Thomas, Paul [Sanford]	Graves, Francis Cleo [Sanford]	31 May 1927	6/ 519
Thomas, Robert	Brown, Ethel	1 Jul 1933	8/ 320
Thomas, Robert Smith	Mason, Margaret Ferris	30 Apr 1933	8/ 294
Thomas, V. Artie	Fulton, Verdell	7 Aug 1934	8/ 519
Thomas, Walter Wesley	Singleton, Geraldine Lubertha	8 Dec 1930	7/ 528
Thomas, William [Apopka]	Gardner, Queenie V. [Ocala]	21 Oct 1925	6/ 68

Thomas, Wimer [Orlando]	Glenn, Ethel Irene [Orlando]	14 Aug 1926	6/ 308
Thompson, Arthur Jr.	King, Mary Essie	4 Oct 1933	8/ 348
Thompson, Bonny [Orlando]	Young, Nellie Lee [Orlando]	27 Oct 1925	6/ 70
Thompson, Jasper	Morgan, Susie	2 Feb 1929	7/ 239
Thompson, John Daniel [B] [Conway]	Farris, Cora [Taft]	4 Jun 1925	5/ 598
Thompson, Leslie	Deese, Marie Zelia	18 May 1926	6/ 241
Thompson, Nathaniel	Garrett, Willie Mae	30 Oct 1932	8/ 211
Thompson, Reuben	McGiven, Lissie	4 Sep 1929	7/ 339
Thompson, Robert Bruce [Winter Park]	Ribby, Lena Delia [Winter Park]	20 Apr 1926	6/ 217
Thompson, Robert Lee	Johnson, Callie Mae	19 Apr 1930	7/ 441
Thompson, Wayne Garren	Watts, Evelyn Mabel	2 Jul 1933	8/ 319
Thompson, William Chester	Shealy, Grace Alberta	28 May 1931	8/ 6
Thompson, William Robert	Mathews, Mary A.	14 Jan 1929	7/ 230
Thompson, William Wiley [W] [Ocoee]	Howell, Alma Arlena [Bushnell, GA]	5 Mar 1925	5/ 535
Thornton, Edwin Burton	Hoeltke, Emma Louise	26 Aug 1928	7/ 178
Thornton, George [B] [Orlando]	Harrison, Stella [Orlando]	25 Jul 1925	6/ 24
Thornton, Marion Calloway	Julian, Ora Cecil	30 Jul 1934	8/ 516
Thorpe, Alonzo	Kirby, Alice	12 Aug 1929	7/ 331
Thrailkill, John William [W] [Sanford]	Kent, Geraldine [Sanford]	5 Jan 1925	5/ 508
Thuemling, A. Julius [W] [Chicago, IL]	Heise, Rose [Chicago, IL]	12 Mar 1925	5/ 538
Thurmond, Harold Hale	Sewell, Vera Irene	29 May 1928	7/ 122
Tibbits, Walace Fay	Johnson, Gladys Zell	19 Feb 1929	7/ 248
Tibbs, Edwin Almond [W] [Arvada, WY]	Griffin, Mamie Viola [Arvada, WY]	14 Jan 1926	6/ 134
Tichenor, Maurice Stafford	James, Edna Joy	19 May 1934	8/ 480
Tiedeman, Herbert Alonzo	Zeigler, Gertrude	8 Feb 1933	8/ 256
Tigg, McKinley [W] [Taft]	Alford, Ella Marie	7 Dec 1925	6/ 96
Tigner, Urban Cooper	Shuts, Kathryn Alfreda	19 Jan 1931	7/ 552
Tiller, William H. [W] [Orlando]	Arvin, Mary W. [Orlando]	28 Mar 1925	5/ 548
Tillman, Dennis	Drake, Rosa	2 Oct 1929	7/ 352
Tillman, Joe [Orlando]	Turner, Tuell [Orlando]	20 Mar 1926	6/ 183
Tillman, Robert	Richardson, Bertha	6 Feb 1931	7/ 552
Tillman, Robert [Winter Garden]	Boise, Maggie [Winter Garden]	2 Dec 1926	6/ 397
Timberlake, Jerald Dean	Bolden, Sarah	8 Dec 1927	7/ 21
Timmons, Henry [B] [Orlando]	Wesley, Geneva [Orlando]	16 May 1925	5/ 574
Timoor, Charles [W] [Los Angeles CA]	Larian, Emma Bay [Orlando]	11 Jul 1925	6/ 15
Tindall, Claude Alfred	Veronee, Alma	13 Apr 1933	8/ 283
Tindall, Guy Cleveland	Eldridge, Beatrice Alice	23 Dec 1933	8/ 392
Tindall, James Clay	Statter, Thelma Elaine	14 Jun 1931	8/ 19
Tindall, Maxwell B.	Toops, Marthelle Gwenevere	4 Feb 1933	8/ 264
Tindell, Rolland James	Jacobs, Mertie Irene	21 Aug 1930	7/ 492
Tinker, Joseph Bert, Jr.	Barnes, Susan Yowell	14 Feb 1931	7/ 555
Tinsley, Jerry	Spencer, E. Lillian	3 Apr 1928	7/ 127
Tinsley, Joe [B] [Orlando]	McCullouch, Rosa Lee [Orlando]	23 Jul 1925	6/ 23
Tipple, Ross [Union City IN]	White, Dollie [Orlando]	31 Oct 1925	6/ 72
Tips, Walter Henry [New York NY]	Marr, Mildred Grace [Hampten Highlands M_?]	23 Jul 1926	6/ 276
Tison, Owen E.	Fields, Zudie E.	22 Sep 1928	7/ 186
Todd, John Edward	Williams, Rae H.	18 Jul 1934	8/ 511
Todd, Meyrl [Willsville, OH]	Anderson, Ethel Jane [Huntington, WV]	2 Nov 1926	6/ 372
Tolbert, John William	Hoyt, Mildred Virginia	12 Nov 1933	8/ 364

Toles, Francis Henry Joseph	Thomas, Katherine Louise	25 Nov 1933	8/ 375
Tomer, William Albert	Taylor, Susie Alice	4 Feb 1934	8/ 427
Tomey, Willian N. [W] [Groveland]	Tomey, Anna C. [Groveland]	21 Jun 1925	6/ 3
Tomlin, Andrew	Corbett, Fronnie	28 Feb 1932	8/ 120
Tomlinson, Carleton Young	Adams, Myrtle Frances	18 Feb 1933	8/ 259
Tomlinson, Joe [Orlando]	Davis, Essie [Orlando]	30 Jun 1926	6/ 253
Tomlinson, Thomas Webb	Parrish, Edith Irene	27 Jul 1931	8/ 36
Tomlinson, Walter Harris	Lee, Laura Alberta	22 Sep 1928	7/ 188
Tompkins, Clyde [Orlando]	Sapp, Dora [Orlando]	21 Apr 1926	6/ 206
Toms, Warner Scott	Partin, Beatrice Burnel	22 Dec 1931	8/ 93
Toole, Allen G.	Olson, Anna S.	10 Sep 1927	6/ 578
Toole, Samuel Westcott [Orlando]	Decker, Dorothy Judson [Orlando]	26 Sep 1925	6/ 62
Toomer, James	Battle, Leanne	6 Jan 1930	7/ 396
Tornstrom, John Leonard	Collins, Helen Elsie	8 Dec 1932	8/ 228
Torrence, Thaddie	Terrell, Addean L.	23 Aug 1933	8/ 338
Torrisi, Frank [Orlando]	Geraci, Concettina [Orlando]	30 Mar 1926	6/ 194
Toussaint, Richard [Orlando]	Canada, Erma [Orlando]	18 Sep 1926	6/ 342
Townsend, Ivan Ibert	Young, Elizabeth Harriet	3 Feb 1932	8/ 112
Townsend, Leon	Purcell, Lillie	26 Feb 1933	8/ 262
Townsend, Lucius V.	Roberts, Ruth Raynor	3 Jul 1929	7/ 318
Townsend, Thomas Seabrook	Clark, Marian Naomi	21 Apr 1934	8/ 468
Toy, James	Jones, Rachel	21 Sep 1928	7/ 185
Toy, James [B] [Orlando]	Myrick, Minnie Lee [Orlando]	14 Feb 1925	5/ 532
Trask, Paul Theodore [Apopka]	Vaden, Dorothy Mildred [Apopka]	1 Jan 1927	6/ 434
Travis, E. H. [Orlando]	Guzman, Amelia J.	5 Oct 1926	6/ 366
Travit, Dave [Winter Garden]	Sheffield, Malissia [Winter Garden]	6 Dec 1926	6/ 400
Treat, Ferris Sylvester	Hansel, Hilda Beatrice	20 Jan 1934	8/ 416
Trishier, Wiley [Taft]	Smith, Arletha [Taft]	25 Oct 1926	6/ 363
Trousdale, Wesley	Duggar, Addie	22 Dec 1929	7/ 388
Trovillion, Harry Rodman [Winter Park]	Fraser, Ruth [Orlando]	28 Apr 1926	6/ 229
Trowell, William Joseph	Hall, Catherine	27 Feb 1928	7/ 70
Truelson, Thomas	Andrews, Dorothy	9 May 1930	7/ 452
Truesdale, Harry M. [W] [Glen Falls NY]	Westcott, Pauline [Glen Falls, NY]	17 Jan 1925	5/ 515
Trusk, Leonard [W] [Apopka]	Arnert, Dora [Orlando]	7 Jan 1926	6/ 143
Tucker, Avery Dewey	Burgess, Julia Alma	19 May 1934	8/ 478
Tucker, Frank L. [Providence, RI]	Walker, Flossie Anita [Graysville, TN]	12 Apr 1926	6/ 208
Tucker, Herbert Oliver	Ponder, Vera Mae	18 Nov 1933	8/ 369
Tucker, J. C. [Orlando]	Santo, Mabel [Orlando]	13 Jun 1927	6/ 532
Tucker, Leon	Osteen, Mary	12 Jun 1928	7/ 138
Tucker, Otto Brown	Sales, Jessie Elva	26 Jul 1928	7/ 174
Tucker, Park Elliot	Weeks, Anita	24 Dec 1932	8/ 235
Tucker, Robert	Parkhurst, Hazel	6 Nov 1927	7/ 8
Tuggle, Emmett Milton [Orlando]	Durich, Lois Johnson [Orlando]	25 Sep 1926	6/ 350
Tullis, Buford Bill	Tucker, Mary Ann	1 Oct 1931	8/ 54
Tunick, Edward Nathan [Orlando]	Strause, Doris Vivian	3 Nov 1926	6/ 374
Tupper, Ferdinand Green	McInnes, Estelle Mulvoy	24 Oct 1927	7/ 2
Turner, Earl Asa	Fletcher, Minnie Evelyn	21 Apr 1934	8/ 466
Turner, J. W.	Johns, Willie Mae	21 Sep 1931	8/ 52
Turner, James Frank	Sanders, Dorothy Hammond	14 Nov 1933	8/ 368
Turner, Jim	Browning, Mattie Lou	29 Jun 1928	7/ 151
Turner, John [Gotha]	Wise, Mamie [Orlando]	23 Oct 1926	6/ 362
Turner, Luther G. [W] [Tampa]	Fountain, Lela [Tampa]	14 Aug 1925	6/ 32

Turner, Morrison J. [Toledo, OH]	Denning, May [Winter Park]	12 Jun 1927	6/ 535
Turner, Roman	Dyke, Erma	9 Jul 1932	8/ 178
Turner, Roman	Hunter, Emma	1 May 1928	7/ 107
Turner, Roy [Orlando]	Record, Muyell [Orlando]	18 Apr 1927	6/ 494
Turner, William Henry	Driggers, Dosia	19 Apr 1934	8/ 464
Turner, William Henry	Keene, Mable	21 Nov 1927	7/ 14
Turrentine, Loer Leonidest	Ellison, Jacqueline Grace	14 Jul 1934	8/ 510
Tuthill, Benjamin Palmer [Orlando]	Dobson, Edelweiss Fennell [Orlando]	13 Jun 1926	6/ 271
Tuttle, Harry Ethelbert Jr.	Weston, Stella Hyde	28 May 1931	8/ 9
Tuttle, Paul Anson	Douglas, Margaret McIver	27 Apr 1933	8/ 287
Tuttle, Ralph Hewlett	Byk, Florence Mildred	23 Jan 1933	8/ 254
Tyler, John Wesley [Kissimmee]	Caskey, Eugenia Elizabeth [Winter Garden]	2 May 1927	6/ 500
Tyner, Edward Rayford	McLaughman, Harriet Louise	7 Oct 1931	8/ 56
Tyner, Fulwood Henry	Paddock, Meda Mae	10 Mar 1928	7/ 78
Tyson, C.	White, Jessie Lee	14 Feb 1933	8/ 257
Tyson, Johnnie [Oviedo]	McAlister, Pauline [Oviedo]	2 Apr 1927	6/ 487
Tyson, June G. [Orlando]	Zemke, Nettie [Orlando]	23 Sep 1925	6/ 48

U

Ufer, Frank Benjamin	Ludwick, Lorna	18 Jun 1932	8/ 172
Ullrich, Frederick	Cecil, Dorothy	20 Nov 1928	7/ 211
Umberger, Joseph Strong	Klinger, Fay Opal	27 Feb 1929	7/ 252
Umberger, Joseph Stronge	Brown, Leila	12 Dec 1930	7/ 529
Underwood, D. [Ocoee]	Parrish, Elizabeth [Ocoee]	6 Mar 1926	6/ 170
Underwood, James R. W. [W] [Orlando]	Napiorkowski, Charlotte [Lockhart]	31 Mar 1925	5/ 550
Unger, Richard	Crawford, Katherine Mary	10 Feb 1933	8/ 256
Usher, Carl Freeland [W] [Geneva, OH]	Jennings, Marjorie [Mansfield, OH]	12 Mar 1925	5/ 542
Ussery, Brady Francis	O'Neal, Ruthie	24 Dec 1931	8/ 96
Ussery, Raymond Cleo [Winter Garden]	Danford, Arlevy [Winter Garden]	1 May 1926	6/ 224

V

Vail, Clarence G.	Hanush, Martha	7 Mar 1930	7/ 424
Van Armer, Jacob Huelings [Altoona, PA]	Richards, Ruth Ozell [Orlando]	28 May 1927	6/ 519
Van Houten, Herbert Milton [Orlando]	Brackett, Alla Mae [Orlando]	1 Sep 1927	6/ 577
Vance, Ira [B] [Orlando]	Davis, Mary [Orlando]	24 Nov 1925	6/ 91
Vance, Samuel	McNair, Ella Fair	24 Sep 1931	8/ 53
Vanderpool, Earnest [Winter Garden]	Moulder, Lorene [Winter Garden]	16 Dec 1926	6/ 410
Vann, Floyd [Orlando]	Blake, Ethel Lee [Orlando]	21 Nov 1926	6/ 390
Vann, Nicholas Nathaniel	Williams, Alline Mae	20 Jun 1928	7/ 150
Vannerson, Howard Edward	Harnage, Edith Dorothy	5 Jul 1933	8/ 321
VanTassel, Kenneth Avery [Astabula, OH]	May, Bessie Katherine [Centralia IL]	1 Mar 1926	6/ 173
Varn, Julian Alton [Sanford]	Darrow, Evelyn Louise	16 Dec 1926	6/ 409
Varrieur, Joseph R. [W] [Orlando]	Luescher, Emma [Lincoln, RI]	22 Dec 1925	6/ 110
Vaughan, Clarence Buford	Heirkner, Mary Lee	23 Nov 1929	7/ 376
Vaughan, James M. [Winter Park]	Wendland, Pauline E. [Winter Park]	30 Aug 1925	6/ 39
Vaughn, Andrew	May, Elizabeth	25 Jun 1928	7/ 147
Veagey, Thomas C. [Ocoee]	Truitt, Venson W. [Ocoee]	15 Mar 1927	6/ 482
Veley, Coydon Alexander [Orlando]	Tresher, Edith Janet [Orlando]	8 Oct 1925	6/ 60

Veo, Walter Henry	Turner, Marian Marguerite	26 Jul 1929	7/ 326
Verigan, William R.	Ford, Doris	3 Jun 1929	7/ 301
Vervaet, Peter Frank	Payne, Louise Elizabeth	20 Aug 1932	8/ 186
Viehman, William Elroy	Mills, Mary Marguerite	30 Jun 1931	8/ 27
Vigenton, Leonard	McDaniel, Myrtle	31 Jan 1929	7/ 238
Vines, Robert Eslie Bryant [Winter Garden]	Baggett, Lola Beatrice [Orlando]	10 Mar 1927	6/ 474
Vining, George Washington [Winter Garden]	Davis, Eula Delilah [Winter Garden]	11 Oct 1925	6/ 63
Vinson, Willie	Lawrence, Levina	27 May 1929	7/ 298
Vogt, Wittie Delmas	Evans, Jessie Seveda	21 Dec 1929	7/ 391
Volf, John [Orlando]	Nash, Margaret [Lockhart]	25 May 1925	5/ 579
Volley, Adolphus	Burns, Carrie	18 Mar 1931	7/ 568
Vollrath, Lawrence Carl	Herring, Eunice Marie	5 Aug 1933	8/ 332
Vollrath, Otto Adelbert	Hecht, Esther Marie	7 Oct 1933	8/ 349
Voss, Wm. Oather	Giles, Sallie Mae	28 May 1931	8/ 8

W

Waddle, William Benson [Orlando]	Buchanan, Flora Ethel [Orlando]	4 Nov 1926	6/ 373
Wade, Andrew	Henderson, Viola	9 Feb 1928	7/ 61
Wade, Calvin Coleman	Adams, Estella	25 May 1933	8/ 304
Wade, James	Brown, Arecena	10 Sep 1927	6/ 590
Wadkins, Alonzo Allen	Carroll, Irene	17 May 1931	8/ 4
Wagoner, Louis Clay	Schafer, Ethel South	7 Apr 1934	8/ 458
Wainright, Thomas Edward	Lee, Josephine	27 Jan 1929	7/ 236
Waite, Porer	Scott, Beulah	18 Jun 1930	7/ 468
Waiters, Frank	Mathews, Rosa Lee	3 Nov 1928	7/ 201
Walaskey, John	Dinda, Helen	21 Oct 1931	8/ 65
Wald, Willie [Orlando]	Clemons, Rosetta [Orlando]	26 Jan 1927	6/ 446
Walden, Jesse [B] [Orlando]	Harvey, Josie Bell [Thomasville, GA]	22 Apr 1925	5/ 563
Walden, Stanley John [Pontiac, MI]	Hunter, Annie Marion [Wildwood, NJ]	22 Mar 1926	6/ 186
Walder, Clarence	Davis, Willie Mae	28 Jan 1932	8/ 109
Walker, Chester C. [Winter Park]	Hickman, Jessie Lee [Winter Park]	8 Mar 1927	6/ 472
Walker, Claude	Jordan, Ester	28 Mar 1932	8/ 135
Walker, Eugene [Orlando]	Prather, Julia [Orlando]	2 Mar 1926	6/ 167
Walker, Evan Fessett [Orlando]	Kepler, Luennia [Orlando]	19 Jun 1926	6/ 273
Walker, Harris	Jones, Annie	16 Jul 1930	7/ 479
Walker, Harry Cameron [Orlando]	Wagoner, Mary Rae [Indianapolis, IN]	15 Oct 1925	6/ 63
Walker, James	Thomas, Rosie	26 Dec 1929	7/ 389
Walker, James Henry	Jefferson, Nettie Pearl	17 Apr 1934	8/ 462
Walker, L. E.	Johnson, Julia Louise	19 Jun 1934	8/ 497
Walker, Lamar Spafford	McDaniel, Frances Elizabeth	17 Apr 1928	7/ 99
Walker, Linton	Demps, Mae Ola	18 May 1931	8/ 3
Walker, Parker [Orlando]	Murphy, Cora [Orlando]	6 Jul 1926	6/ 289
Walker, Robert Daniel	Vining, Mable Virginia	13 Feb 1934	8/ 432
Walker, Sim	Simmons, Mattie Lou	3 Jul 1929	7/ 319
Walker, William	Graves, Rosa	8 Nov 1930	7/ 519
Walker, Willie [Orlando]	Davis, Mary [Orlando]	24 Oct 1926	6/ 367
Walker, Willie Thomas	Ruddell, Kathryn	2 Jun 1929	7/ 306
Wall, Alton Joseph	Dingley, Ada Porter	16 Jun 1932	8/ 170
Wall, Eliha W. [Orlando]	Patrick, Hattie E. [Knoxville, TN]	5 Jan 1927	6/ 431
Wall, Harold Lyman	Nelson, Florence Charlotte	28 Oct 1933	8/ 358
Wallace, Ernest Quinn	Caldwell, Mildred Grace	15 May 1933	8/ 299

Wallace, James [Orlando]	Roberts, Chanie Lee [Orlando]	13 Jun 1927	6/ 536
Wallace, Lewis Andrew	Drake, Addie L.	4 Dec 1927	7/ 19
Wallace, Madrick	Ivory, Minnie	28 May 1934	8/ 483
Wallace, Marcellus [B] [Orlando]	Johnson, Georgia Lee [Orlando]	25 Nov 1925	6/ 93
Wallace, William C. [Pinecastle]	Drawdy, Mamie Alice [Pinecastle]	4 Aug 1927	6/ 558
Wallace, William Clancy	Hogan, Martha Jo	23 Apr 1932	8/ 150
Walling, Henry Talmadge [Elberton, GA]	Fuller, Lois [Orlando]	23 Apr 1926	6/ 222
Walls, Benjamin Carmage	Dobbs, Odessa Lee	7 Jun 1928	7/ 132
Walsh, Thomas Walter	Elrod, Emma Lucy	18 Jan 1928	7/ 48
Walsh, Tilden Charles [Maitland]	Mann, Josephine [Orlando]	20 Apr 1927	6/ 495
Walters, Claude L. [Hendersonville, NC]	Falkner, Evie F. [Cullman, AL]	10 Sep 1925	6/ 43
Walterson, Julius V., Jr.	Kolbe, Louise	4 Dec 1929	7/ 380
Walton, Oscar	Flowers, Jessie Mae	3 Nov 1928	7/ 201
Walton, R. T.	McLendon, Angie	14 Apr 1929	7/ 278
Ward, Benjamin Franklin	Sweat, Willie Lee	19 May 1928	7/ 121
Ward, Dexter Elmer	Burks, Emma Morgan	29 May 1933	8/ 307
Ward, Harold Ancon, Jr.	Michael, Elizabeth	11 Aug 1929	7/ 332
Ward, Kenneth Lee [W] [Orlando]	Tharrett, Luella Frances [Orlando]	16 Dec 1925	6/ 102
Ward, Monroe	Manigault, Annie Victoria	3 Aug 1931	8/ 41
Ward, Raymond Orrin [Winter Park]	McQuarters, Eva Catherine	18 Feb 1926	6/ 160
Ward/Word, Oliver	Mathies, Lottie Mae	11 Jun 1928	7/ 136
Ware, Benjamin [Orlando]	Willis, Ola [Orlando]	13 Sep 1926	6/ 336
Ware, Daniel	Grant, Amanda	17 Feb 1928	7/ 66
Ware, Eddie [B] [Orlando]	Johnson, Mattie [Orlando]	3 Aug 1925	6/ 28
Ware, Fred [Orlando]	James, Claudia [Orlando]	15 Sep 1926	6/ 337
Ware, William Holloway	Thomas, Dorothy Reed	28 Mar 1932	8/ 134
Waring, Robert Donald, Jr.	Moors, Bernice Ethel	1 Apr 1934	8/ 459
Waring, William	Dingley, Mary Elizabeth	28 Oct 1928	7/ 200
Warner, Edward Martin	Linnell, Charlotte	6 Dec 1928	7/ 212
Warren, Benjamin A. [W] [Apopka]	Smith, Ethel Pearl [Apopka]	5 Dec 1925	6/ 104
Warren, Carlin	Jackson, Minnie Lee	13 Feb 1931	7/ 554
Warren, Jesse James	Pearson, Marget	2 Nov 1929	7/ 365
Warren, John Laws, Jr [W] [Orlando]	Helmick, Fannig Marian [Apopka]	31 Dec 1925	6/ 127
Warren, Nathaniel James	Ivory, Ora	11 Mar 1931	7/ 566
Warren, Raymond Leon	Harris, Cassie Belle	9 Dec 1933	8/ 381
Wasem, Charles Arthur [Orlando]	Richerson, Laura Alice [W. Frankfurt, IL]	11 Jan 1927	6/ 435
Washington, Booker T.	Brown, Lillie Mae	31 Dec 1927	7/ 37
Washington, Booker T.	Beauford, Ossie	13 May 1932	8/ 154
Washington, Curtis [B] [Orlando]	Martin, Minnie Lee [Orlando]	11 Jul 1925	6/ 19
Washington, Earl	Hooks, Ella Eunice	15 Apr 1933	8/ 283
Washington, Eddie [Orlando]	Jenkins, Hattie [Orlando]	13 Jun 1927	6/ 539
Washington, George William [Orlando]	Simpkins, Willie Mae [Orlando]	25 Sep 1926	6/ 344
Washington, James [Winter Garden]	Williams, Nellie Mae [Winter Garden]	9 Apr 1927	6/ 489
Washington, Jeff [B] [Orlando]	Garnett, Naomi [Orlando]	2 Jan 1926	6/ 129
Washington, Quilla	Grant, Mabell	13 Aug 1934	8/ 521
Washington, Roy	Milton, Eleanor	17 Dec 1926	6/ 409
Wasmund, Benjamin Edward	Barksdale, Clara Mae	4 Apr 1931	7/ 575
Waters, Clarence	Cleveland, Ophelia	27 Apr 1929	7/ 284
Waters, Ernest E. [W] [Orlando]	Goolsbee, Mary I. [Orlando]	No Date	6/ 120
Waters, Willie [Orlando]	Davies, Jerry Lee [Orlando]	9 Jun 1927	6/ 531

Watford, Johnie	McCant, Sadie	8 Dec 1928	7/ 213
Watkins, Henry Carlyle [Ft. Myers]	Green, Clarice Elizabeth [Branford]	30 Sep 1926	6/ 345
Watkins, Herbert	Canaday, Arilla	2 Mar 1928	7/ 73
Watkins, J. L. [Columbus, OH]	Reasor, Lois	17 Jan 1927	6/ 439
Watson, Henry [Sanford]	Simmons, Dora [Sanford]	17 May 1910	6/ 585
Watson, James Odis	Phillips, Bonnie Lou	24 Jun 1934	8/ 499
Watson, Marion H. [W] [Maitland]	Connell, Zona Lee [Maitland]	7 Nov 1925	6/ 78
Watts, Bethel	Bowers, Idella	6 Jun 1933	8/ 310
Watts, Cory	Williams, Helen	22 Feb 1928	7/ 71
Watts, Henry [Bainbridge, GA]	Moody, Gladys [Russelville, AL]	10 Jul 1926	6/ 315
Watts, Zulius [Orlando]	Jones, Ruby [Jacksonville]	21 Mar 1927	6/ 480
Weathers, Ollie [Sanford]	Williams, Susie [Orlando]	14 Oct 1925	6/ 62
Weaver, Mack	Lybass, Roberta	12 Nov 1930	7/ 520
Weaver, Raymond C. [W] [Orlando]	Mayne, Catheryn [Orlando]	31 Mar 1925	5/ 554
Weaver, Tillis Belton	Willingham, Grace Delorian	24 Dec 1933	8/ 403
Weaver, Welmer W.	Luckie, Marguerite E.	11 Jan 1930	7/ 400
Webb, Albert Clifton	Johnson, Emma Lee	21 Nov 1931	8/ 76
Webb, Calvin W. [Orlando]	Jacobs, Hazel Velma [Chuluota]	24 Sep 1925	6/ 53
Webb, Daniel Booker	Trapp, Elsa Johanna Meta	16 Oct 1932	8/ 204
Webb, Gary Alton [Winter Garden]	Lewis, Elsie May [Orlando]	2 Jun 1927	6/ 524
Webb, Hubert Postell	Akins, Ruby Myrtle	11 Jun 1932	8/ 169
Webb, Hutchins Boyington [Orlando]	Salter, Mary Louise [Bambridge, GA]	2 Jul 1927	6/ 559
Webb, William Levi [W. Tampa]	Brown, Annie Glynne [Kissimmee]	26 Oct 1925	6/ 71
Weber, Theodore Henry	Tanner, Juanita Fay	20 Jul 1933	8/ 327
Websking, Henry Robert	Shaldahl, Virginia Maxine	18 Oct 1930	7/ 510
Weeks, George Frank	Norcross, Lotta Mae	21 Dec 1933	8/ 389
Weeks, Walter Brooker [Orlando]	Dann, Ardis Jeannette [Clarcona]	3 Jun 1927	6/ 524
Weeks, William Berry [Ocoee]	Turner, Selma Florrie [Ocoee]	6 Aug 1927	6/ 560
Weippert, Henry McKim	Sallas, Pearl	22 Feb 1930	7/ 419
Welch, Allen	Taylor, Ruby	24 May 1930	7/ 459
Welch, Carl Lynwood	Flourney, Catherine	2 Oct 1928	7/ 189
Welch, J. P.	Futch, Bessie	15 Oct 1927	7/ 1
Welch, James [Orlando]	Boddie, Irene [Orlando]	21 Feb 1927	6/ 465
Welch, Joseph	May, Alberta	8 Nov 1930	7/ 518
Wells, Charlie [B] [Orlando]	Jackson, Hattie [Orlando]	28 Jan 1925	5/ 518
Wells, Fred Charles	Pennington, Mildred Cordelia	20 Apr 1932	8/ 147
Wells, George Donald	Orcutt, Ruth Evelyn	16 Apr 1933	8/ 285
Wells, Harry [Orlando]	Shackleford, Nora Lee [Orlando]	13 Mar 1926	6/ 178
Wells, Henry Irvin [Orlando]	Johnson, Vera [Orlando]	13 Feb 1926	6/ 156
Wells, Taylor	Wilson, Aretha	16 Apr 1928	7/ 99
Welsh, David George [Orlando]	Gay, Robin Stuart [Orlando]	5 Dec 1926	6/ 404
Wenger, Theodore Emanuel	Lowery, Esther	27 Dec 1930	7/ 538
Wentz, Phillip Arthur	Ayers, Kathleen	4 Sep 1932	8/ 196
Werline, Eugene Henry	Warner, Hazel Catherine	13 May 1933	8/ 298
Werline, Leon	Hooker, Claudey	18 Feb 1929	7/ 247
Wertz, John Alexander [Maitland]	Vabor, Katherine [Orlando]	30 May 1927	6/ 518
Wesley, Alfred	Brown, Clara	16 Feb 1934	8/ 430
Wesley, John	Porter, Alice	24 Feb 1930	7/ 419
Wesley, Thomas [B] [Orlando]	Brown, Ella V. [Orlando]	23 Dec 1925	6/ 119
Wesson, Horace Holloman	Routh, Florida Wilma	28 Nov 1933	8/ 381
West, Addison Tinsley	Rand, Ruth Catherine	2 Aug 1933	8/ 331
West, Daniel	Hornes, Elizabeth	16 Jun 1928	7/ 139

West, Elijah	Brown, Maggie	6 Apr 19313	7/ 575
West, Hugh Lee	Cornell, Lorene	14 Jul 1934	8/ 513
West, Isaiah	Frederick, Jammie Sammie	26 Nov 1931	8/ 81
West, Lester William [Orla Vista]	Webb, Edna Kathryn [Orla Vista]	17 Jan 1927	6/ 444
West, Ollie B. [Bartow]	Clayton, Anna Belle [Bartow]	26 Nov 1926	6/ 393
Westcott, William Emerson	Moore, Mary Louise	9 Jun 1929	7/ 307
Westover, Robert James	Hadden, Margaret Evelyn	9 Mar 1929	7/ 259
Whalen, Andrew Clarence	Brockman, Ada	30 Jan 1928	7/ 55
Wheatley, Claude I.	Scott, Marion E.	28 Mar 1928	7/ 88
Wheeler, J. H. [Ft Christmas]	Vickery, Belle [Ft Christmas]	17 Oct 1925	6/ 64
Wheeler, Joe F.	Brown, Claudie	27 Dec 1928	7/ 223
Wheeler, McConnell	Carr, Beatrice	23 Feb 1929	7/ 264
Wheeler, Perry [W] [Winter Garden]	Liles, Mattie [Winter Garden]	11 Apr 1925	5/ 558
Wheeless, C. W. [W] [Orlando]	Dempsey, Anna [Orlando]	1 Jan 1926	6/ 124
Whelan, John Robert	Foley, Isabel	30 Dec 1932	8/ 236
Whiddon, David Waldo	Wilkerson, Velma	21 Dec 1929	7/ 386
Whilden, Arthur Dewey	Jones, Vera Ann	9 Mar 1934	8/ 446
Whilden, Eldred Morris	Bates, Oney	9 Jun 1928	7/ 134
Whipp, Shannon Leslie	Simmons, Margaret Elizabeth	18 May 1930	7/ 462
Whipper, Sam	Merriett, Elsie	9 Apr 1931	7/ 577
White, Clinton Emery [Orlando]	Lonze, Nellie [Orlando]	20 Jul 1926	6/ 297
White, Earl Godlonton	Hanson, Adeline	5 Jul 1929	7/ 319
White, Elvin [Lake Mary]	Janus, Elizabeth [Lake Mary]	21 Mar 1927	6/ 480
White, Frederick Preston	Birch, Elizabeth Emma	30 Sep 1933	8/ 347
White, Grover Cleveland	McQueen, Beatrice	3 Mar 1931	7/ 563
White, Henry Ervin	Anderson, Panzy	18 Jul 1929	7/ 323
White, Hugh Zenas	Cumbus, Annie Powell	14 Feb 1932	8/ 116
White, Irvin [Orlando]	Brown, Daisy [Orlando]	3 Feb 1927	6/ 450
White, Joe	Kendricks, Lottie	4 Dec 1928	7/ 211
White, John [Orlando]	Ladler, Gertrude [Orlando]	5 Apr 1926	6/ 198
White, Johnny James	Mickens, Etta	27 Apr 1933	8/ 287
White, Louis [W] [Orlando]	Lemmon, Margaret Alice [Orlando]	11Mar 1925	5/ 543
White, Mathew Harrison [B] [Orlando]	Ross, Earline [Orlando]	6 Jul 1925	6/ 12
White, Richard	Leonard, Lillian	9 Jan 1933	8/ 240
White, Richard [B] [Orlando]	Long, Mary [Orlando]	10 Aug 1925	6/ 31
White, Robert	Crow, Marjorie	19 Nov 1932	8/ 218
White, Roscoe [Orlando]	Pinkney, Roberta [Orlando]	8 Mar 1926	6/ 174
White, Rufus [B] [Winter Park]	Phillip, Annie [Winter Park]	20 Jul 1925	6/ 20
White, Thomas Preston [W] [Charlotte, NC]	Tucker, Henrietta Preston [Lexington, KY]	21 Mar 1925	5/ 546
White, Victor Lee [W] [Orlando]	Inabnit, Daisy Belle [Orlando]	11 Aug 1925	6/ 31
White, William [B] [Orlando]	Logue, Beatrice [Orlando]	28 Feb 1925	5/ 533
Whitlock, Derrie [Winter Garden]	Sapp, Virgie [Winter Garden]	6 Aug 1927	6/ 559
Whitlow, Robert	Arnette, Aquilla	22 Apr 1929	7/ 282
Whitney, Howard A. [W] [Taft]	Collier, Ella Mae [Taft]	5 Jan 1925	5/ 508
Whitney, Kenneth [Clermont]	Welch, Margaret [Clermont]	13 Oct 1926	6/ 353
Whittaker, John	Weaver, Johnnie May	21 Apr 1932	8/ 145
Whitted, Ray Frederick [Apopka]	Rogers, Dorothy Grace [Clarcona]	6 Jan 1926	6/ 142
Whitten, Rufus Claude	Rotunde, Marie Katherine	16 May 1930	7/ 455
Whittington, Alvie [Orlando]	Smith, Allie Mae	9 May 1927	6/ 505
Whittington, Curtis	McLendon, Mattie	9 Oct 1931	8/ 59

Wickman, Erich Louis	Stainmaker, Kezzie	8 Aug 1930	7/ 487
Wideman, Frank [B] [Woodbridge]	Tombridge, Essie [Woodbridge]	30 Jan 1926	6/ 144
Wiercisdki, Theodore [Sanford]	Daoust, Adele [Winter Park]	18 Apr 1927	6/ 496
Wiggins, Glenn Duncan	Haynie, Flossie	30 Sep 1930	7/ 504
Wiggins, James Jackson	Shirley, Pearl Frances	1 Nov 1930	7/ 516
Wiggins, James Millard	Harris, Glessie Mae	29 Nov 1932	8/ 222
Wigginton, Archie Barnett [St Cloud]	Landiss, Nina Lue [St Cloud]	24 Jul 1926	6/ 276
Wilcox, George William [Orlando]	Siler, Eva [Apopka]	12 Mar 1926	6/ 177
Wilcox, Jefferson	Adams, Anna Belle Parker	5 Jan 1928	7/ 44
Wilda, James Blanton [Orlando]	Dettner, Lydia Louise	28 Aug 1926	6/ 325
Wilder, Emmett Frank	Gillis, Loreter	26 Feb 1934	8/ 437
Wilder, Oliver	Smith, Daisy	16 Aug 1931	8/ 43
Wilder, William Julius	Carroll, Thelma	20 Aug 1932	8/ 186
Wiles, William	James, Ada	3 Mar 1930	7/ 423
Wiley, Madison	Craft, Ollie	6 Dec 1932	8/ 226
Wiley, Robert	Lovett, Leslie	5 Jun 1934	8/ 489
Wiley, Willie	Cunningham, Phennie Mae	5 Nov 1932	8/ 216
Wilkerson, I. V.	Marsh, Bessie	2 Jun 1934	8/ 487
Wilkerson, James	Harrison, Willie Mae	25 Feb 1933	8/ 261
Wilkerson, John R.	Whiddon, Idzial	21 Dec 1929	7/ 386
Wilkerson, William Platers [New Smyrna]	Mitchell, Emerine Edgerly [Miami]	25 May 1927	6/ 516
Wilkes, Louie [Orlando]	Nickerson, Flosill [Orlando]	7 Dec 1926	6/ 402
Wilkinson, Allen [St Cloud]	Rogers, Annie [Kissimmee]	20 Feb 1926	6/ 159
Wilkinson, John Calhoun	Drawdy, Ernestine	7 Apr 1934	8/ 458
Willard, John Edward	Gentry, Lucille	26 Dec 1927	7/ 31
Willett, William Buifield	Venning, Ethel Victoria	29 Jan 19331	7/ 551
William, B. W.	McCauley, Lula	8 Sep 1929	7/ 346
William, Collie	Marshall, Carrie	12 Jan 1928	7/ 43
Williams, A. B.	Shavis, Sarah	7 Nov 1929	7/ 367
Williams, A. J. [Orlando]	Proctor, Sarah [Orlando]	18 Dec 1926	6/ 411
Williams, Alan	Parker, Johnnie Mae	18 May 1929	7/ 296
Williams, Alonzo	Widener, Sadie Elizabeth	27 Jun 1928	7/ 148
Williams, Anderson	Calhoun, Mabelle	8 Jun 1929	7/ 306
Williams, Anthony	Foster, Nora	19 Mar 1928	7/ 82
Williams, Arnette Franklin	James, Melita D.	30 Apr 1929	7/ 289
Williams, Arthur	Kelly, Rosa	13 Sep 1930	7/ 496
Williams, Arthur	Brown, Sallie	20 Nov 1927	7/ 13
Williams, Ben [Orlando]	Scurry, Martha [Orlando]	18 Sep 1926	6/ 341
Williams, Ben [Orlando]	Isabell, Sonia [Orlando]	22 Oct 1926	6/ 359
Williams, Bennie Albertus [B][Winter Garden]	Benbow, Clara [Winter Garden]	14 Jan 1926	6/ 138
Williams, Bill Claude	Allen, Rutha Mae	16 Dec 1933	8/ 385
Williams, Charles Louis	Ware, Mildred Kathryn	14 Oct 1932	8/ 205
Williams, Charles Slocume	Williams, Frieda	30 Jan 1928	7/ 56
Williams, Clarence Nunn	Little, Betty Barr	23 Oct 1931	8/ 64
Williams, Claude	Bolden, Henrietta	7 May 1934	8/ 474
Williams, Claudie	Jones, Willie Mae	19 Apr 1930	7/ 441
Williams, Clifford Foster	Rocks, Emma Mae	19 Jun 1933	8/ 314
Williams, Clyde	Shepard, Ida	3 Aug 1931	8/ 40
Williams, Cornel [Orlando]	Johnson, Lizzie [Orlando]	2 Jan 1927	6/ 431
Williams, David Jacob [B] [Sanford]	Johnson, Isabelle [Sanford]	29 May 1925	5/ 582
Williams, Dixie [B] [Orlando]	Frazier, Janie [Orlando]	30 Jun 1925	6/ 7
Williams, Earl	Sawyer, Louise	5 Dec 1932	8/ 225

Williams, Eben	White, Mary Lee	5 Nov 1931	8/ 71
Williams, Ed [Orlando]	Hatcher, Anna Belle [Orlando]	3 Jan 1927	6/ 427
Williams, Eissie [Orlando]	Holland, Elizabeth [Orlando]	24 Jan 1927	6/ 442
Williams, Ernest [Benson Springs]	Kirby, Eva [Benson Springs]	26 Apr 1926	6/ 219
Williams, Fate	Jerry, Sadie	16 May 1931	8/ 3
Williams, Filmore [Orlando]	Brown, Falara [Orlando]	25 Jul 1927	6/ 554
Williams, Florzell	Webb, Mary Alice	17 Jan 1931	7/ 544
Williams, Frank [Orlando]	Nobles, Edith [Orlando]	31 May 1926	6/ 293
Williams, George Washington	Roberts, Lesby	30 May 1931	8/ 8
Williams, Gernie Edward	Hickson, Viola Mae	21 Oct 1931	8/ 63
Williams, Harry [W] [Winter Park]	Hopson, Oviedo [Orlando]	24 Dec 1925	6/ 117
Williams, Harry [Orlando]	Wallace, Viola [Orlando]	8 May 1926	6/ 231
Williams, Henry [Winter Garden]	Body, Ethel [Winter Garden]	13 Sep 1926	6/ 336
Williams, Herbert [Sanford]	McClinton, Alice [Conway]	13 Feb 1927	6/ 456
Williams, Herbert [Orlando]	Williams, Sarah Jane [Orlando]	17 May 1926	6/ 237
Williams, Horace [B] [Orlando]	Goff, Mamie [Orlando]	2 May 1925	5/ 566
Williams, Horton	Thompson, Drennie	9 Feb 1931	8/ 114
Williams, James	Grover, Stella	30 Apr 1929	7/ 285
Williams, James	Jones, Ollie Mae	1 Dec 1930	7/ 524
Williams, James [Orlando]	Hart, Idell [Orlando]	15 Dec 1926	6/ 408
Williams, Jasper Moses [Winter Park]	Lee, Irma [Adison,GA]	25 Oct 1926	6/ 363
Williams, Jimmie	Williams, Ruth	7 Feb 1928	7/ 57
Williams, Jimmie	Fields, Martha	22 Apr 1929	7/ 281
Williams, Joe	McCloud, Gertrude	6 May 1934	8/ 473
Williams, Joe [Winter Park]	Hutchins, Easter [Winter Park]	20 Mar 1926	6/ 183
Williams, John	Anderson, Leora	21 Jan 1928	7/ 49
Williams, John	Kinsey, Evelyn	10 Oct 1931	8/ 58
Williams, John Samuel	Artis, Arlein Inez	31 Jul 1930	7/ 485
Williams, John Wesley	Lancaster, Margaret	25 Dec 1929	7/ 392
Williams, Joseph [Orlando]	Long, Annie [Orlando]	6 Dec 1926	6/ 400
Williams, Joseph Washington	Henry, Dorothy Mae	2 Nov 1931	8/ 69
Williams, Junrous	Woodbury, Carrie	17 Mar 1930	7/ 427
Williams, Leroy	Wooden, Alberta	24 Feb 1932	8/ 118
Williams, LeRoy	Harris, Gladys	4 Jun 1928	7/ 126
Williams, Leroy [Orlando]	Banks, Susie May [Orlando]	23 Oct 1926	6/ 360
Williams, Leslie	Robinson, Hattie	14 Mar 1929	7/ 264
Williams, Lewis C. [B] [Orlando]	Reeves, Sarah [Orlando]	30 Jul 1925	6/ 29
Williams, Lewis Rogers [Orlando]	Foote, Katie Mae [Orlando]	31 Jul 1927	6/ 556
Williams, Lloyd	Brown, Mamie	9 Sep 1931	8/ 48
Williams, Lonnie [B] [Orlando]	Hammond, Katherine [Orlando]	15 Apr 1925	5/ 560
Williams, Lou Curtis	Davis, Dallie Lou	23 Dec 1932	8/ 242
Williams, Louis	Fuller, Ines	18 Feb 1934	8/ 432
Williams, Nathan	Lampkins, Lettie	3 Jan 1930	7/ 395
Williams, Nathan Jewell	England, Inez Kathleen	18 Apr 1934	8/ 465
Williams, Occie	Wilson, Ada	3 Jan 1930	7/ 394
Williams, Omar R. [Frostproof, FL]	Bird, Emma Jeasine	1 Jan 1927	6/ 425
Williams, Otha B.	Stewart, Mary	10 Dec 1927	7/ 22
Williams, Otis Benjamin	Saylor, Dorothy	7 Jul 1930	7/ 477
Williams, Peter [Sanford]	Roberts, Louisa [Mrs](Sanford)	30 Apr 1910	6/ 585
Williams, Phil [Orlando]	Swains, Julie [Orlando]	9 Oct 1926	6/ 351

Williams, Ralph [Brooksville]	Aaron, Nellie May [Winter Garden]	22 May 1926	6/ 243
Williams, Richard Coley [W] [Winter Park]	Riner, Alberta Melvera [Winter Park]	11 Jul 1925	6/ 13
Williams, Robert [B] [Taft]	Davis, Lucinda [Taft]	1 Aug 1925	6/ 27
Williams, Roosevelt	Buford, Ruby Mae	16 Jun 1928	7/ 139
Williams, Ruthford Buchard	Watkins, Annie Belle	7 Jun 1933	8/ 311
Williams, Sam	Johnson, Louise	13 May 1929	7/ 293
Williams, Sammie Joe	Carswell, Katherine	16 Jul 1934	8/ 509
Williams, Samuel	Morris, Lucile	21 Nov 1931	8/ 77
Williams, Sandy	Clarke, Estella	3 Sep 1927	6/ 573
Williams, Shepart	Brown, Albertha	6 Dec 1930	7/ 527
Williams, Sidney	Jackson, Frances	29 Apr 1933	8/ 288
Williams, Silas [B] [Zellwood]	Fennel, Eva [Zellwood]	20 Feb 1925	5/ 528
Williams, Solomon	Palmer, Daisy	17 Oct 1932	8/ 204
Williams, Thomas	Stanley, Rosalie	18 Mar 1933	8/ 272
Williams, Thomas [B] [Orlando]	Woodbury, Ruby [Orlando]	8 Apr 1925	5/ 556
Williams, Thomas Allen	Shepherd, Ruth Elizabeth	27 Sep 1933	8/ 346
Williams, Tom	Jones, Lizzie Lee	11 Nov 1928	7/ 204
Williams, W. W. [Orlando]	Calloway, Lotie [Orlando] [Holloway on return]	12 Dec 1925	6/ 99
Williams, Wesley	Mathews, Carrie	6 May 1928	7/ 110
Williams, William Isaac [Tampa Shores]	Dekle, Mary Louise [Tampa]	19 Jun 1926	6/ 280
Williams, Willie	Reddick, Lucy	23 Oct 1929	7/ 360
Williams, Willie	Neason, Annie May	6 Jan 1934	8/ 401
Williams, Zeke [B] [Winter Garden]	Edwards, Hattie [Winter Garden]	17 Mar 1925	5/ 541
Williamson, Roy Thomas	Parrish, Ella May	11 May 1929	7/ 293
Williamson, Will [Oakland]	Perkins, Winifred [Lancaster KY]	22 Mar 1926	6/ 187
Williamson, Wm. Henry Hubert [W] [Florence, SC]	Dobbs, Amy Iduma [Orlando]	23 Nov 1925	6/ 91
Willie, Lee [Orlando]	Morris, Willie May [Orlando]	27 Nov 1926	6/ 392
Williford, Hamp [Orlando]	Taylor, Annie [Orlando]	5 Jun 1926	6/ 258
Willingham, Grant [Orlando]	Woodley, Carrie [Orlando]	16 Oct 1926	6/ 356
Willis, Carl	Bryant, Thelma Lee	19 Feb 1931	7/ 558
Willis, Cecil Manker	Perdue, Ruth Elizabeth	20 Sep 1930	7/ 498
Willis, Durward [W] [Miami]	Brown, Dorothy Mae [Orlando]	6 Feb 1925	5/ 528
Willis, Edgar Lynn	Owen, Ida Frances	30 Jun 1929	7/ 317
Willis, James	Hylick, Addie Lee	23 Dec 1929	7/ 388
Willis, Wilbur Amos	Smith, Mildred Eva	29 Apr 1932	8/ 150
Willoughby, George	Clack, Maud Opal	23 Dec 1931	8/ 93
Willoughby, James	Talton, Stella Delain	7 Apr 1928	7/ 93
Wills, Harrold Stanley	Mahrt, Juanita Maria	4 Dec 1930	7/ 526
Wills, LeRoy	Whitfield, Rosetta	16 Sep 1929	7/ 346
Willsey, Clarence William [Lockhart]	Neurlet, Mary Elizabeth [Lockhart]	2 Oct 1926	6/ 349
Willsey, Herbert David	Burr, Patricia	13 Jun 1932	8/ 169
Willsey, Sumner Alton	Beasley, Leona	24 May 1930	7/ 460
Wilson, Alfonzo	Murry, Lottie	20 Dec 1932	8/ 230
Wilson, Arthur Reynolds [Orlando]	Smith, Lucile [Orlando]	11 Jun 1927	6/ 534
Wilson, Bennie Mosley	Bruner, Omie Marguerite	25 Oct 1933	8/ 354
Wilson, Eddie [Orlando]	Heath, Haseltine [Orlando]	23 May 1927	6/ 514
Wilson, Edgar Sherrard [Winter Park]	Smith, Viola Vandelores [Winter Park]	7 Aug 1926	6/ 310
Wilson, Freeman [Orlando]	Crocker, Willie Lee [Orlando]	5 Apr 1926	6/ 200
Wilson, George	Wilkerson, Every May	21 Aug 1926	6/ 317
Wilson, George [Cocoa]	Manyham, Winifred [Cocoa]	23 Feb 1926	6/ 163

Wilson, Glenn Ressegue [Orlando]	Laire, Ada E. [Orlando]	15 Feb 1926	6/ 155
Wilson, Henry	Spencer, Hattie Louise	25 May 1933	8/ 306
Wilson, Ira Lamar	Cornell, Willie Mae	12 Dec 1931	8/ 86
Wilson, James	Mathews, Geraldine	14 Jun 1930	7/ 467
Wilson, James [Lakeland]	Hill, Pearl [Winter Park]	1 Oct 1925	6/ 54
Wilson, James	Gerett, Amelia	11 Feb 1930	7/ 417
Wilson, James Reese	Parker, Margaret Evelyn	11 Nov 1933	8/ 368
Wilson, Jesse [Orlando]	Hodge, Sally [Orlando]	15 Mar 1926	6/ 178
Wilson, John H. [W] [Port Chester NY]	Reese, Olga [Tampa]	11 Apr 1925	5/ 561
Wilson, Napoleon [B] [Winter Garden]	Williams, Mary [Winter Garden]	5 Jun 1925	6/ 10
Wilson, Norman Eugene [Orlando]	Patterson, Helen Williams [Orlando]	4 Apr 1926	6/ 197
Wilson, Ransome [Orlando]	Bell, Eliza	23 Oct 1926	6/ 362
Wilson, Reese	Gamble, Madie	20 Jan 1928	7/ 48
Wilson, Samuel	Jackson, Aggie Mae	2 Jul 1928	7/ 154
Wilson, Samuel L.	Cocowitch, Gladys	5 May 1934	8/ 474
Wilson, Thomas Glenn	Russell, Lillian Jean	29 Feb 1932	8/ 121
Wilson, Walter Herman [Christianburg, VA]	Cusler, Lucy Elizabeth [Pearisburg VA]	1 Jun 1926	6/ 256
Wilson, William Luther [Ocala]	Thomas, Lakie Marie [Apopka]	16 Mar 1927	6/ 477
Wilson, Willie	Smith, Mildred	26 Sep 1927	6/ 586
Wilson, Willie [Orlando]	Williams, Alberta [Orlando]	17 Oct 1926	6/ 356
Wimberley, Harry Oscar [Orlando]	Drawdy, Elsie Louise	15 Jul 1926	6/ 298
Wimberly, Homer [B] [Winter Park]	Green, Willie Belle [Winter Park]	2 Feb 1925	5/ 520
Wimberly, Patrick Rogers	Jones, Dorothea Mae	2 Mar 1930	7/ 423
Winchester, Everett	McKinzie, Norma Rue	11 Apr 1932	8/ 140
Winchester, Zan Levander	Miller, Essie Mae	4 Jun 1934	8/ 487
Windham, Claude Arleigh [Lakeland]	Lee, Violet [Lakeland]	2 Jan 1927	6/ 444
Windham, Henry Grady	McFarland, Martha Jane	23 Dec 1929	7/ 391
Winegard, Charles Henry	Mosley, Leola	1 May 1929	7/ 288
Winegard, George Asman [Orlando]	Arnett, Flora Elizabeth [Orlando]	24 Feb 1927	6/ 465
Wingert, Floyd Milton	Byers, Carrie Louise	27 Jun 1929	7/ 320
Winkler, Cornie	Schleifenbaum, Florence Martha	30 Apr 1929	7/ 286
Winn, William H.	Routh, Aura	28 Dec 1929	7/ 391
Winter, Henry Kenneth [Oakland]	Michael, Alpha Evelyn	16 Sep 1926	6/ 341
Winter, Karl Clifton [Orlando]	Latimer, Alice Leigh [Orlando]	4 Apr 1926	6/ 207
Wise, Earle C.	Howard, Viona C.	21 Apr 1928	7/ 101
Wise, Jewell Vaughan	Stewart, Francis	28 Jan 1931	7/ 548
Wite, Irving McKinley [W] [Arcadia]	James, Opal Ellen Marguerete [Arcadia]	11 Jan 1926	6/ 133
Witherow, Winfred Glenn	King, Quilla	21 Jan 1931	7/ 546
Witman, A. C.	Polete, Annie	9 Apr 1928	7/ 94
Wofford, Phillip [W] [Miami]	Farless, Maggie [Orlando]	5 Nov 1925	6/ 75
Wofforf, Lee Vernon	Brown, Edna	4 Feb 1933	8/ 253
Wolf, William F. [Mascoutah, IL]	Hilton, Mary C. [Knoxville, TN]	9 May 1927	6/ 505
Wolfe, James	Angel, Frances	12 Jun 1928	7/ 138
Wolfe, Sidney Alexander [Orlando]	Connor, Amy Donovan [Akron, OH]	12 Nov 1926	6/ 381
Womack, Joseph Samuel	Martin, Agnes	12 Jul 1933	8/ 324
Wood, Joe Brinton	Slavik, Margaret Freda	28 Jun 1934	8/ 503
Wood, Neil	Moffat, Mary Kate	2 Jun 1933	8/ 310
Wood, Richard Harris [Orlando]	Polk, Rozzie [Orlando]	21 Jun 1927	6/ 540
Wood, Samuel D. [Orlando]	Frye, Sarah [Oklahoma City, OK]	6 Aug 1926	6/ 311
Wood, Samuel David	Kamp, Jennie	26 Oct 1927	7/ 3

Wood, Stewart	Long, Jocelyn	27 Jan 1928	7/ 62
Wood, Thomas Jefferson [W] [Ft Christmas]	Streb, Katie Inez [Palatka]	27 Jan 1926	6/ 144
Woodard, Douglas Odelle	Walden, Marguerite Katherine	5 Sep 1931	8/ 49
Woodberry, Ed [B] [Orlando]	Neely, Georgia [Orlando]	11 Aug 1925	6/ 31
Wooden, George [Orlando]	Gallon, Elizabeth [Orlando]	30 Jul 1927	6/ 556
Woodham, Brady	Shoemaker, Nellia	3 Dec 1932	8/ 223
Woodham, Omar Vincent	Patton, Ruth	25 May 1931	8/ 6
Woodley, Henry [B] [Orlando]	Clark, Hattie [Orlando]	28 Dec 1925	6/ 118
Woodley, Mace [B] [Orlando]	Spivey, Laura [Orlando]	8 Aug 1925	6/ 30
Woodley, William Alvie	Anderson, Mildred Luverne	30 Apr 1932	8/ 149
Woodruff, Charles Alexander	McRoy, Willie Virginia	6 Nov 1933	8/ 360
Woodruff, Grover [B] [Orlando]	Tolliver, Evelyn [Orlando]	28 Mar 1925	5/ 548
Woods, Alonzo	Lolley, Matilda	22 Jun 1930	7/ 471
Woods, Charles [Orlando]	Arnold, Carrie Lou [Orlando]	25 May 1927	6/ 517
Woods, Elder	Adams, Susie Mae	9 Oct 1928	7/ 191
Woods, James Martin	Strickland, Mary Janettie	7 May 1932	8/ 188
Woods, Reddy William	Hilliard, Ruby Mildred	24 Sep 1931	8/ 52
Woods, Robert	Doyle, Olivia	7 Jan 1931	7/ 540
Woods, William Madison [Mascott]	Grover, Elizabeth [Mascott]	28 Mar 1927	6/ 482
Woodside, Clarence Oscar [W] [Lakeland]	Haynes, Nell Rae	21 Jan 1926	6/ 141
Woodward, Elton	Johnson, Maria	21 Aug 1932	8/ 186
Woodward, James	Pope, Beaulah Mae	7 May 1931	7/ 595
Woody, Robert H.	Wills, Louise	3 Jun 1929	7/ 303
Woolston, Samuel [Tampa]	McGee, Leila Mae [Miami]	28 Feb 1927	6/ 471
Woolverton, Wilford B. [W] [Orlando]	Hamrick, Maggie M. [Orlando]	7 May 1925	5/ 570
Wooton, John [Sanford]	Perks, Ella [Orlando]	17 Jul 1927	7/ 8
Wootten, John Frank	Shadburn, Betty	14 Jun 1929	7/ 309
Worthy, Jack [B] [Winter Park]	Churnn, Ella Mae [Winter Park]	14 Feb 1925	5/ 525
Wright, Atthur Jr.	Brown, Rose Lee	5 Sep 1931	8/ 46
Wright, Charlie	Wallace, Pinkie	13 Apr 1928	7/ 96
Wright, Dotsey	Jackson, Georgia	15 Mar 1931	7/ 567
Wright, Ed	Mobley, N. E.	13 Jan 1930	7/ 420
Wright, Edward Thomas [Orlando]	Zuber, Kathleen [Orlando]	10 Aug 1927	6/ 565
Wright, Frank McCormick	McMaster, Mary Parshall	25 Aug 1933	8/ 336
Wright, Frederick Donald [Sherrill, NY]	Gilch, Annie [Buffalo, NY]	18 May 1926	6/ 242
Wright, George Henry	Roberts, Sallie	20 Sep 1930	7/ 499
Wright, George Lester	Shafter, Georgie	15 Jul 1933	8/ 326
Wright, James	Oliver, Bessie	22 Mar 1929	7/ 265
Wright, James Anderson	Zachary, Margaret	26 Dec 1931	8/ 101
Wright, Jas. Sam'l	Amos, Jeannine	12 Nov 1927	7/ 10
Wright, Joe, Jr.	Johnson, Maggie Lee	15 Mar 1929	7/ 263
Wright, John [B] [Orlando]	Phillips, Viola [Winter Park]	13 May 1925	5/ 572
Wright, Levy William	White, Frances Amanda	22 Mar 1930	7/ 433
Wright, Otho [Winter Garden]	Wells, Lila [Winter Garden]	5 Feb 1927	6/ 450
Wright, Robert	Washington, Angie	26 Aug 1926	6/ 320
Wrye, Richard Edison	Woods, Annie Belle	5 Sep 1931	8/ 47
Wylie, Carl Herbert [Sringfield, OH]	Stewart, Ethel Lee [Orlando]	17 Nov 1926	6/ 385
Wynn, Lawrence	Dunlap, Dosie Bell	5 Aug 1934	8/ 520
Wynn, Phillip	Jackson, Georgia	19 Jan 1932	8/ 105

Y

Yake, Keith L. [Orlando]	Branden, Catherine Opal	2 Sep 1926	6/ 334
Yancey, Thomas Allen	Hancock, Lillie Gertrude	31 Jan 1931	7/ 551
Yarbrough, Claude Lee	Stockton, Joda	25 Mar 1933	8/ 276
Yarbrough, George N. L.	Rogers, Hattie	4 Mar 1930	7/ 422
Yarbrough, George N. L.	Helms, Daisy	7 Nov 1932	8/ 214
Yarbrough, James Edgar	Darlington, Hazel Sfell	15 Jul 1928	7/ 164
Yarbrough, Joseph Guy	Wren, Hester Rozell	17 Jul 1934	8/ 511
Yarbrough, Theodore Turnbull [Tallahassee]	Wadell, Winnifred Roberta [Winter Park]	1 Jun 1926	6/ 256
Yard, Edward Lewis	Lockridge, Idell	18 Feb 1928	7/ 66
Yates, Elbert Lee	Hatch, Julia Virginia	14 Apr 1934	8/ 460
Yates, Everett	Hart, Josie	30 Aug 1933	8/ 337
Yates, Frank [Pinecastle]	Thomas, Minnie [Pinecastle]	25 Sep 1925	6/ 50
Yates, Jeffrey David [Orlando]	Milton, Margie Mageline	1 Jul 1927	6/ 542
Yates, Joe	Buchnan, Elsie	21 Jul 1928	7/ 163
Yates, Luther Earl	Ayers, Kimmie Ellen	22 Mar 1928	7/ 85
Yates, Moses E.	Yates, Mary F.	8 Sep 1930	7/ 495
Yates, Williams	Gordan, Allins	4 Jan 1930	7/ 394
Yeager, Allen Cunningham	Stewart, Mary Margaret	30 Oct 1931	8/ 67
Yearts, Alton B.	Chesshire, Zelda	10 Dec 1928	7/ 213
Yewell, Eb Vernon	Anderson, Hope Alice	6 Jun 1933	8/ 310
Youman, Bue	Staten, Matilda C.	24 Dec 1932	8/ 233
Young, E. Van	Reed, Eula Lee	25 May 1929	7/ 298
Young, Ernest	Williams, Jewell Virginia	20 Feb 1933	8/ 259
Young, Garfield	Tillman, Nancy	2 Nov 1929	7/ 364
Young, George	Jackson, Marie Netha	15 Jul 1932	8/ 178
Young, Johnnie	Hall, Sarah Lee	14 Apr 1930	7/ 438
Young, Lot	Parker, Kate	2 Apr 1929	7/ 271
Young, Sylvester [Orlando]	Sampson, Willie Mae [Orlando]	11 Jun 1927	6/ 550
Youngblood, Earl [W] [Winter Garden]	Slone, Lucille [Ocoee]	19 Apr 1925	5/ 561
Younger, Nathaniel	Williams, Norah	13 Mar 1928	7/ 81
Youtsey, James Oliver	Deaning, Winifred	25 Aug 1928	7/ 176
Yowler, Lee	Long, Mildred Louise	16 Dec 1933	8/ 386

Z

Zanders, Randall	Huff, Hattie	5 Jul 1929	7/ 320
Zates, Albert [Ft. Christmas]	Carver, Daisy [Bithlo]	18 Dec 1926	6/ 411
Zebedon, Floyd	Linthicum, Ruby Alice	24 Sep 1927	6/ 584
Zeigler, Louis William	Gelm, Josephine Caroline	3 Jun 1931	8/ 12
Zimmerman, Carl Augustus [Apopka]	Schafer, Rose Agnes [Apopka]	26 Apr 1926	6/ 220
Zink, William James [Birmingham, AL]	Young, Sadie [New York, NY]	25 Mar 1926	6/ 189
Zipperer, Henry Eustis	Morgan, Maggie	28 Feb 1931	7/ 561
Zittrower, Lance Griffin [Orlando]	Knight, Della Vera [Orlando]	19 Feb 1927	6/ 487

Index

Ayers
- Corinne Hamilton. 20
- Irene. 20
- Kathleen. 102
- Kimmie Ellen. 109
- Marion. 4
- Roy. 4

Aymard
- Abbie Viola. 13

Babb
- Millard Grady. 4
- Roberta. 57
- Willie. 4

Babbitt
- E. E.. 4
- Earl. 4

Bach
- Agnes Hewitt. 21

Bachman
- Richard. 4

Bachmann
- Ernest Edward.. 4

Backes
- Emma Louise. 15

Backster
- Adelinda. 59

Bagett
- Luella. 32

Baggett
- Earth Clayton. 4
- Julian Herman.. 4
- Lola Beatrice.. 100
- Roberta. 58
- Selma. 76

Baidy
- Arthur. 4

Bailey
- Ada Alton. 57
- Alice Louise. 62
- Arthur. 4
- Benjamin Herman.. 4
- Bessie Adell. 65
- Burrell Francis. 4
- Dewey Asa. 4
- Edith May. 29
- Eleanor. 14
- Eva. 10
- Hance V.. 4
- Henry William. 4
- Imogene. 34, 50

Bailey cont..
- Josephine. 43
- Julia Dowell. 19
- Margaret. 83
- Robert. 4
- W. H., Jr 4
- Walter Burton.. 4
- William Herbert. 4

Baily
- Mary Fanida. 25

Baines
- Emma Jane. 9
- Lucius. 4
- Robert. 4

Baity
- Abraham Jeff 4

Baken
- Jimmie Lee. 4

Baker
- Ada. 95
- Albert J.. 4
- Alice. 61
- Allen Nathaniel.. 4
- Belle. 88
- Clare. 49
- Dorothy Marie. 28
- Ella Lou. 67
- Esop Willie.. 4
- Fannie. 12
- Frances Virginia. 96
- Hardy. 4
- Harry Edward. 4
- Horace Benjamin. 4
- Irene. 30
- Jake Granville.. 4
- Jerry Lee. 4
- John Caldwell.. 4
- John G.. 4
- Leola. 18
- Lillie. 48
- Mamie.. 17
- Martha.. 84
- Mary. 41
- Maude. 20
- Mozel. 4
- Nellie Evans. 20
- Opal. 16
- Raymond.. 4
- Susie. 49
- Ulyseese. 4
- Vernon E.. 4

Baldo
- Leslie Joseph.. 4

Baldwin
- Lillian Taylor. 92
- Minor C.. 4

Bales
- Jack. 4

Balian
- Hetoum. 4

Ball
- Hayward. 4
- J. F.. 4
- Lee. 4
- Sidney C.. 5

Ballard
- Lena. 82
- Marion. 86

Ballentine
- Mattis. 5

Bandy
- Elmer Earl.. 5
- Lena McCown. 1
- Olie Sherman. 5
- Virginia Lee. 42

Banker
- Lillie Mae. 57

Bankley
- Henry E.. 5

Banknight
- Adell Jackson. 5

Banks
- Caster. 5
- Elmer Gerard. 5
- Rosa. 6
- Susie May. 105

Bankston
- Katie May 35
- Susie. 12
- Willie. 5

Barber
- Ada. . . . . -81-
- Adeline. 40
- Aubrey DeWitt. 5
- Eva. 49
- John William.. 5
- Maggie S.. 59
- William. 5

Barco
- Erma. 69

Barden
- Howard Walton.. 5
- Masalea.. 66

114

137

148

149

162

163

185

Volley
Adolphus.............. 100
Vollrath
Lawrence Carl........... 100
Otto Adelbert. 100
Von Dauber
Hazel................ 18
Von Oehlhoff
Jane Tudor. 70
Vose
Margie Lavell. 31
Voss
Wm. Oather. 100

Waddell
Frances Marian.......... 25
Waddle
William Benson. 100
Wade
Andrew............... 100
Blanche.............. 7
Calvin Coleman. 100
James. 100
Jerry Blythe............ 65
Lillie Mae............ 89
Mary Jane............. 70
Ophilia Thereas........... 7
Wadell
Winnifred Roberta. 109
Wadkins
Alonzo Allen. 100
Waehaus
Margaret............... 20
Waggoner
Marie Louise............ 50
Wagner
Jean Wallace........... 87
Nellie. 66
Wagoner
Louis Clay............. 100
Mary Rae. 100
Wainer
Inez.................. 73
Wainright
Thomas Edward. 100
Waite
Porer................. 100
Waiters
Frank................. 100
Waitman
Gertrude. 46

Wakeman
Caroline Alice........... 55
Walaskay
Annie. 26
Walaskey
John.................. 100
Wald
Willie................ 100
Walden
Alice................. 65
Jesse................ 100
Marguerite Katherine...... 108
Mollie. 12
Stanley John. 100
Walder
Chester C. 100
Clarence.............. 100
Claude............... 100
Eugene. 100
Evan Fessett. 100
Harris............... 100
Harry Cameron.......... 100
James............... 100
L. E................. 100
Lamar Spafford.......... 100
Linton................ 100
Parker................ 100
Robert Daniel. 100
Sim. 100
William............... 100
Willie. 100
Willie Thomas. 100
Walker
Alice Rebecca........... 54
Alloria............... 39
Carolyn............... 90
Cordie................ 35
Elinor Selbourne......... 27
Estelle................ 65
Ethel................ 28
Flossie Anita............ 98
Helen Florence. 66
Jimmie............... 62
Luellor. 69
Mabelle Love. 9
Margaret Alice........... 82
Mary E. 63
Mildred Molina.......... 71
Mildred Pauline. 14

Wall
Alton Joseph............ 100
Annie. 76
Della Ernestine. 14
Eliha W................ 100
Harold Lyman........... 100
Wallace
Belle................. 11
Ernest Quinn........... 101
Ethel Mae............ 82
James. 101
Jeanie Dorothy. 91
Jimmie Lee............. 93
Lewis Andrew........... 101
Lottie E................ 22
Madrick............... 101
Marcellus. 101
Mary Belle. 45
Pinkie. 6, 108
Sophia................ 43
Viola................. 105
William C.............. 101
William Clancy.......... 101
Waller
Norah. 64
Wallett
Bessie LeDerle. 84
Walling
Henry Talmadge......... 101
Walls
Benjamin Carmage....... 101
Elsie. 42
Illa Mae............... 55
Mary Emma. 76
Walsh
Alma.................. 4
Emma Lucy............. 85
Thomas Walter.......... 101
Tilden Charles.......... 101
Walter
Sadie................. 95
Walters
Claude L............... 101
Lillie Mae.............. 24
Walterson
Julius V., Jr............. 101
Walton
Minnie May. 19
Oscar................. 101
R. T.................. 101

Notes

www.ingramcontent.com/pod-product-compliance
Lightning Source LLC
Chambersburg PA
CBHW080409290526
45791CB00008BA/2209